Learn Japanese: College Text, Volume I

Mazamaza to

Amerika ni miru

Atarashiki

Mono e no hiyaku ni

Ikiru inochi o

— *Nyozekan* —

LEARN JAPANESE

COLLEGE TEXT VOLUME I

By John Young and Kimiko Nakajima

Published for
University College, University of Maryland

The University Press of Hawaii 🏃
Honolulu

This volume is another in a series of Japanese language textbooks prepared by the Far East Division of the University College, University of Maryland and published by The University Press of Hawaii. It was first published and copyrighted in Japan under the Universal Copyright Convention. This edition is an authorized U.S. reprint.

First published by the East-West Center Press 1967
Second printing 1968
Third printing 1969
Fourth printing 1970
Fifth printing by The University Press of Hawaii 1972
Sixth printing 1972
Seventh printing 1973
Eighth printing 1974
Ninth printing 1975
Tenth printing 1977
Eleventh printing 1978
Twelfth printing 1979
Thirteenth printing 1980
Fourteenth printing 1981

Library of Congress Catalog Card Number 67-64871
ISBN 0-8248-0061-3
Manufactured in the United States of America

Table of Contents

ACKNOWLEDGMENTS

The authors are deeply indebted to the Japanese language faculty and administrative staff members of the University of Maryland's Far East Division and of the University of Hawaii who assisted in the preparation of this book.

We especially wish to mention the following people whose assistance was the most valuable:

Miss Yoshiko Ando, who assisted us in preparing the text and enriched it with her practical and valuable suggestions.

Dr. Ivan Benson, who edited the English portion of the text, and also for his valuable suggestions.

Mr. Keiichiro Okutsu, who reviewed our notes and gave us his valuable suggestions.

Mr. Setsuo Sugimura, for his fine illustrations.

Mr. Shozo Kurokawa and Mr. Keiichiro Okutsu, who gave us permission to use freely and adapt the content of LEARN JAPANESE — *Pattern Approach*.

Yuku kumo ya

Hotaka no mine no

Nokori yuki

— Seien —

Clouds drifting
Over the mountains of Hotaka
Snow lingers

INTRODUCTION

1. PURPOSE

Since the Second World War, the teaching of languages has undergone a significant change in the United States, with primary stress now placed upon oral communication as the basis for learning a foreign language. This new emphasis resulted partly from new and improved methods of teaching a spoken language based on descriptive linguistic analysis of the target language and from a realization that there is among Americans a general and immediate need for an oral language capability. It was in line with these considerations that LEARN JAPANESE — *College Text* was prepared.

LEARN JAPANESE — *College Text* was originally written, under the title of LEARN JAPANESE — *Pattern Approach,* for the University of Maryland's Far East Division, where the students have a unique opportunity to use Japanese outside of the classroom. However, in its revised form, the text has been adapted for use in regular university classes, with special emphasis on use in accelerated or intensive language programs.

2. APPROACH

The Japanese presented herein represents the language most acceptable and widely adopted within Japan; i.e., the dialect that may be more or less defined as being spoken by native speakers of a middle-class background, with a college education, residents of the YAMANOTE area of Tokyo and roughly falling into the 25-45 age group. Although certain vocabulary items or minor patterns may vary from locality to locality, no difficulty in communication should result from adhering to the materials presented here.

The "pattern approach" used in this text should not be confused with that used in other texts in this field. In essence, this text goes beyond the "formula-application" approach and develops a whole new presentation based upon association and repetition. There is no need to reiterate here the importance of repetition in language study, but repetition should not be enforced in isolation. We emphasize both association and repetition. Association reflects the connecting links between modes of utterances or patterns. Repetition formulates habits in uttering sentence patterns. A "pattern" is not a single item, occurring independently or to be learned in isolation. Rather, it is a structure related to other structures, and consequently must be associated with them in order to achieve complete mastery of the language. Associating these structures, or moving from one structure to another, is accomplished through principles of "transformation," utilized extensively in this text.

Additionally, a strong association is maintained between the patterns presented and the language as it is used in living situations. The pattern is associated, then, with its functional role as a means of transferring ideas in real conversational situations as well as with its part in the structure of the language.

Furthermore, the material presented is based upon a contrastive study of English and Japanese structure, but effort has been made to relegate the differences to their proper places in the language. The grading of the material presented herein is based upon the degree of difficulty of learning it from the standpoint of English speakers. But the most difficult items are not necessarily the most important items, and they should not be unduly stressed or increased out of proportion.

A dialog serves as the core of each lesson, and, in turn, the patterns introduced in each lesson serve as the backbone of the dialog. New patterns are introduced in each lesson in a natural and functional manner and are analyzed graphically. They are developed in the drills or exercises to the extent that the student should achieve a level of mastery reflected by almost automatic response.

The drills constitute an essential part of each lesson. It is through the drills that the student is given the opportunity to produce his own Japanese; the systematic transformation and expansion of the Japanese sentence structure are the vehicles through which the student absorbs the language for his own use. Too much emphasis cannot be given them nor can the necessity for always maintaining normal speed in the responses be ignored. Constant review also should be kept in mind as a means of insuring that the student has actually mastered the respective points of the drills. Going ahead too rapidly, before the student has completely mastered the point, must be avoided. Each successive pattern is dependent on the preceding material and presupposes an understanding of all that comes before it.

It should be borne in mind that the use of English in the classroom should be limited to the essentials. Valuable class time should be devoted to producing Japanese, not to explaining the logic of the language in English. Logic doesn't necessarily determine what is accepted in the language.

3. LESSON ARRANGEMENT

Volume I of LEARN JAPANESE consists of fifteen lessons, each of which requires a minimum of three hours of classroom work. The first two lessons provide an introduction to Japanese pronunciation and seek to emphasize creating a foundation in correct pronunciation, accent, and intonation habits. Some useful classroom and daily expressions are introduced in these two lessons mainly for the purpose of practicing pronunciation. In addition to the lessons that constitute the main body of the text, there are special systematic review lessons, lessons 6, 10, and 13, which cover the materials in the preceding lessons. Lesson 14 provides the student with an opportunity to review, through the use of *kana* (*hiragana* and *katakana*), what he has become familiarized with. It also introduces the rules of Japanese orthography. The last lesson, Lesson 15, provides a general review exercise of the entire textbook and prepares the student for the final exam.

Other than in the phonology and review lessons, the following format is followed:

Part 1.   Useful Expressions

These are contemporary expressions which are used idiomatically in conversation. They are not usually included in any pattern classification presented but are necessary for conversational purposes. They should be memorized.

Part 2.   Dialog

Each dialog consists of a realistic conversation incorporating useful expressions and sentences based upon patterns either introduced in the respective lesson or in previous lessons. The student's first contact with the dialog should not be visual, but aural. The "mim-mem" method — mimicking the instructor or tape, and thus memorizing — is recommended. After the drill work, the student should again repeat the dialog, memorize it, and develop his own controlled but situation-centered conversation.

Part 3.   Pattern Sentences

New "pattern sentences" are broken down graphically into their respective components and the "structural" elements involved in a pattern are illustrated visually without subjecting the student to the intricacies of traditional grammar. These pattern sentences are fundamental to a rapid mastery of the oral language and should be memorized by the student.

Part 4.   Notes

Brief structural explanations as well as other explanations are contained in this section. The student should familiarize himself with this section so that the instructor may concentrate upon drills during the class sessions. In this section, an arrow indicates modification: a box followed by an arrow always shows that it modifies the box following an arrow. In other words, the box before an arrow is the Predicate Modifier and the box after an arrow is the Predicate. When two or more Predicate Modifiers are positioned vertically, it means that the sequence of these Predicate Modifiers can be relatively changed, while horizontally-arranged Predicate Modifiers show that their sequence is absolute. The analysis of the structure is to be considered as an aid to the student and should not be treated as an item to be memorized. Japanese words or phrases occurring within an English context will be indicated in italics, as will the English words that occasionally occur in Japanese contexts in the notes. Also, English translations or equivalents, for Japanese expressions, occurring in an English context are noted by quotation marks.

Part 5. Vocabulary

New words and phrases appearing in the dialog, notes, and drills are given their English equivalents in this section. It should be noted, however, that vocabulary items are normally not used independently. They are used as part of a sentence and their independent meanings should not be overemphasized.

Part 6. Hiragana Practice

Hiragana is introduced in certain of the vocabulary words already acquired by the student. This is merely intended to familiarize the student somewhat with the Japanese *hiragana* writing system. The student is not responsible for mastering the *hiragana* presented Lessons 3 through 12.

Part 7. Drills

Various types of drills are included in this section, depending upon the language aspect being stressed. The left-hand column is for the instructor, and the right-hand column suggests varied responses which may be given by the student. The textbook should not be used by the student during the drills; the student should listen to the instructor carefully and respond according to instruction. The use of English should be limited to the English cues given in the E-J drill. New vocabulary items may also be added in this section so that sufficient or more realistic drill might be effected.

A. Pronunciation Drill

This section is based upon the words and phrases in the lesson and stresses correct pronunciation. The purpose is to let the student understand the stream of sounds, hear the distinctive sound features and approximate their production. The importance of understanding the language at a normal speed and of facilitating good pronunciation habits should not be underemphasized at any stage.

B. Pattern Drill

This drill consists of important pattern sentences from the dialog. They should be repeated by the student until he has memorized them and can reproduce them automatically. Automatic habit formulation in the use of Japanese is the target of this drill.

C. Substitution Drill

A code sentence is given first by the instructor. After mastering the pattern, the student substitutes that part of the sentence shown in italics by other words or phrases. This is a highly controlled drill and rapid response as well as good pronunciation should be stressed at all times.

D. Expansion Drill

This drill starts with short sentences which the student expands by adding words, Relationals, or phrases.

E. Transformation Drill

This is a drill wherein the student makes changes of a structural transformation nature in the sentences given him.

F. Response Drill

This is a question and answer drill designed to encourage the student to respond utilizing his own Japanese as opposed to the previous drills, which were highly controlled in that the student was limited to producing one particular item or phrase.

G. Mixed Drill

This includes any drill that combines elements of substitution or transformation with any of the other types of drills. It is a complicated type of drill, forcing the student to cope with several changes or structural differences simultaneously.

H. Combination Drill

Two or more sentences are given by the instructor for the student to combine into one sentence. This is designed to affect the student's ability to formulate complicated sentences.

I. E-J Drill (English-Japanese Drill)

In this drill, the instructor, after giving the code sentence, gives the cues in English. The student should quickly respond with the Japanese sentence modeled on the code sentence. Should there be such a need, the instructor may convert other types of drill into this type by giving the cues in English. This drill is effective when used as a review drill. In this drill, substitution or transformation is signaled in English.

J. Relational Checking Drill

This drill is meant to check the use of Relationals. The student should complete a sentence by inserting a proper Relational.

K. Review Drill

This drill deals with the pattern sentences introduced in this particular lesson as well as those covered in previous lessons.

Part 8. Exercises

This part may be covered in the classroom or outside the classroom, depending upon the difficulty of the pattern sentences to be learned. Normally the student is expected to do the review exercises outside the classroom.

4. OTHER CONSIDERATIONS

The above description of the various component parts of each lesson is designed to facilitate their most efficient and effective use by both the student and the instructor. There are several basic principles of application which should be constantly borne in mind by the instructor as well as the student.

First, in view of the fact that the students using these texts for the first time represent a wide range of proficiency in Japanese — from "zero" to a relatively fair degree — the contents of the lessons have been separated into two categories, one for "active" learning and the other for "passive" learning.

For our purposes, "active" learning reflects those portions of the lessons that should be thoroughly learned by the student, to the point where they can be both *recognized* and *produced* by him easily and naturally. This includes, for example, Useful Expressions, Dialogs, Pattern Sentences, and the contents of the drill portions of each lesson. "Passive" learning represents those parts that are included as supplementary information and should be learned by the student to the point where they can be *recognized* and *understood* by him. *Reproduction* will not be required. The parts for "passive" learning, for example, are Hiragana Practice in Volume I, the analysis section included in the appendices, etc. The student is responsible for a thorough knowledge of all the materials contained in the "active" learning category but the material contained in the "passive category will not be included in examinations.

As a second general principle, the instructor should adhere to the sequence of presentation followed in each lesson, moving on to the next part only when he is satisfied that the students have a thorough grasp of and facility with that particular material. The instructor may supplement the examples given in the drills but should exercise great caution not to burden the student with extra vocabulary items nor unconsciously introduce structural forms unfamiliar to the student. In the review lessons, however, the instructor is free to exercise his discretion in emphasizing or de-emphasizing certain points, depending on his appraisal of the students' facility with that particular item.

Further, it is desirable that the textbook should be closed at all times in the classroom. The instructor is urged to avoid giving redundant explanations or directions for the various drills. For example, the simple term "substitute" followed by hand signals should be enough to effect a fast-moving substitution drill, as opposed to lengthy explanations about how the drill should be conducted. The importance of maintaining a fast pace and not letting the class lag is fundamental. In the event that a student cannot answer in a reasonably short interval, the instructor should not hesitate to give further cues or hints rather than permitting the classroom atmosphere to become interrupted.

5. ROMANIZATION

The romanization system herein is the Hepburn system, together with two modifications. It was felt that the system used in *Beginning Japanese* by Dr. Jorden was superior from the standpoint of effecting an easier transition to the written language as well as facilitating morpho-phonemic and structural descriptions, but it was realized that a large number of students are already familiar with the Hepburn system and a sudden change to the Beginning Japanese system might create some initial confusion. As a result, the Hepburn system with the following two modifications was adopted for this text:

1. Long vowels are written as *aa, ii, uu, ei, oo* in this text. However, long vowel *ē* in a foreign word and three words — Sentence Interjective *ee*, Sentence Particle *nee* and Nominative *oneesan* — are written as *ee*.

	Hepburn	Learn Japanese
e.g.	ōkii	*oo*kii
	kyū	ky*uu*
	okāsan	ok*aa*san
	bīru	b*ii*ru
	tait*ei*	tait*ei*
	onēsan	on*ee*san

2. Within a word, the non-final syllabic *n* will be written as *n'*:

e.g.   gen'in   kon'ban   shin'bun

At the same time, however, the following convention, distinguished by / / symbols, is adopted in explaining phonological and structural rules:

1) /t/ represents *t, ts,* and *ch;*

2) /s/ represents *s* and *sh;*

3) /h/ represents *f* and *h*; and

4) /z/ represents *j* and *z* (*j* covers /zy/ before *a, u,* or *o*).

LESSON 1

1.1 USEFUL EXPRESSIONS

Ohayoo gozaimasu. — "Good morning." This expression is a formal or polite greeting used in the morning. Informally, *Ohayoo* is used. The literal meaning is "It is early." Consequently, this expression may not be used later than 10 or 11 a.m.

Kon'nichi wa — "Hello." "Good day." This expression may be used roughly from 10 or 11 a.m. to 5 or 6 p.m. when it gets dark. Do not use this expression when you leave.

Kon'ban wa — "Good evening." This expression literally means "Tonight," and may be used after it gets dark. This greeting is not to be used when one leaves.

Sayoonara. — "Goodbye." This expression is sometimes contracted to *Sayonara*.

Oyasumi nasai. — "Good night." The literal meaning is "Rest," or "Go to sleep." Therefore, you use this expression when you leave if it is dark enough to go to sleep at night or if you are going to sleep, or if you see someone going to sleep in the daytime. The contracted form is *Oyasumi*.

Wakarimasu ka / — "Do you understand?" "Is that clear?"

(Hai,) wakarimasu. — "(Yes,) I understand."

(Iie,) wakarimasen. — "(No,) I do not understand."

Yoku dekimashita. — "Very good." "You did a good job." This is a compliment for good accomplishment.

Moo ichido itte kudasai. — "Please say it once more."

Ato o tsukete itte kudasai. — "Please repeat after me."

Yoku kiite kudasai. — "Please listen carefully."

Yon'de kudasai. — "Please read it."

Kaite kudasai. — "Please write it."

Hanashite kudasai. — "Please speak." "Please talk."

*1.3.5

Gopeeji o akete kudasai.   "Please open [the book on] page five."

Hon o tojite kudasai.   "Please close your book."

Chotto matte kudasai.   "Please wait for a moment."

1.2 PRONUNCIATION NOTES

1.2.1 Syllables

The Tōkyō dialect has, for the purpose of this text, 5 vowels, 13 consonants and 2 semi-vowels. They formulate 105 syllables. Each syllable should be pronounced with equal length and more or less even stress, although some syllables may be pronounced with more prominence.

Syllables are formulated in one of the following ways:

1)	Vowel	5
2)	Consonant	5
3)	Consonant+Vowel	58
4)	Consonant+/y/*+Vowel	33
5)	/y/ or /w/+Vowel	4
	Total:	105

* The symbol / / is used to indicate a phoneme.

Chart 1   Syllables of Japanese

initial \ final	/a/	/i/	/u/	/e/	/o/	/ya/	/yu/	/yo/	/wa/	ZERO
ZERO	a	i	u	e	o	ya	yu	yo	wa	/
/p/	pa	pi	pu	pe	po	pya	pyu	pyo	/	p
/b/	ba	bi	bu	be	bo	bya	byu	byo	/	/
/t/	ta	chi	tsu	te	to	cha	chu	cho	/	t
/d/	da	/	/	de	do	/	/	/	/	/
/k/	ka	ki	ku	ke	ko	kya	kyu	kyo	/	k
/g/	ga	gi	gu	ge	go	gya	gyu	gyo	/	/
/s/	sa	shi	su	se	so	sha	shu	sho	/	s
/z/	za	ji	zu	ze	zo	ja	ju	jo	/	/
/h/	ha	hi	fu	he	ho	hya	hyu	hyo	/	/
/m/	ma	mi	mu	me	mo	mya	myu	myo	/	/
/n/	na	ni	nu	ne	no	nya	nyu	nyo	/	/
/r/	ra	ri	ru	re	ro	rya	ryu	ryo	/	/
/n'/	/	/	/	/	/	/	/	/	/	n'

1.2.2 Vowels and Semi-Vowels

There are five vowels /a/, /i/, /u/, /e/, and /o/, and two semi-vowels /y/ and /w/ in Japanese. Vowels are pronounced in the mouth as shown in the following:

Chart 2   Vowels

	FRONT	CENTRAL	BACK
HIGH	i		u
MID	e		o
LOW		a	

1.2.3 Single Vowels

/a/ is pronounced like "a" in "father," but it must be shorter.
/i/ is pronounced like "i" in "machine," but it has to be shorter and clearer. Its sound is entirely different
    from "i" in "knit," which occurs as a short "i" in English.
/u/ is pronounced like "oo" in "hook." Japanese /u/ is produced without the lip-rounding.
/e/ is pronounced like "e" in "pet," but it is shorter.
/o/ is pronounced like "o" in "horse," but it is shorter and clearer.

1.2.4 Vowels in Sequence

Since a single vowel can be a syllable by itself in Japanese, a vowel can be followed by another vowel, and in pronunciation each vowel is to be short, clear and even in length. Consecutive vowels can be different, such as /ai/, /ue/, /ie/, and /oi/, or the same, such as /aa/, /ii/, /uu/, /ee/, and /oo/. In the latter case, the vowels are called long vowels.

English-speaking people tend to pronounce the second of a two-different-vowels sequence, especially "i" and "u," in an off-glide manner.

Compare:

ka-u . . . . cow	*o-u* . . . . owe	*ba-i* . . . . buy	*ma-i* . . . . my
ha-i . . . . high	*a-i* I	*so-u* . . . . sew	*to-i* . . . . toy

1.2.5 Long Vowels

English-speaking people often neglect to distinguish between long and short vowels but the distinction is extremely important in Japanese, as the length of the vowel may change the meaning of the word.

ooi   aa   iie   seeru   kuuki   Tookyoo

4

Compare:

ojisan   "uncle"   ....ojiisan   "grandfather" or "old man"

obasan   "aunt"   ....obaasan   "grandmother" or "old woman"

beru   "bell"   ....beeru   "veil"

biru   "building"   ....biiru   "beer"

Soko ni arimasu.   "It's there."   ....Sooko ni arimasu.   "It's in the warehouse."

1.2.6 Semi-Vowels

/y/ may be placed either in the initial position or between a consonant and a vowel in a syllable. /y/
appears only before /a/, /u/, and /o/.
/y/ is pronounced approximately like "y" in "year," but it is more fully voiced.

yama   yuki   yoi   kyaku   kyuukoo   ryokan

/w/ is placed only at the initial position of a syllable. /w/ appears only before /a/.
/w/ is pronounced like "w" in "want," but it is fully voiced.

warui   watakushi   kawa

1.2.7 Voiceless Vowels

Whenever an /i/ or /u/ vowel is placed between two of the voiceless consonants /k/, /s/, /t/, /p/ or
/h/, the /i/ or /u/ becomes voiceless or is lost unless it is accented. In some cases, this phenomenon
may occur when either *i* or *u* is placed between a voiceless consonant and a period.

s(u)-su-mu   ts(u)-ka-u   ma-ts(u)

Ko-re wa ho-n de-s(u).   Sh(i)-te imas(u).

Wa-ta-k(u)-shi mo i-ki-ma-s(u).

Chart 3   Consonants

manner of articulation \ point of articulation		labial	apical	palatal	velar	glottal	others
plosive	voiceless	p	t -a -e -o		k		
plosive	voiced	b	d -a -e -o		g		
affricate			t (ts)* -u	t (ch) -i			
fricative	voiceless	h (f) -u	s -a -u -e -o	s (sh) -i	h -i	h -a -e -o	
fricative	voiced	w	z -a -u -e -o	y z (j) -i			
nasal	non-syllabic	m	n		g		
nasal	syllabic						n'
flap			r				

* Spellings in parentheses are those used in this text.

1.2.8   Consonants

There are 13 consonants in Japanese. All of these, except /n'/, may form syllables in combination with a vowel or a semi-vowel plus a vowel. However, of these 13 consonants, 5 do not necessarily require a combination of a vowel or semi-vowel to form a syllable. There are 58 cases of Consonant+Vowel syllables and 33 cases of Consonant+Semi-Vowel+Vowel combinations.

1.2.9   Single Consonant Syllables

The five consonants that can formulate a syllable alone are /k/, /s/, /t/, /p/ and /n'/. /k/, /s/, /t/ or /p/ as a syllabic consonant comes only before another identical consonant; that is, /kk/, /ss/, /tt/ or /pp/. These are conventionally called "double consonants," and are often difficult for English-speaking people to pronounce correctly. The tongue position for the pronunciation of the first consonant is held for one syllable beat before the tongue starts to move to produce the second consonant. The consonant syllable /n'/ will be explained later.

hakkiri   chotto   assari   yappari   massugu

6

Compare:

saka	"slope"	....	sakka	"writer"
ito	"thread"	....	itto	"one *to*"
keshi	"poppy"	....	kesshi	" 'do-or-die' spirit"
ita	"was (in a place)"	....	itta	"went"
ichi	"one"	....	itchi	"agreement"

1.2.10 Consonant + (Semi-Vowel) + Vowel Syllables

/p/ formulates nine syllables, *p, pa, pi, pu, pe, po, pya, pyu,* and *pyo.*
/p/ before *a, u, e,* or *o* is pronounced like "p" in "poor" with less aspiration.
/p/ before *i, ya, yu,* or *yo* is pronounced like "p" in "pure."

> apaato   piano   ippuu   peeji   ippo   ippyoo   pyuu

/b/ formulates eight syllables, *ba, bi, bu, be, bo, bya, byu,* and *byo.* It is pronounced like English "b,"
    except that it is more fully voiced.
/b/ before *a, u, e,* or *o* is pronounced like "b" in "rebel," and *b* before *i, ya, yu,* or *yo* is pronounced like
    "b" in "abuse."

> bai   tabi   byooki   byakuya

/t/ formulates nine syllables, *t, ta, chi, tsu, te, to, cha, chu,* and *cho.*
/t/ before *a, e,* or *o* is pronounced like "t" in "top," but the tongue touches the teeth. It has less aspiration
    than English "t."

> taitei   ittoo   ittai

/t/ with /u/ is spelled *tsu* and /t/ is pronounced like "ts" in "cats." *Tsu* is one of the most difficult
    Japanese sounds for English-speaking people. Put your tongue in the position of producing English *t,*
    and before you pronounce *u* give a slight hiss. If you forget to start with *t,* it will sound like *su.*

Compare:

> tsu .... su   tsumi .... sumi
> utsu .... usu   tsuki .... suki

/t/ with /i/, /ya/, /yu/, or /yo/ is spelled *chi, cha, chu,* or *cho,* and /t/ is pronounced like "ch" in "cheap."

> chichi   bachi   chittomo   itchi   itchaku   chotto

/d/ formulates three syllables, *da, de,* and *do.* /d/ is made by touching the alveolar ridge (behind the teeth) with the wider part of the tongue right behind the tip, but not as close to the tip as when one is sounding the English "d." To Americans Japanese /d/ and /r/ may sound alike.

eda   ude   doko   kodomo

/k/ formulates nine syllables, *k, ka, ki, ku, ke, ko, kya, kyu,* and *kyo.*
/k/ is less aspirated than English "k." /k/ before *a, u, e,* or *o* is pronounced like "c" in "coot."
/k/ before *i, ya, yu,* or *yo* is pronounced like "c" in "cute."

kokkai   kikyoo   iku   dake   kyaku   kekkyoku

/g/ formulates eight syllables, *ga, gi, gu, ge, go, gya, gyu,* and *gyo.*
/g/ is pronounced similarly to the hard English "g," when it is in initial position, but it is more fully voiced than in English.
/g/ before *a, u, e,* or *o* is pronounced approximately like "g" in "begone."
/g/ before *i, ya, yu,* or *yo* is pronounced like "g" in "regular," but it is more fully voiced.

gyaku   gyuunyuu   gyookai   geki

gakkoo   gikei   guchi   gochisoo

When /g/ appears in any other position than the initial, plosive /g/ changes into nasal /g/, the sound similar to "ng" in "singer." This is also true of the Relational *ga.* Although nasal /g/ is prominent in the Tōkyō speech of Japanese, there are quite a few Tōkyō people who don't use nasal /g/. Therefore, it isn't absolutely necessary to be able to pronounce it, but you should be able to recognize it.

nagai   sugi   sugu   eigo   sagyoo   kaigyaku   toogyuu

Kore ga hon desu.

/h/ formulates eight syllables, *ha, hi, fu, he, ho, hya, hyu,* and *hyo.*
/h/ before *i, ya, yu,* or *yo* is pronounced like "h" in "human," but it is more fricative.

hito   koohii   hyaku   hyuuzu   hyooshi

/h/ before *a, e,* or *o* is pronounced like "h" in "hot."

haha   heta   hoshi   chihoo

/h/ with *u* is spelled *fu* and produced with the lips close together and then by letting air come out in a puff. Since the upper teeth are not used at all, this pronunciation is unlike that of the English "f."

fuufu   fuyu   fuchi   Koofu   Fujisan

/s/ formulates nine syllables, *s, sa, shi, su, se, so, sha, shu,* and *sho.*
/s/ before *a, u, e,* or *o* is pronounced like "s" in "see," but it is produced farther forward in the mouth.

asa   sasa   susuki   gassaku   issei   soko

/s/ with /i/, /ya/, /yu/, or /yo/ is spelled *shi, sha, shu,* or *sho,* and /s/ is pronounced like "sh" in "she." But this is more aspirated than the above /s/.

shichi   shishi   kushi   kesshite   shashoo   isshuu

/z/ formulates eight syllables, *za, ji, zu, ze, zo, ja, ju,* and *jo.*

/z/ with /i/, /ya/, /yu/, or /yo/ is spelled *ji, ja, ju,* and *jo* respectively, and /z/ is pronounced like "j" in "reject." But usually it is pronounced as if it were spelled "dz."

/z/ before *a, u, e,* or *o* is pronounced like "z" in "bazaar," but it is more fully voiced.

jiko   jaa   kuji   juuji   koojoo

zaseki   hazu   zehi   kazoku

/m/ formulates eight syllables, *ma, mi, mu, me, mo, mya, myu,* and *myo.*

/m/ is close to English "m," except for being more fully voiced.

/m/ before *a, u, e,* or *o* is pronounced like "m" in "mine," and /m/ before *i, ya, yu,* or *yo* is pronounced like "m" in "amuse."

mado   mimi   yomu   kome   motsu

myaku   Myuuzu   kimyoo

/n/ formulates eight syllables, *na, ni, nu, ne, no, nya, nyu,* and *nyo.*

/n/ before *a, u, e,* or *o* is pronounced like "n" in "deny" with the tongue touching the teeth and is fully voiced.

funa   inu   mune   kono

/n/ before *i, ya, yu,* or *yo* is pronounced like "n" in "menu."

nyooboo   niku   han'nya   gyuunyuu

/n'/, syllabic nasal, immediately before *p, b,* or *m,* is pronounced as a long "m."

en'pitsu   Shin'bashi   kin'mu

/n'/ immediately before /t/, /d/, /z/, /n/, or /r/ is pronounced as a long "n."

hon'too   san'ji   don'na   en'ryo   hon'dai

/n'/ before *k* or *g* is pronounced like the prolonged "ng" sound in "singer."

nan'gai   ben'kyoo   Ogen'ki desu ka /

Elsewhere, that is, before vowels, before *y, w,* glottal *h, s,* or at the end of a word, *n'* is pronounced with long nasalization. /n'/ at the end of a word is spelled *n* in this text.

hon   ten'in   kan'shin

/r/ formulates eight syllables, *ra, ri, ru, re, ro, rya, ryu,* and *ryo.* The Japanese /r/ is a flap /r/, made by flicking the tip of the tongue against the alveolar ridge.

Therefore, it is entirely different from American English "r," but is more like "l." This is rather similar to the British English pronunciation of "r" in "very."

raku   urusai   iroiro   rin'go   kirei   ryokan   Ryuukyuu

To American-English-speaking people, the Japanese /r/ may sound like /d/, but Japanese /r/ is shorter than /d/, and in producing /r/, the tip of the tongue touches the alveolar ridge, whereas in the production of /d/, the area of the tongue immediately behind the tip touches the upper teeth.

Compare:

Hara ... hada   sore .... sode   raku .... daku

roku .... doku

1.3 DRILLS

1.3.1 General Pronunciation Drill

1) a ai au aoi i ii iie ie u ue uo o oi ooi

2) kau kao ou sou hai bai aiai taikai

3) tooi soo kookoo ookii tootoo

4) taitei seito sen'sei keisei meiji

5) yaya iya yuuki yuki yoi iwa waei

6) s(u)sumu mats(u) watak(u)shi ikimas(u) sh(i)tte imas(u)

7) sakka hassha happun tokkyo Hattori

8) gopeeji ippon pianisuto depaato

9) tabi byooki byuu shibai

*   *   *   *   *   *   *   *   *   *   *   *

Tongue Twister: Tonari no kyaku wa yoku kaki kuu kyaku da

Boozu ga byoobu ni joozu ni boozu no e o kaita.

Nama mugi, nama gome, nama tamago.

10) tatami totemo moto

11) Doozo dete kudasai.

12) kaki hokkyoku kyaku kyuukoo kokki kyoo

13) gaku Gin'za guchi geta goi gyaku gyuu gyookai

14) uchi ichi chakusoo chuui chotto

15) tsuyoi kutsu tsuru itsutsu tsutsu motsu yottsu

16) fuku fuufu fuuboo Fujisan yoofuku furui saifu

17) sesoo sasu issai issei

18) shichi yasashii shishakai shussho issho

19) hitotsu hima koohii hyaku hihyoo hyoohi hyuuzu

20) hachi heta fuhei

21) zasshi mazui zehi soozoo

22) jiko kujaku oji josei juuji

23) mada kumi muzukashii gimei

24) nani nuno nemasu gyuunyuu nyooboo

25) akan'boo kan'byoo shin'pai en'pitsu san'mai kin'mu Kon'nichi wa.

26) hon'too san'ji en'ryo kon'do ben'jo han'nyuu

27) nagai migi sugu agemasu gogo kaigyaku toogyuu sagyoo

28) nan'gai ben'kyoo hon'ki

29) hon ten'in kan'shin han'ei kan'sha hon'ya

30) raku kirai rin'go kuri rusu uru ren'shuu kore Roshia mochiron ryaku ryuukoo ichiryuu
ryokoo kyooryoku ryooriya

1.3.2 Contrast Drill (Single Vowels *vs.* Long Vowels)

obasan	....	obaasan		seru	....	seeru
ojisan	....	ojiisan		beru	....	beeru
nisan	....	niisan		soko	....	sookoo
chizu	....	chiizu		toshin	....	tooshin
yuki	....	yuuki		yoko	....	yokoo
shuki	....	shuuki				

1.3.3 Contrast Drill (Consonant + Vowel Syllable vs. Syllabic Consonant)

ika	....	ikka	gaka	....	gakka
iku	....	ikku	isho	....	issho
saka	....	sakka	futa	....	futta
asari	....	assari	haka	....	hakka
kasai	....	kassai	bushi	....	busshi
nishi	....	nisshi	kita	....	kitta
heta	....	hetta	Okanai desu.	....	Okkanai desu.
kata	....	katta	Ito desu ka /	....	Itto desu ka /
soto	....	sotto	Ite kudasai.	....	Itte kudasai.

1.3.4 Sounds to be distinguished

a. (shi)   (chi)

ishi	....	ichi	tashimasu	....	tachimasu
kashi	....	kachi	Hashi desu.	....	Hachi desu.
kushi	....	kuchi	Shikai desu ka /	......	Chikai desu ka /
toshi	....	tochi	Ushi o kaimasu.	......	Uchi o kaimasu.
jishin	....	jichin			

b. (su)   (tsu)

kasu	....	katsu	sukimashita	....	tsukimashita
suru	....	tsuru	Are wa suki desu.	.....	Are wa tsuki desu.
suika	....	tsuika	Den'sha ga sukimasu.	....	Den'sha ga tsukimasu.
sumi	....	tsumi	Suna ga arimasu ka /	..	Tsuna ga arimasu ka /
basu	....	batsu			

12

c.   (d)   (r)

doku	....	roku		muda	....	mura
eda	....	era		sode	....	sore
kodomo	....	koromo		yudemasu	....	yuremasu
kokuden	....	kokuren		Hidoi desu nee.	......	Hiroi desu nee.
hadan	....	haran		Tada desu.	....	Tara desu.

d.   (i)   (e)

mai	....	mae		kaimasu	....	kaemasu
aimasu	....	aemasu		kaerimasu	....	kaeremasu
ikimasu	....	ikemasu				

e.   (i)   (hi)

iru	....	hiru		jii	....	jihi
iso	....	hiso		ikimasu	....	hikimasu
mai	....	mahi				

f. (/y/ in the syllabic   (/y/ in the syllabic
     initial position)   non-initial position)

kiyoo	....	kyoo		kiyaku	....	kyaku
hiyoo	....	hyoo		hiyaku	....	hyaku
riyoo	....	ryoo		shiyoo	....	shoo
biyooin	....	byooin				

g. (syllabic /n'/)   (/n/)

bun'an	....	bunan		ken'en	....	kenen
gen'an	....	genan		kin'en	....	kinen
shin'an	....	shinan				

1.3.5 Pronunciation Drill (Practice the following numerals to familiarize yourself with them.)

page number

a.	1	....	ichi	ippeeji; ichipeeji
	2	....	ni	nipeeji
	3	....	san	san'peeji
	4	....	shi; yon	yon'peeji
	5	....	go	gopeeji
	6	....	roku	rokupeeji
	7	....	shichi; nana	shichipeeji; nanapeeji
	8	....	hachi	happeeji; hachipeeji
	9	....	ku; kyuu	kyuupeeji
	10	....	juu	jippeeji; juppeeji
	11	....	juuichi	juuichipeeji; juuippeeji
	12	....	juuni	juunipeeji
	13	....	juusan	juusan'peeji
	14	....	juushi; juuyon	juuyon'peeji
	15	....	juugo	juugopeeji
	16	....	juuroku	juurokupeeji
	17	....	juushichi; juunana	juushichipeeji; juunanapeeji
	18	....	juuhachi	juuhappeeji; juuhachipeeji
	19	....	juuku; juukyuu	juukyuupeeji
	20	....	nijuu	nijippeeji; nijuppeeji

21	. . . .	nijuuichi	nijuu ichipeeji
⋮	⋮	⋮	⋮
30	. . . .	san'juu	san'jippeeji; san'juppeeji
40	. . . .	yon'juu	yon'jippeeji; yon'juppeeji
50	. . . .	gojuu	gojippeeji; gojuppeeji
60	. . . .	rokujuu	rokujippeeji; rokujuppeeji
70	. . . .	shichijuu; nanajuu	shichijippeeji; nanajuppeeji
80	. . . .	hachijuu	hachijippeeji; hachijuppeeji
90	. . . .	kyuujuu	kyuujippeeji; kyuujuppeeji
100	. . . .	hyaku	hyakupeeji
200	. . . .	nihyaku	nihyakupeeji
300	. . . .	san'byaku	san'byakupeeji
400	. . . .	yon'hyaku	yon'hyakupeeji
500	. . . .	gohyaku	gohyakupeeji
600	. . . .	roppyaku	roppyakupeeji
700	. . . .	nanahyaku	nanahyakupeeji
800	. . . .	happyaku	happyakupeeji
900	. . . .	kyuuhyaku	kyuuhyakupeeji
1,000	. . . .	sen	sen'peeji

b.
1	. . . . hitotsu	5	. . . . itsutsu	9	. . . . kokonotsu
2	. . . . futatsu	6	. . . . muttsu	10	. . . . too
3	. . . . mittsu	7	. . . . nanatsu		
4	. . . . yottsu	8	. . . . yattsu		

1.4 EXERCISES

1.4.1 One of the following words or expressions in each group will be pronounced by your instructor. Listen and underline the one pronounced.

a.	obasan	obaasan	n.	kodomo	koromo
b.	nisan	niisan	o.	hadan	haran
c.	yuki	yuuki	p.	mai	mae
d.	soko	sooko	q.	kaimasu	kaemasu
e.	saka	sakka	r.	iru	hiru
f.	kasai	kassai	s.	ikimasu	hikimasu
g.	heta	hetta	t.	kiyoo	kyoo
h.	bushi	busshi	u.	biyooin	byooin
i.	hiyoo	hyoo	v.	Ite kudasai.	Itte kudasai.
j.	kushi	kuchi	w.	Ushi o kaimasu.	Uchi o kaimasu.
k.	kin'en	kinen	x.	Shikai desu.	Chikai desu.
l.	suika	tsuika	y.	Hidoi desu nee.	Hiroi desu nee.
m.	kaerimasu	kaeremasu	z.	Den'sha ga sukimasu.	Den'sha ga tsukimasu.

1.4.2 In each group three words or expressions will be pronounced by your instructor. One of the three words or expressions is different from the other two. Work on this exercise with your book closed. Write the number representing the different word or expression.

> Note: The following list is only for the use of the instructor. It is recommended that the instructor change the word order in each group to make this exercise effective. The instructor is also encouraged to make new lists based on the idea shown in the list.

a.	(1)	chizu	(2)	chizu	(3)	chiizu
b.	(1)	ojisan	(2)	ojiisan	(3)	ojisan
c.	(1)	asari	(2)	assari	(3)	assari
d.	(1)	gakka	(2)	gaka	(3)	gakka
e.	(1)	tochi	(2)	tochi	(3)	toshi
f.	(1)	Hashi desu.	(2)	Hachi desu.	(3)	Hashi desu.
g.	(1)	basu	(2)	basu	(3)	batsu
h.	(1)	kokuden	(2)	kokuren	(3)	kokuden
i.	(1)	muda	(2)	mura	(3)	muda
j.	(1)	sode	(2)	sode	(3)	sore
k.	(1)	aimasu	(2)	aimasu	(3)	aemasu
l.	(1)	iru	(2)	hiru	(3)	hiru
m.	(1)	biyooin	(2)	biyooin	(3)	byooin
n.	(1)	hiyaku	(2)	hyaku	(3)	hiyaku
o.	(1)	bun'an	(2)	bun'an	(3)	bunan

LESSON 2

2.1 USEFUL EXPRESSIONS

Doomo arigatoo gozaimasu.
"Thank you very much." This is a formal expression of thanks. Depending upon the degree of politeness, some parts of this expression may be omitted. Here are expressions of thanks listed from the formal to less formal:
Doomo arigatoo gozaimasu.
Arigatoo gozaimasu.
Doomo arigatoo.
Arigatoo.
Doomo.

Doomo sumimasen.
"I am very sorry for what I am now doing, or I am going to do, or for what I have done." "Thanks a lot." Informally, the contracted form *Doomo* may be used. Originally, this expression was merely that of apology, but it is now common practice to use it as an expression of gratitude.

Gomen nasai.
"Forgive me." This expression is used as a colloquial expression of apology. Compared with *Sumimasen,* which is broad in use, *Gomen nasai* is used as a somewhat more hearty apology, usually on less formal occasions, and is somewhat more colloquial.

Doo itashimashite.
"Don't mention it." "Not at all." This expression is used as a formal reply not only to expressions of gratitude but also to those of apology. Sometimes, *Iie* "No" will precede this expression. In the most informal cases, only *Iie* is used.

Gomen kudasai.
"Pardon me." "Excuse me." This expression is commonly used by a visitor to someone's home to attract the resident's attention to the fact that the visitor is at the door. Or it may be used by a customer in a store to attract the sales clerk's attention. To answer this, *Hai* "Yes" is used.

Irasshai (mase).
"I am glad that you came." "Welcome." This expression is used for greeting a customer entering a store. *Irasshaimase* is more polite than *Irasshai* and is used by women, and by employees of stores, restaurants, hotels, etc.

Tadaima
"I've come home now." This expression literally means "Just now," and it implies that the speaker has safely come home.

Okaeri nasai.
"Welcome home." "I am glad to see you back." This expression is used by a person who is at home, as a reply to *Tadaima.* Informally, *Okaeri* is used.

Itadakimasu.
"I am going to eat or drink." This expression is used when a person is going to eat or drink. Literally it means "I will receive."

Gochisoo sama deshita.	"It was a feast." This expression is used after a person has eaten or drunk something and expresses his gratitude for it. *Deshita* may be omitted.
Onegai shimasu.	The literal translation is "I make a request." This expression is polite. Depending upon the context, this expression can be translated into various expressions in English, such as "Please do it for me," "Please take care of things," etc.
Omedetoo gozaimasu.	"Congratulations." This expression is used when someone has a birthday, has been promoted, or has had some other happy experience. It is also used as a New Year greeting. Informally, *Omedetoo* is used.

2.2 SYLLABIC LENGTH, ACCENT & INTONATION NOTES

2.2.1 Syllabic Length

One of the most outstanding features in pronouncing Japanese is its syllabic length. A phrase or a sentence should be pronounced with an even and regular rhythm consisting of many beats, uttered with the same length. These beats are called syllables. About the same amount of time must be spent for each syllable. There is neither a speeding up nor a slowing down.

to-ko-ro	to-ki-do-ki	Yo-ko-ha-ma	ko-n'-ni-chi-wa
ki-t-to	yu-k-ku-ri	Na-ga-sa-ki	ko-n'-ba-n-wa

2.2.2 Accent

In English, if a syllable is accented, it shows that the accented syllable is produced with a strong stress. Therefore, English accent is called STRESS ACCENT. Furthermore, English vowels in a phrase or a sentence are not pronounced with the same duration. This contrasts with the Japanese language distinctly.

In English the stressed syllable is much more clearly uttered than others, and it is longer in time duration.

> an Énglishman   an Américan

On the other hand, Japanese syllables are pronounced with more or less equal length and stress. Although some syllables are given more prominence, this has more to do with pitch than stress. Therefore, Japanese accent is called PITCH ACCENT.

2.2.3 Pitch Levels

For the purpose of this book two levels of pitch will be discussed, namely HIGHER PITCH and LOWER PITCH. They are not absolute pitch levels. They are higher or lower, relative to each other. Within one accent unit, syllables with higher pitch level will be marked by a horizontal bar over them.

> yoofuku   den'wa

When there is a fall in pitch within one accent unit, a small superscript hook symbol will be attached to the end of the horizontal bar over the higher pitched level syllables. Any word with such a hook is called an accented word. Conversely, any word without such a hook is called an unaccented word.

tatemono   chookyori den'wa

However, when there is no fall in pitch within one accent unit, the superscript hook will not be attached to the superscript bar.

yoofuku   den'wa

2.2.4 Tokyo Pitch

In Tōkyō, pitch levels in one accent unit are governed by the following two conventions:

(1) the pitch level of the first syllable must be different from that of the second syllable. Therefore, if the first syllable is higher in pitch, the second must be lower, and vice versa;
(2) within one accent unit, whether it is a word, a phrase, or a clause, higher-pitched syllables can never be interrupted by any lower-pitched syllable.

Thus:

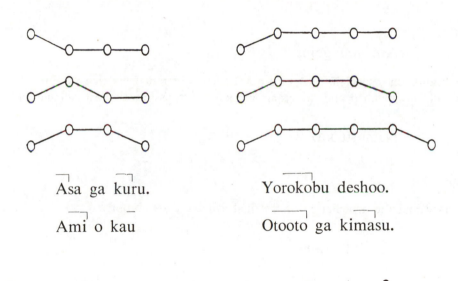

Asa ga kuru.   Yorokobu deshoo.

Ami o kau   Otooto ga kimasu.

But never

2.2.5 Accent Variation

Many accented words lose their accent when used with other words forming one accent unit. Conversely, many accented words gain the accent when used with other words forming one accent unit.

arigatoo + gozaimasu = arigatoo gozaimasu

kaki + kata = kakikata

2.2.6 Intonation

The following marks are applicable only to useful expressions and dialogs.

1. Period (.)

This mark indicates that the final syllable of an utterance is pronounced with falling intonation. This is used at the end of a statement, a proposition, or an indirect question.

Soo desu.

Kabukiza de aimashoo ka.

Soo shimashoo.

2. Rising Intonation (____/)

When a sentence or a phrase is uttered as a question or ends with a Sentence Particle *yo* or *ne,* etc., the final syllable is more or less pronounced in rising intonation.

English speakers tend to raise the pitch of the last several syllables or words in a gradually heightening pitch manner.

Are you going?

Thus, Japanese intonation, especially that of a question, is different from that of English. The syllable next to the last is usually low-pitched and the rising intonation creeps into the last syllable while it is produced.

Ikimasu ka/

3. Exclamation (!)

This mark indicates that the articulation of the final syllable ends abruptly.

Yamada san!

4. Comma (,)

A comma indicates a break within the utterance. Therefore, when you see a comma after a word, a phrase, or a clause, you can pause between the expression and the word following.

Hai, wakarimasu.

2.3 DRILLS

2.3.1 General Accent Drill

a. e .... E ga arimasu.   tomodachi .... Tomodachi ni au.

   uchi .... Uchi ga arimasu.   murasakiiro .... Murasakiiro no hana

   unagi .... Unagi o taberu.

b. e .... E ga arimasu.   yoi .... Yoi deshoo.

   asa .... Asa ga suki desu.   Fujisan .... Fujisan ga mieru.

c. ike .... Ike ga aru.   okaasan .... Okaasan ni iimasu.

   aoi .... Aoi iro desu.   uma .... Uma ni norimasu.

d. otoko .... Otoko ga imasu.   yorokobu .... Yorokobu deshoo.

   ureshii .... Ureshii desu.   kodomotachi .... Kodomotachi ga kimasu.

e. otooto .... Otooto deshita.   hazukashii .... Hazukashii desu.

   dokukeshi .... Dokukeshi o nomu.   atatakai .... Atatakai tokoro.

2.3.2 General Intonation Drill

a. Ohayoo gozaimasu.   Gomen nasai.   Itadakimasu.

   Sayoonara.   Gomen kudasai.   Onegai shimasu.

   Oyasumi nasai.   Okaeri nasai.   Omedetoo gozaimasu.

b. Soo desu ka /   Ikimasen ka /   Moo naraimashita ne /   Gakkoo desu ne /

   Ogen'ki desu ka /   Doko e ikimasu ka /   Soo desu ne /   Moshi moshi /

c. A!   Moshi moshi!   Kon'nichi wa!

   Sayoonara!   Soo desu yo!

d. Gochisoo sama   Kon'ban wa   Irasshai

   Tadaima   Iie   Kon'nichi wa

2.3.3 Contrastive Word Accent Drill

(The instructor may indicate the difference in meaning.)

ika	. . . .	ika	ichi	. . . .	ichi
uki	. . . .	uki	tsuma	. . . .	tsuma
kaki	. . . .	kaki	kami	. . . .	kami
yooki	. . . .	yooki	kame	. . . .	kame
sake	. . . .	sake	kiri	. . . .	kiri
asa	. . . .	asa	iji	. . . .	iji
ishi	. . . .	ishi	igai	. . . .	igai
hashi	. . . .	hashi	suzu	. . . .	suzu
kachi	. . . .	kachi	tabi	. . . .	tabi

2.3.4 Contrastive Sentence Accent Drill

(The instructor may indicate the difference in meaning.)

a. E o mochimasu. . . . . E o mochimasu.

b. Kaki o tabemasu. . . . . Kaki o tabemasu.

c. Sake desu ne / . . . . Sake desu ne /

d. Kame desu ka / . . . . Kame desu ka /

e. Atsui mono desu. . . . . Atsui mono desu.

f. Hana ga akai . . . . Hana ga akai

g. Kono hashi desu. . . . . Kono hashi desu.

h. Kore o kaite kudasai. . . . . Kore o kaite kudasai.

i. Otte kudasai. . . . . Otte kudasai.

j. Fuite kudasai. . . . . Fuite kudasai.

k. Yon'de kudasai. . . . . Yon'de kudasai.

l. Harete kimashita ne / . . . . Harete kimashita ne /

m. Kite kudasai. .... Kite kudasai.

n. Ima desu ka / .... Ima desu ka /

o. Koori o kaimasu. .... Koori o kaimasu.

2.3.5 Contrastive Intonation Drill

a. Soo desu ka.   Soo desu ka /

b. Soo desu ne /   Soo desu ne.   Soo desu nee.

c. Soo desu yo.   Soo desu yo /

d. Moshi moshi.   Moshi moshi /   Moshi moshi !

e. Kabukiza deshoo.   Kabukiza deshoo /

f. Goji han goro aimashoo ka.   Goji han goro aimashoo ka /

g. Ikeda san   Ikeda san !

2.4 EXERCISES

2.4.1 Accent

In each group, three words or expressions will be pronounced by your instructor. Two types are included in this exercise:

(A) In some groups two words or expressions are identical, while (B) in other groups three words are identical.

Write on your paper the numbers representing the identical items.

Example :   A. (1) ika   (2) ika   (3) ika

Write on your paper :   (1)   (2)

Example :   B. (1) sake   (2) sake   (3) sake

Write on your paper :   (1)   (2)   (3)

  Note: The following list is for the use of the instructor. It is suggested that he change the word order or create
       new lists to make this exercise effective.

a. (1) ishi   (2) ishi   (3) ishi

b. (1) maku   (2) maku   (3) maku

c. (1) asa   (2) asa   (3) asa

d. (1) hashi   (2) hashi   (3) hashi

e. (1) ichi   (2) ichi   (3) ichi

f. (1) kame   (2) kame   (3) kame

g. (1) toshi   (2) toshi   (3) toshi

h. (1) suru   (2) suru   (3) suru

i. (1) Kaki ga arimasu yo.   (2) Kaki ga arimasu yo.   (3) Kaki ga arimasu yo.

j. (1) Atsui mono desu.   (2) Atsui mono desu.   (3) Atsui mono desu.

k. (1) Kame desu.   (2) Kame desu.   (3) Kame desu.

. (1) Yon'de kudasai.   (2) Yon'de kudasai.   (3) Yon'de kudasai.

m. (1) Kite kudasai.   (2) Kite kudasai.   (3) Kite kudasai.

n. (1) Ki ga tsukimashita.   (2) Ki ga tsukimashita.   (3) Ki ga tsukimashita.

o. (1) Ima desu ka /   (2) Ima desu ka /   (3) Ima desu ka /

2.4.2 Accent

One of the two words or expressions listed in each group will be pronounced by your instructor. Listen and check the right one with "X."

a. (1) uki   (2) uki

b. (1) kaki   (2) kaki

c. (1) kami   (2) kami

d. (1) suzu   (2) suzu

e. (1) tabi   (2) tabi

f. (1) Nihon desu ka /   (2) Nihon desu ka /

g. (1) Otte kudasai.   (2) Otte kudasai.

h. (1) Kono hashi desu.   (2) Kono hashi desu.

i. (1) Dare ga matte imasu ka /   (2) Dare ga matte imasu ka /

j. (1) Nani o katte imasu ka /   (2) Nani o katte imasu ka /

2.4.3 Intonation

One of the two words or expressions listed in each group will be pronounced by your instructor. Listen and check the right one with "X."

a. (1) Soo desu ka.   (2) Soo desu ka /

b. (1) Kirei desu yo /   (2) Kirei desu yo.

c. (1) A.   (2) A !

d. (1) Dooshite /   (2) Dooshite.

e. (1) Yoku wakarimashita ne /   (2) Yoku wakarimashita nee.

LESSON 3

3.1 USEFUL EXPRESSIONS

Itte (i)rasshai.

"Hurry back." This expression is used when seeing someone off. Literally this means "Go and come back." *Itte irasshai* is often contracted to *Itte rasshai*. In polite speech *Itte (i)rasshaimase* may be heard.

Itte mairimasu.

"I'm going." This expression is used by a person who is leaving, in reply to the above expression *Itte (i)rasshai*, and vice versa. Literally this means "I am going and will come back."

3.2 DIALOG

— After class, leaving the classroom —

Mr. Yamada : Ishii san,*1 sugu*2 uchi e*3 kaerimasu*4 ka*5*6/

Miss Ishii : Iie,*7 sugu kaerimasen.*8

Mr. Yamada : Doko*9 e ikimasu*10 ka /

Miss Ishii : Kan'da e ikimasu.

Mr. Yamada : Kan'da e*11/

Miss Ishii : Ee,*7 hon o*12 kaimasu.

Mr. Yamada : Sore kara, nani*9 o shimasu ka /

Miss Ishii : Resutoran de*13 gohan o tabemasu. Soshite, uchi e kaerimasu.

Anata wa*14/

Mr. Yamada : Sugu uchi e kaerimasu.

Miss Ishii : Ashita*15 gakkoo e kimasu*10 ka /

Mr. Yamada : Ee, mainichi*15 kimasu. Jaa, itte irasshai.

Miss Ishii : Itte mairimasu.

3.3 PATTERN SENTENCES

3.3.1

N	R
Gohan	o

*3.4.16

V	(SP)
tabemasu	ka

$\longrightarrow$

"Are [you] going to have a meal?"

3.3.2

N	R
Uchi	e

$\longrightarrow$

V
kaerimasen

"[I] am not going back home."

3.4 NOTES

3.4.1 The -san* in *Ishii san* is a dependent Nominative attached to a family name or to the first name of someone else. With a family name it may mean either Mr., Mrs., or Miss. Note also that in Japanese one's family name is always said first.

Yamada san	"Mr., Mrs., or Miss Yamada"
Ikuo san	"Ikuo" (male's first name)
Yamada Ikuo san	"Mr. Ikuo Yamada"

Do not use the -san with your name.

* A hyphen before or after a word indicates that the word is used dependently.

3.4.2 *Sugu* is an Adverb meaning "soon." The use of Adverbs will be explained in Note 7.4.1.

Sugu uchi e kaerimasu ka ?	"Are [you] going [back] home soon?"
Sugu gohan o tabemasen.	"[I] am not going to have a meal right away."

3.4.3 The *e* is a Relational that denotes direction, and is equivalent to the English Preposition "to" as in "to (a place)." It follows a place Nominative or a Nominative that may indicate a place. The place Nominative followed by *e* formulates a Predicate Modifier that modifies a Predicate following. The Predicate following this Predicate Modifier is always a verbal Predicate, and particularly that of motion Verbs, such as *ikimasu* "go," *kimasu* "come," *kaerimasu* "go (come) back," etc.

motion Verb ⟶ place Nominative + *e* + motion Verb

$$\left.\begin{array}{l}\text{ikimasu}\\\text{kimasu}\\\text{kaerimasu}\end{array}\right\} \longrightarrow \left.\begin{array}{l}\text{Amerika}\\\text{Nihon}\\\text{Hawai}\\\text{Tookyoo}\\\text{Gin'za}\\\text{Kan'da}\\\text{gakkoo}\\\text{uchi}\end{array}\right\} + e + \left\{\begin{array}{l}\text{ikimasu}\\\text{kimasu}\\\text{kaerimasu}\end{array}\right.$$

Uchi e kaerimasu.	"[I] am going [back] home."
Gin'za e ikimasu.	"[I] am going to the Ginza."
Nihon e kimasu.	"[He] is coming to Japan."

3.4.4 The *-masu* as in *kaerimasu* occurs in a normal style statement as the affirmative imperfect* tense form ending of a verbal Predicate. The *-masu* is a verbal Derivative and represents either a future action or a habitual action, depending on the circumstance. With such time expressions as *ashita* "tomorrow," *kaerimasu* means "[I] am going back," or "[I] will go back," and *kaerimasu* with *mainichi* "every day" will mean "[I] go back" as a habitual action.

Ashita uchi e kaerimasu.	"[I] am going [back] home tomorrow."
Mainichi uchi e kaerimasu.	"[I] go [back] home every day."
Ashita gakkoo e ikimasu.	"[I] am going to school tomorrow."
Mainichi gakkoo e ikimasu.	"[I] go to school every day."

* The imperfect tense form (some books call it the present tense) shows that an action has not been completed. The perfect tense form (some books call it the past tense) means that the action has been completed. More details will be explained later.

3.4.5 In changing a statement into a question, it is not necessary in Japanese to change the word order as one does in English. The addition of the Sentence Particle *ka* to the end of a statement turns it into an interrogative sentence.

Predicate ⟶ Predicate + *ka* ?

Uchi e kaerimasu.   ⟶   Uchi e kaerimasu ka ?

  "[I] am going home."   "Are [you] going home ?"

Gin'za e ikimasu.   ⟶   Gin'za e ikimasu ka ?

  "[I] am going to the Ginza."   "Are [you] going to the Ginza ?"

3.4.6 In Japanese the subject of a sentence such as "I," "you," "he," "she," etc., is optional: it may be expressed, or it may be omitted when it is understood. *Ikimasu* may be either "I go," "You go," "He goes," etc., and the situation usually makes it clear which person the speaker is referring to.

3.4.7 In most cases the Sentence Interjective *iie* corresponds to "no" and *ee* to "yes." *Ee* has a more formal equivalent, *hai*. *Ee* is more commonly used than *hai* in conversation, but *hai* should be used to answer a knock at the door or the calling of one's name.

Uchi e kaerimasu ka ?　　　　"Are [you] going [back] home?"

Ee, (uchi e) kaerimasu.　　　"Yes, [I] am going [back] (home)."

Iie, (uchi e) kaerimasen.　　　"No, [I] am not going [back] (home)."

Teacher :　Yamada san !　　　"Mr. Yamada!"

Yamada :　Hai !　　　　　　"Yes!"

The different uses of *ee* and *iie* will be explained in Note 9.4.3.

3.4.8 The *-masen* in *kaerimasen* is the negative of *-masu*, which has been introduced in Note 3.4.4. The *-masen* also represents either a future action or a habitual action.

Verb(-*masu*) ⟶ Verb(-*masen*)

Uchi e kaerimasu.　　　⟶　Uchi e kaerimasen.

　"[I] am going [back] home."　　　"[I] am not going [back] home."

Nihon e kimasu.　　　⟶　Nihon e kimasen.

　"[He] will come to Japan."　　　"[He] will not come to Japan."

3.4.9 *Doko* "what place?" and *nani* "what?" are interrogative Nominatives. An interrogative sentence with an interrogative Nominative is formed by replacing a Nominative with a corresponding interrogative Nominative.

Nominative + Relational + Predicate + *ka* ? → interrogative Nominative + Relational + Predicate + *ka* ?

Gakkoo e ikimasu ka ?　　⟶　*Doko* e ikimasu ka ?

　"Are [you] going to school?"　　　"Where are [you] going?"

Ten'pura o tabemasu ka ?　⟶　*Nani* o tabemasu ka ?

　"Are [you] going to eat *tempura*?"　　　"What are [you] going to eat?"

3.4.10 The use of *ikimasu* and *kimasu* is a little different from that of English "go," and "come." *Ikimasu* means motion away from the speaker's position, and *kimasu* always means motion toward the speaker. Therefore, "I will come to (your) house" will be (*Anata no*) *uchi e ikimasu*, when the speaker is not at the house, but if he is there, he should say (*Anata no*) *uchi e kimasu.*

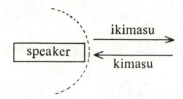

Kaerimasu, however, may mean either "go back" or "come back."

3.4.11 In speaking Japanese, as with English, you may sometimes repeat part of the other speaker's speech with rising intonation when you get unexpected information, or you can use just part of a sentence when the rest of the sentence is understood.

Gin'za e ikimasu.	"[I] am going to the Ginza."
Gin'za e ?	"To the Ginza?"
Ashita Amerika e ikimasu.	"[I] am going to the States tomorrow."
Ashita ?	"Tomorrow?"
Amerika e ?	"To the States?"

3.4.12 Verbs such as *ikimasu* "go," *kaerimasu* "go back," *kimasu* "come" normally occur with the direction Relational *e* "to," according to the nature of the Verbs. Likewise, there are Verbs that normally occur with the Relational *o*, and they will be called transitive Verbs. The Relational *o* presented in this lesson indicates that the preceding Nominative is the direct object of a transitive Verb, such as *kaimasu* "buy," *shimasu* "do," *nomimasu* "drink," *tabemasu* "eat," etc.

transitive Verb ⟶ Nominative + *o* + transitive Verb
  (object)

tabemasu
nomimasu
kaimasu   ⟶ OBJECT + o +   tabemasu
shimasu   nomimasu
                               kaimasu
                               shimasu

Taipuraitaa o kaimasu.	"[I] am going to buy a typewriter."
Nani o shimasu ka ?	"What are [you] going to do?"
Mizu o nomimasu.	"[I] will drink water."
Ten'pura o tabemasu ka ?	"Are [you] going to eat *tempura*?"

Note that some Japanese transitive Verbs do not correspond to English transitive verbs, and vice versa. Those Verbs will be noted when they appear.

3.4.13 A place Nominative followed by the Relational *de* indicates the place where an action takes place.

This Relational will be explained in Note 4.4.8.

Resutoran de gohan o tabemasu.   "[I]" am going to have a meal at a restaurant."

Gin'za de kamera o kaimasu.   "[I] am going to buy a camera at the Ginza."

3.4.14 *Anata wa?* means "How about you?" *Anata wa doko e ikimasu ka?* has been shortened because *doko e ikimasu ka?* is understood. The use of *wa* will be explained in Note 5.4.3.

3.4.15 The use of such time Nominatives as *ashita* "tomorrow," *mainichi* "every day," and *kyoo* "today" will be explained in Note 9.4.1.

Ashita gakkoo e kimasu ka ?   "Are [you] coming to school tomorrow?"

Mainichi ikimasu.   "[I] go [there] every day."

Kyoo jisho o kaimasu.   "[I] am going to buy a dictionary today."

3.4.16 As you see in the PATTERN SENTENCES, a Predicate in Japanese occurs at the end of a sentence, and Predicate Modifiers such as *gohan o* precede the Predicate.

3.5 VOCABULARY

Dialog

Yamada	. . . .	N	family name
Ishii	. . . .	N	family name
-san	. . . .	Nd	Mr.; Mrs.; Miss (see 3.4.1)
sugu	. . . .	Adv.	soon (see 3.4.2)
uchi	. . . .	N	home; house
e	. . . .	R	to (a place) (see 3.4.3)
kaerimasu	. . . .	V	go back; come back (normal form of *kaeru*)
ka	. . . .	SP	(see 3.4.5)
iie	. . . .	SI	no (see 3.4.7)
kaerimasen	. . . .	V	do not go (come) back (negative of *kaerimasu* ⟵ *kaeru*)
doko	. . . .	Ni	what place?; where?
ikimasu	. . . .	V	go (normal form of *iku*)
Kan'da	. . . .	N	Kanda Street or book center of Tōkyō
ee	. . . .	SI	yes (see 3.4.7)
hon	. . . .	N	book
o	. . . .	R	(see 3.4.12)

kaimasu	....	V	buy (normal form of *kau*)
sore kara	....	SI	afterward; and (then)
nani	....	Ni	what? (see 3.4.9)
shimasu	....	V	do (normal form of *suru*)
resutoran	....	N	restaurant
de	....	R	(see 3.4.13)
gohan	....	N	meal; boiled rice
tabemasu	....	V	eat (normal form of *taberu*)
soshite	....	SI	and
anata	....	N	you
wa	....	R	(see 3.4.14)
ashita	....	N	tomorrow (see 3.4.15)
gakkoo	....	N	school
kimasu	....	V	come (normal form of *kuru*)
mainichi	....	N	every day
jaa	....	SI	well

Notes

Ikuo	....	N	boy's first name
Amerika	....	N	the United States of America; America
Nihon	....	N	Japan
Hawai	....	N	Hawaii
Tookyoo	....	N	capital of Japan
Gin'za	....	N	Ginza Street or a shopping center of Tōkyō
-masu	....	Dv	(see 3.4.4)
hai	....	SI	yes (formal equivalent of *ee*) (see 3.4.7)
-masen	....	Dv	(see 3.4.8)
kimasen	....	V	do not come (negative of *kimasu* ⟵ *kuru*)
ten'pura	....	N	*tempura*; Japanese fry; fritter
nomimasu	....	V	drink (normal form of *nomu*)
taipuraitaa	....	N	typewriter
mizu	....	N	water
kamera	....	N	camera
kyoo	....	N	today
jisho	....	N	dictionary

Drills

koohii	....	N	coffee

bifuteki	. . . .	N	beefsteak
gyuunyuu	. . . .	N	cow's milk
ocha	. . . .	N	(green) tea
pan	. . . .	N	bread
biiru	. . . .	N	beer

3.6 HIRAGANA PRACTICE

3.6.1 Recognize the difference or similarity between two *hiragana* in each of the following pairs:

へ·····へ   く·····ん   く·····し   い·····い
へ·····く   つ·····つ   て·····ん   り·····い
つ·····へ   つ·····て   ん·····ん   り·····り
く·····く   て·····て   し·····ん   り·····こ
て·····く   し·····し   こ·····こ
つ·····く   し·····つ   い·····こ

3.6.2 Practice writing the following *hiragana*:

1. へ [he] へ へ へ
2. く [ku] く く く
3. つ [tsu] つ つ つ
4. て [te] て て て
5. ん [n'] ん ん ん ん
6. し [shi] し し し
7. こ [ko] こ こ こ
8. い [i] い い い
9. り [ri] り り り

3.7 DRILLS

3.7.1 Pronunciation Drill

kaerimasu	taipuraitaa	sore kara	resutoran	Itte irasshai.
Amerika	kamera	ten'pura	Itte mairimasu.	

3.7.2 Pattern Drill

1. Sugu uchi e kaerimasu ka?
2. Iie, sugu kaerimasen.
3. Doko e ikimasu ka?
4. Kan'da e ikimasu.
5. Hon o kaimasu.
6. Nani o shimasu ka?
7. Resutoran de gohan o tabemasu.
8. Ashita gakkoo e kimasu ka?
9. Ee, mainichi kimasu.

3.7.3 Response Drill (negative response)

1. Gin'za e *ikimasu* ka? .... *Iie, ikimasen.*
2. Koohii o nomimasu ka? .... Iie, nomimasen.
3. Gakkoo e kimasu ka? .... Iie, kimasen.
4. Amerika e kaerimasu ka?... Iie, kaerimasen.
5. Jisho o kaimasu ka? .... Iie, kaimasen.
6. Nihon e kimasu ka? .... Iie, kimasen.
7. Mizu o nomimasu ka? .... Iie, nomimasen.
8. Uchi e kaerimasu ka? .... Iie, kaerimasen.
9. Bifuteki o tabemasu ka?... Iie, tabemasen.
10. Gakkoo e ikimasu ka? .... Iie, ikimasen.
11. Hon o kaimasu ka? .... Iie, kaimasen.
12. Gohan o tabemasu ka?.... Iie, tabemasen.

3.7.4 Transformation Drill (statement ⟶ question)

1. Uchi e kaerimasu. ⟶ Uchi e kaerimasu *ka*?
2. Gohan o tabemasu. ⟶ Gohan o tabemasu ka?
3. Nihon e ikimasu. ⟶ Nihon e ikimasu ka?
4. Hon o kaimasu. ⟶ Hon o kaimasu ka?
5. Gakkoo e ikimasu. ⟶ Gakkoo e ikimasu ka?
6. Koohii o nomimasu. ⟶ Koohii o nomimasu ka?
7. Bifuteki o tabemasu. ⟶ Bifuteki o tabemasu ka?
8. Amerika e kimasu. ⟶ Amerika e kimasu ka?
9. Mizu o nomimasu. ⟶ Mizu o nomimasu ka?
10. Nihon e kimasu. ⟶ Nihon e kimasu ka?
11. Jisho o kaimasu. ⟶ Jisho o kaimasu ka?
12. Gin'za e ikimasu. ⟶ Gin'za e ikimasu ka?
13. Gakkoo e kaerimasu. ⟶ Gakkoo e kaerimasu ka?

36

3.7.5 Transformation Drill (N ⟶ Ni)

1. *Gakkoo* e ikimasu. ⟶ *Doko* e ikimasu ka?
2. Bifuteki o tabemasu. ⟶ *Nani* o tabemasu ka?
3. Gyuunyuu o nomimasu. ⟶ Nani o nomimasu ka?
4. Uchi e kaerimasu. ⟶ Doko e kaerimasu ka?
5. Jisho o kaimasu. ⟶ Nani o kaimasu ka?
6. Uchi e kimasu. ⟶ Doko e kimasu ka?
7. Koohii o nomimasu. ⟶ Nani o nomimasu ka?
8. Ten'pura o tabemasu. ⟶ Nani o tabemasu ka?
9. Amerika e kaerimasu. ⟶ Doko e kaerimasu ka?
10. Nihon e ikimasu. ⟶ Doko e ikimasu ka?
11. Hon o kaimasu. ⟶ Nani o kaimasu ka?
12. Ocha o nomimasu. ⟶ Nani o nomimasu ka?
13. Gakkoo e kimasu. ⟶ Doko e kimasu ka?

3.7.6 Substitution Drill

Gakkoo e *ikimasu.*

1. *Tookyoo* ....*Tookyoo* e ikimasu.
2. *kimasu* ....Tookyoo e *kimasu.*
3. uchi ....Uchi e kimasu.
4. kaerimasu ....Uchi e kaerimasu.
5. Nihon ....Nihon e kaerimasu.
6. ikimasu ....Nihon e ikimasu.
7. ikimasen ....Nihon e ikimasen.
8. gakkoo ....Gakkoo e ikimasen.
9. kimasen ....Gakkoo e kimasen.
10. Amerika ....Amerika e kimasen.
11. kaerimasen ....Amerika e kaerimasen.
12. uchi ....Uchi e kaerimasen.
13. ikimasu ka? ....Uchi e ikimasu ka?
14. Tookyoo ....Tookyoo e ikimasu ka?
15. kimasu ka? ....Tookyoo e kimasu ka?
16. uchi ....Uchi e kimasu ka?
17. kaerimasu ka? ....Uchi e kaerimasu ka?
18. Nihon ....Nihon e kaerimasu ka?
19. doko ....Doko e kaerimasu ka?
20. ikimasu ka? ....Doko e ikimasu ka?

3.7.7 Substitution Drill

Jisho o *kaimasu.*

1. *pan* ......Pan o kaimasu.
2. koohii ......Koohii o kaimasu.
3. nomimasu ......Koohii o nomimasu.
4. mizu ......Mizu o nomimasu.
5. nomimasen ......Mizu o nomimasen.
6. ocha ......Ocha o nomimasen.

7. kaimasen	......Ocha o kaimasen.	13. tabemasu ka?	......Gohan o tabemasu ka?
8. ten'pura	......Ten'pura o kaimasen.	14. nani	......Nani o tabemasu ka?
9. tabemasu	......Ten'pura o tabemasu.	15. nomimasu ka?	......Nani o nomimasu ka?
10. bifuteki	......Bifuteki o tabemasu.	16. kaimasu ka?	......Nani o kaimasu ka?
11. tabemasen	......Bifuteki o tabemasen.	17. shimasu ka?	......Nani o shimasu ka?
12. gohan	......Gohan o tabemasen.		

3.7.8 Response Drill

1. Kyoo doko e ikimasu ka? / Tookyoo ...... (Kyoo) Tookyoo e ikimasu.

2. Koohii o nomimasu ka? / ee ...... Ee, (koohii o) nomimasu.

3. Nani o tabemasu ka? / ten'pura ...... Ten'pura o tabemasu.

4. Mainichi gakkoo e kimasu ka? / ee ...... Ee, (mainichi gakkoo e) kimasu.

5. Ashita uchi e kaerimasu ka? / iie ...... Iie, (ashita uchi e) kaerimasen.

6. Nani o kaimasu ka? / hon ...... Hon o kaimasu.

7. Ashita kimasu ka? / iie ...... Iie, (ashita) kimasen.

8. Amerika e kaerimasu ka? / iie ...... Iie, (Amerika e) kaerimasen.

9. Kyoo nani o shimasu ka? / gakkoo e ikimasu ...... (Kyoo) gakkoo e ikimasu.

10. Nani o nomimasu ka? / mizu ...... Mizu o nomimasu.

11. Doko e ikimasu ka? / uchi ...... Uchi e ikimasu.

3.7.9 Expansion Drill

1. Ikimasu. ...... Ikimasu.

    Kan'da e ...... Kan'da e ikimasu.

    ashita ...... Ashita Kan'da e ikimasu.

2. Tabemasen. ...... Tabemasen.

    gohan o ...... Gohan o tabemasen.

    kyoo ...... Kyoo gohan o tabemasen.

3. Ikimasu ka ? ...... Ikimasu ka ?

    doko e ...... Doko e ikimasu ka ?

    mainichi ...... Mainichi doko e ikimasu ka ?

4. Kaimasu ka ? ...... Kaimasu ka ?

nani o   ..... Nani o kaimasu ka?

kyoo   ..... Kyoo nani o kaimasu ka?

5. Kaerimasen. ..... Kaerimasen.

uchi e   ..... Uchi e kaerimasen.

kyoo   ..... Kyoo uchi e kaerimasen.

6. Kimasu ka? ..... Kimasu ka?

gakkoo e   ..... Gakkoo e kimasu ka?

mainichi   ..... Mainichi gakkoo e kimasu ka?

7. Shimasu ka? ..... Shimasu ka?

nani o   ..... Nani o shimasu ka?

ashita   ..... Ashita nani o shimasu ka?

8. Nomimasu. ..... Nomimasu.

biiru o   ..... Biiru o nomimasu.

mainichi   ..... Mainichi biiru o nomimasu.

3.7.10 Relational Checking Drill

1. Tookyoo, ikimasu ... Tookyoo e ikimasu.

2. mizu, nomimasu .... Mizu o nomimasu.

3. uchi, kaerimasen .... Uchi e kaerimasen.

4. nani, shimasu ka? ... Nani o shimasu ka?

5. gohan, tabemasu .... Gohan o tabemasu.

6. doko, ikimasu ka? ... Doko e ikimasu ka?

7. jisho, kaimasu   .... Jisho o kaimasu.

8. ocha, nomimasu ka? .. Ocha o nomimasu ka?

9. uchi, kimasen   .... Uchi e kimasen.

10. nani, tabemasu ka? .. Nani o tabemasu ka?

11. kamera, kaimasen ... Kamera o kaimasen.

12. doko, kaerimasu ka?.. Doko e kaerimasu ka?

13. Hawai, ikimasen .... Hawai e ikimasen.

3.7.11 Combination Drill (*sore kara*)

1. Tookyoo e ikimasu.
   Uchi e kaerimasu.   } ⟶ Tookyoo e ikimasu. Sore kara, uchi e kaerimasu.

2. Gohan o tabemasu.
   Gakkoo e ikimasu.   } ⟶ Gohan o tabemasu. Sore kara, gakkoo e ikimasu.

3. Amerika e ikimasu.
   Nihon e kimasu.   } ⟶ Amerika e ikimasu. Sore kara, Nihon e kimasu.

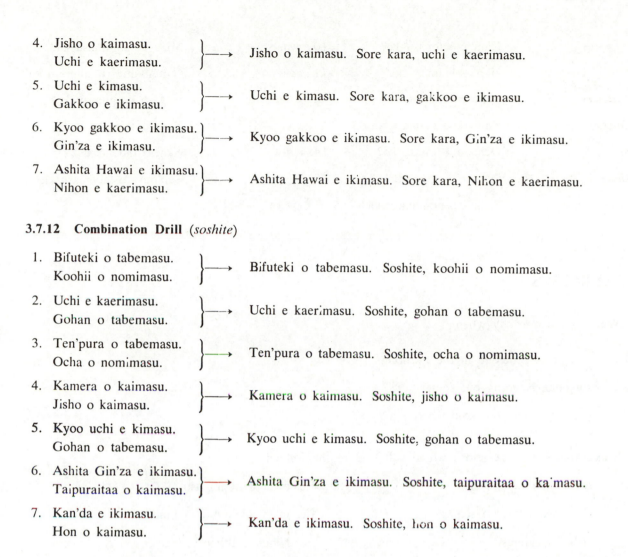

4. Jisho o kaimasu.
   Uchi e kaerimasu. }⟶ Jisho o kaimasu. Sore kara, uchi e kaerimasu.

5. Uchi e kimasu.
   Gakkoo e ikimasu. }⟶ Uchi e kimasu. Sore kara, gakkoo e ikimasu.

6. Kyoo gakkoo e ikimasu.
   Gin'za e ikimasu. }⟶ Kyoo gakkoo e ikimasu. Sore kara, Gin'za e ikimasu.

7. Ashita Hawai e ikimasu.
   Nihon e kaerimasu. }⟶ Ashita Hawai e ikimasu. Sore kara, Nihon e kaerimasu.

3.7.12 Combination Drill (*soshite*)

1. Bifuteki o tabemasu.
   Koohii o nomimasu. }⟶ Bifuteki o tabemasu. Soshite, koohii o nomimasu.

2. Uchi e kaerimasu.
   Gohan o tabemasu. }⟶ Uchi e kaerimasu. Soshite, gohan o tabemasu.

3. Ten'pura o tabemasu.
   Ocha o nomimasu. }⟶ Ten'pura o tabemasu. Soshite, ocha o nomimasu.

4. Kamera o kaimasu.
   Jisho o kaimasu. }⟶ Kamera o kaimasu. Soshite, jisho o kaimasu.

5. Kyoo uchi e kimasu.
   Gohan o tabemasu. }⟶ Kyoo uchi e kimasu. Soshite, gohan o tabemasu.

6. Ashita Gin'za e ikimasu.
   Taipuraitaa o kaimasu. }⟶ Ashita Gin'za e ikimasu. Soshite, taipuraitaa o kaimasu.

7. Kan'da e ikimasu.
   Hon o kaimasu. }⟶ Kan'da e ikimasu. Soshite, hon o kaimasu.

3.7.13 E-J Substitution Drill

Gakkoo e *ikimasu* ka?

1. *to the States* . . . . . . Amerika e ikimasu ka?
2. *return* . . . . . . Amerika e kaerimasu ka?
3. *home* . . . . . . Uchi e kaerimasu ka?
4. *come* . . . . . . Uchi e kimasu ka?
5. *go* . . . . . . Uchi e ikimasu ka?
6. *to Hawaii* . . . . . . Hawai e ikimasu ka?
7. *to Japan* . . . . . . Nihon e ikimasu ka?

8. *return* . . . . . . Nihon e kaerimasu ka?
9. *to Tōkyō* . . . . . Tookyoo e kaerimasu ka?
10. *come* . . . . . . Tookyoo e kimasu ka?
11. *to the Ginza* . . . . . Gin'za e kimasu ka?
12. *where* . . . . . . Doko e kimasu ka?
13. *go* . . . . . . Doko e ikimasu ka?
14. *return* . . . . . . Doko e kaerimasu ka?

3.7.14 E-J Substitution Drill

Gohan o *tabemasu* ka?

1. *beefsteak* . . . . . . Bifuteki o tabemasu ka?   2. *what* . . . . . . Nani o tabemasu ka?

3. *buy*	......	Nani o kaimasu ka?	10. *water*	...... Mizu o nomimasu ka?
4. *book*	......	Hon o kaimasu ka?	11. *cow's milk*	...... Gyuunyuu o nomimasu ka?
5. *dictionary*	......	Jisho o kaimasu ka?	12. *what*	...... Nani o nomimasu ka?
6. *camera*	......	Kamera o kaimasu ka?	13. *do*	...... Nani o shimasu ka?
7. *tea*	......	Ocha o kaimasu ka?	14. *eat*	...... Nani o tabemasu ka?
8. *drink*	......	Ocha o nomimasu ka?	15. *tempura*	...... Ten'pura o tabemasu ka?
9. *coffee*	......	Koohii o nomimasu ka?		

3.8   EXERCISES

3.8.1   What would you say when :

1. you greet someone in the morning ?

2. someone is going out somewhere ?

3. you are going out somewhere ?

3.8.2   Make appropriate questions which will lead to the following answers :

1. Bifuteki o tabemasu.

2. Iie, uchi e kaerimasen.

3. Jisho o kaimasu.

4. Gakkoo e ikimasu.

5. Ee, ocha o nomimasu.

6. Iie, mainichi koohii o nomimasu.

7. Ee, Nihon e ikimasu.

8. Iie, kaimasen.

3.8.3   Insert an appropriate item in each of the following blanks :

1. Doko (   ) kimasu (   ) ?

2. Ocha (   ) nomimasu.

3. Amerika (   ) kaerimasen.

4. Uchi (   ) kaerimasu. (   ), Tookyoo (   ) ikimasu.

5. Nani (   ) shimasu (   ) ?

3.8.4   Carry on the following conversations in Japanese :

1. Ishii: Good morning.

   Yamada: Good morning.

   Ishii: Where are you going today?

Yamada: I am going to Tōkyō. And, I am going to buy a dictionary.

Ishii: After that, what are you going to do?

Yamada: I am going home. How about you?

Ishii: I am going to school today.

2. Ishii: Are you going to have a meal?

Yamada: Yes, I am.

Ishii: What are you going to eat?

Yamada: I am going to eat *tempura*. And, I will drink tea. How about you?

Ishii: I will have beefsteak.

Yamada: Are you going to drink tea?

Ishii: No, I am not. I will drink coffee.

3.8.5 Answer the following questions in Japanese :

1. Ashita gakkoo e ikimasu ka ?

2. Sugu uchi e kaerimasu ka ?

3. Nani o tabemasu ka ?

4. Ocha o nomimasu ka ?

5. Kyoo hon o kaimasu ka ?

6. Doko e ikimasu ka ?

7. Nani o shimasu ka ?

LESSON 4

4.1 USEFUL EXPRESSIONS

Chotto shitsurei.	"Excuse me for a moment." The expression at full length is *Chotto shitsurei shimasu.*
Omachidoo sama	"Sorry to have kept you waiting." The expression at full length is *Omachidoo sama deshita.*
Soo desu ka /	"Is that so?" "Really?" This is one of the expressions used most frequently among Japanese. According to the intonation or situation, this expression is interpreted in various ways.

4.2 DIALOG

— On the street —

Mr. Ueki: Kono hen*1 ni*2 den'wa ga*3 arimasu*4 ka /

Mr. Suzuki: Asoko*5 ni arimasu yo*6 /

Mr. Ueki: Jaa, chotto shitsurei. Sugu kimasu.

....

Mr. Ueki: Omachidoo sama

Mr. Suzuki: Doo itashimashite. Jaa, ikimashoo*7 ka.

Mr. Ueki: Ee, ikimashoo. A, soko ni Yamada san ga imasu*4 yo /

Yamada san, kon'nichi wa

Mr. Suzuki: Kon'nichi wa

Mr. Yamada: Kon'nichi wa

Mr. Ueki: Kinoo eki de*8 anata o mimashita*9 yo / Doko e ikimashita ka /

Mr. Yamada: Shin'juku e ikimashita. Soshite, depaato de kaimono*10 o shimashita.

Soosoo, depaato ni Keiko san to*11 Kazuko san ga imashita yo /

Mr. Ueki :   Soo desu ka /

Mr. Suzuki :   Yamada san, ima ohima*12 ga arimasu*13 ka /

Mr. Yamada : Ee.

Mr. Suzuki :   Ima Ueki san to Itoo san ga uchi e kimasu. Issho ni uchi de

               ban'gohan o tabemashoo.

Mr. Yamada : Ee, arigatoo.

4.3 PATTERN SENTENCES

4.3.1

N	R
Asoko	de

$\longrightarrow$

V
kaimashoo

"Let's buy [it] over there."

4.3.2

*4.4.14

N	R
Depaato	ni

N	R
Keiko san	ga

V
imashita

"Keiko was in the department store."

4.4 NOTES

4.4.1 *Kono hen* means "this vicinity," or "this area." The *-hen* is a dependent Nominative meaning "area." The use of *kono* "this" will be introduced in Note 7.4.2.

Kono hen ni den'wa ga arimasu ka ?   "Is there a telephone in this vicinity?"

Kono hen ni otearai ga arimasu ka ?   "Is there a rest room around here?"

4.4.2 The Relational *ni* used after a place Nominative is the Relational of location. A place Nominative followed by the Relational *ni* denotes the place where something or someone is situated or exists, and usually precedes a verbal expression of existence, living, staying, etc., that are all inactive.

Verb of existence ⟶ **place Nominative + *ni* + Verb of existence**

$$\left.\begin{matrix}\text{arimasu}\\\text{imasu}\end{matrix}\right\} \longrightarrow \left\{\begin{matrix}\text{gakkoo}\\\text{Tookyoo}\\\text{koko}\\\text{soko}\\\text{asoko}\\\text{kono hen}\end{matrix}\right\} + \text{ni} + \left\{\begin{matrix}\text{arimasu}\\\text{imasu}\end{matrix}\right. \quad \text{``is} \left\{\begin{matrix}\text{in school''}\\\text{in Tōkyō''}\\\text{here''}\\\text{there''}\\\text{over there''}\\\text{in this vicinity''}\end{matrix}\right.$$

Kono hen ni arimasu ka?   "Is [it] around here?"

Uchi ni arimasu.   "[It] is in [my] house."

Soko ni imasu.   "[Someone] is there."

Doko ni imasu ka?   "Where is [he]?"

See Note 4.4.4 about the difference between *arimasu* and *imasu*.

4.4.3 The Relational *ga* that stands after a Nominative is the subject Relational, and singles out the Nominative as the subject of the following Predicate. Note that the subject followed by *ga* is equally emphasized as the following Predicate. As for the topic subject, see Note 5.4.3.

Predicate ⟶ **Nominative + *ga* + Predicate**
             (subject)

A Predicate can be a Verb, an Adjective, or a Nominative plus the Copula.

Den'wa ga arimasu.   "There is a telephone."

Yamada san ga uchi e kimasu.   "Mr. Yamada is coming to my house."

4.4.4 *Arimasu* and *imasu* are Verbs meaning "exist." The difference between *arimasu* and *imasu* is that *arimasu* refers to the location of inanimate objects while *imasu* is used with animate objects. In other words, *arimasu* is used to say "(something) is, or is situated (in a place)," and *imasu* is used to say "(someone or an animate object) is (in a place)."

place Nominative + *ni* + $\left\{\begin{matrix}\textbf{animate object + } \textit{ga}\textbf{ + }\textit{imasu}\\\textbf{inanimate object + } \textit{ga}\textbf{ + }\textit{arimasu}\end{matrix}\right.$

$$\left.\begin{matrix}\text{eki}\\\text{uchi}\\\text{koko}\\\text{depaato}\end{matrix}\right\} + \text{ni} + \left\{\begin{matrix}\left.\begin{matrix}\text{Keiko san}\\\text{Kazuko san}\\\text{inu}\\\text{tori}\end{matrix}\right\}+\text{ga}+\text{imasu}\\\left.\begin{matrix}\text{otearai}\\\text{den'wa}\\\text{shokudoo}\end{matrix}\right\}+\text{ga}+\text{arimasu}\end{matrix}\right. \quad \begin{matrix}\text{``Keiko}\\\text{``Kazuko}\\\text{``a dog}\\\text{``a bird}\\\hline\text{``the rest room}\\\text{``a telephone}\\\text{``an eating place}\end{matrix} \Big\} \text{is} \left\{\begin{matrix}\text{in the station''}\\\text{at home''}\\\text{here''}\\\text{in the department store''}\end{matrix}\right.$$

Koko ni den'wa ga arimasu.	"Here is a telephone."
Koko ni Yamada san ga imasu.	"Here is Mr. Yamada."
Soko ni haizara ga arimasu.	"There is an ashtray."
Doko ni inu ga imasu ka?	"Where is the dog?"
Depaato ni nani ga arimasu ka?	"What is in the department store?"

4.4.5   *Asoko* is a Nominative meaning "that place over there." Here are a group of place Nominatives:

koko	"this place" or "here"
soko	"that place" or "there"
asoko	"that place over there" or "over there"
doko	"what place?" or "where?"

Note that these are all Nominatives and are often followed by Relationals, such as *de, ni, e,* or other Relationals.

Koko de kaimasu.	"[I] will buy [it] here."
Soko ni imasen.	"[He] is not there."
Asoko e ikimasu ka?	"Are [you] going over there?"
Doko ni arimasu ka?	"Where is [it]?"

Ko, so, a, and *do* as in *koko, soko, asoko,* and *doko* respectively indicate "this ~," "that ~," "that ~ over there," and "wh~?" Therefore, *ko so, a,* and *do* will occur in various series of words of this kind. See Notes 5.4.8, 7.4.2, 7.4.9.

Ko refers to something close to the speaker, *so* refers to something near the hearer or something that has just been mentioned, and *a* to something at a distance from both the speaker and the hearer. Therefore, when someone asks you about something close to him but away from you, he will say *kore,* but you will say *sore.*

When you compare three things within sight, use *kore* for the thing closest to you, *sore* for the thing next in distance, and *are* for the thing farthest away.

4.4.6   *Yo* is an emphatic Sentence Particle that occurs at the end of a sentence as does *ka,* and is used to call the hearer's attention to a statement giving warning, new information, assurance, etc. It corresponds to English "you know," "I tell you," "say," or "certainly," but sometimes it may not appear in English equivalents and only intonation or stress may imply it.

Asoko ni arimasu yo.	"[It] is over there, [you see]."
Ima Keiko san ga eki ni imasu yo.	"Keiko is now at the station, you know."
Ashita gakkoo e ikimasu ka?	"Are [you] going to school tomorrow?"
Ee, ikimasu yo.	"Yes, [I] certainly will."

4.4.7 The -*mashoo* in *ikimashoo* is the OO form of -*masu*. In this lesson, this form is used propositionally as equivalent for "Let's (do)." Therefore, the -*mashoo* followed by the Sentence Particle *ka* corresponds to "Let's (do), shall we?" or "Shall we (do)?" The use of OO form other than the above will be explained in Note 12.4.8.

Predicate Modifier + Verb(-*masu*) ⟶ Predicate Modifier + Verb(-*mashoo*)

Ikimashoo ka ?	"Shall we go?"
Uchi e kaerimashoo ka ?	"Shall we go [back] home?"
Ee, kaerimashoo.	"Yes, let's go [back]."
Ban'gohan o tabemashoo.	"Let's eat supper."
Depaato de kaimono o shimashoo.	"Let's do [some] shopping at the department store."
Uchi de terebi o mimashoo ka ?	"Shall we watch T.V. at home?"
Ashita eiga o mimashoo.	"Let's see a movie tomorrow."

As this usage of -*mashoo* is limited to the speaker's proposition of doing something with the hearer, *arimashoo* never occurs in this meaning.

4.4.8 A place Nominative followed by the Relational *de* indicates the place where an action takes place. This Relational precedes an action Verb or a Verb of happening. Note that the difference between the Relationals *de* and *ni* introduced in this lesson does not appear in English equivalents, but they should be used to indicate whether a Verb following a place Nominative represents "action," or "existence."

place Nominative + *de* + (∼*o*) + action Verb

Tookyoo		(kaimono o)	shimasu	"do shopping		in Tōkyō"
		(terebi o)	kaimasu	"buy a T.V. set		
shokudoo		(ban'gohan o)	tabemasu	"have supper		at the eating place"
	de	(osake o)	nomimasu	"drink *sake*		
koko		(eiga o) +	mimasu	"see a movie		here"
gakkoo		(tegami o)	kakimasu	"write a letter		at school"
		(hon o)	sagashimasu	"look for a book		at the station"
eki		(Keiko san o)	machimasu	"await Keiko		

Eki de anata o mimashita.	"[I] saw you at the station."
Doko de kaimono o shimasu ka ?	"Where are [you] going shopping?"
Uchi de tegami o kakimashita.	"[I] wrote a letter at home."
Gakkoo de Keiko san o machimasu.	"[I] will await Keiko at school."
Eki de sagashimashita.	"[I] looked for [it] at the station."

Compare:

Soko ni arimasu.	"[It] is there."
Soko de kaimasu.	"[I] will buy [it] there."

4.4.9 The *-mashita* in *mimashita* indicates the perfect tense form or normal TA form of *-masu*.

Predicate Modifier + Verb(-*masu*) ⟶ Predicate Modifier + Verb(-*mashita*)

mimasu	"see"	⎱	mimashita	"saw"
kimasu	"come"	⟶	kimashita	"came"
kakimasu	"write"	⎰	kakimashita	"wrote"

Anata o mimashita.   "[I] saw you."

Kinoo Tookyoo e ikimashita.   "[I] went to Tōkyō yesterday."

Nani ga arimashita ka?   "What was there?"

4.4.10 The Relational *o* in *kaimono o shimasu* is optional. Verbs of this kind will be explained in Note 9.4.5.

4.4.11 The *to* that occurs between Nominatives is a Relational. The Relational *to* joins Nominatives, and is equivalent to "and." When more than two Nominatives are listed, *to* appears more than once.

N1 *to* N2 *to* ...... Nn

Depaato ni Keiko san to Kazuko san   "Keiko and Kazuko were in the department store."
  ga imashita.

Gin'za to Shin'juku e ikimashita.   "[I] went to the Ginza and to Shinjuku."

Kazuko san to Keiko san to Ueki san   "Kazuko, Keiko, and Mr. Ueki are here."
  ga koko ni imasu.

Note that *to* is never used to join sentences or predicates.

4.4.12 The normal word for "free time," or "leisure" is *hima*. When the speaker is referring to someone else's free time, the polite prefix *o-* may be attached to the beginning of *hima* in polite speech. Therefore, *ohima* cannot refer to the speaker's. However, some of the *o-* and Nominative combinations, such as *ocha* "tea," replace the original Nominatives in normal speech. The use of *o-* is more common in women's speech.

mizu	...... omizu	"water"
kane	...... okane	"money"
sake	...... osake	"Japanese rice wine; alcohol"
tearai	...... otearai	"rest room"

Ohima ga arimasu ka?   "Do [you] have (free) time?"

Iie, hima ga arimasen.   "No, [I] don't have free time."

4.4.13 The Verb *arimasu* may be used in a pattern that does not have any place expression. In this case, *arimasu* corresponds to "(someone) has (something)."

Ohima ga arimasu ka?		"Do [you] have free time?"
Okane ga arimasen.		"[I] do not have any money."
Tabako to matchi ga arimasu ka?		"Do [you] have cigarettes and a match?"

4.4.14 Most Japanese sentences have more than one Predicate Modifier.

(1) Kono hen ni   den'wa ga   arimasu ka?
       (PM)   (PM)   (P)

(2) Issho ni   uchi de   ban'gohan o   tabemashoo.
       (PM)   (PM)   (PM)   (P)

Even if the order of the Predicate Modifiers is changed in the above sentences, the sentences will still be grammatically correct, and the meanings of the two sentences will not differ. There will be only a slight change in the place of emphasis. Generally speaking, the Predicate Modifier that is closer to the Predicate will be the more emphatic.

(1) Den'wa ga kono hen ni arimasu ka?

(2) Uchi de issho ni ban'gohan o tabemashoo.
     Ban'gohan o uchi de issho ni tabemashoo.
     Issho ni ban'gohan o uchi de tabemashoo.

This flexible transposition is called "relative sequence." The cases in which the above procedure cannot be applied will be explained in Note 5.4.13.

4.5 VOCABULARY

Dialog

Ueki	....	N	family name
kono	....	PN	this (see 7.4.2)
-hen	....	Nd	area; vicinity
ni	....	R	in; at (see 4.4.2)
den'wa	....	N	telephone
ga	....	R	(see 4.4.3)
arimasu	....	V	is situated (normal form of *aru*) (see 4.4.4)
Suzuki	....	N	family name
asoko	....	N	that place over there; over there (see 4.4.5)
yo	....	SP	(see 4.4.6)
ikimashoo	....	V	let us go (OO form of *ikimasu* ⟵ *iku*) (see 4.4.7)
a	....	SI	oh; ah
soko	....	N	that place; there

50

imasu	. . . .	V	exist (normal form of *iru*) (see 4.4.4)
kinoo	. . . .	N	yesterday (see 9.4.1)
eki	. . . .	N	station
de	. . . .	R	at; in (see 4.4.8)
mimashita	. . . .	V	saw (TA form of *mimasu* ←— *miru* – see or "watch" in "watch T.V.") (see 4.4.9)
ikimashita	. . . .	V	went (TA form of *ikimasu* ←— *iku*)
Shin juku	. . . .	N	a district of Tōkyō
depaato	. . . .	N	department store
kaimono	. . . .	N	shopping
shimashita	. . . .	V	did (TA form of *shimasu* ←— *suru*)
soosoo	. . . .	SI	oh, yes; I remember (this is used when the speaker suddenly recalls something)
Keiko	. . . .	N	girl's first name
to	. . . .	R	and (see 4.4.11)
Kazuko	. . . .	N	girl's first name
imashita	. . . .	V	existed (TA form of *imasu* ←— *iru*)
ima	. . . .	N	now (see 9.4.1)
o-	. . . .	(prefix)	(see 4.4.12)
hima	. . . .	Na	free time
Itoo	. . . .	N	family name
issho ni	. . . .	PM	together; with [me, us, etc.]
ban'gohan	. . . .	N	supper; evening meal
tabemashoo	. . . .	V	let us eat (OO form of *tabemasu* ←— *taberu*)

Notes

(o)tearai	. . . .	N	rest room (literal meaning is "hand washing") (see 4.4.12)
koko	. . . .	N	this place; here
inu	. . . .	N	dog
tori	. . . .	N	bird; chicken (meat)
shokudoo	. . . .	N	dining room (hall); cafeteria; eating place
haizara	. . . .	N	ashtray
-mashoo	. . . .	Dv	OO form of *-masu* (see 4.4.7)
terebi	. . . .	N	television
eiga	. . . .	N	movie
(o)sake	. . . .	N	Japanese rice wine; alcohol
tegami	. . . .	N	letter [correspondence]
kakimasu	. . . .	V	write (normal form of *kaku*)

machimasu	. . . .	V	wait (normal form of *matsu*) (different from the English verb "wait," *machimasu* is a transitive Verb; it follows the direct object Relational *o*)
sagashimasu	. . . .	V	look for (normal form of *sagasu*) (*sagashimasu* is a transitive Verb; it follows the direct object Relational *o*)
-mashita	. . . .	Dv	TA form of -*masu* (see 4.4.9)
kaimono (o) shimasu	. . . .	V	do shopping (normal form of *kaimono* (*o*) *suru*)
(o)kane	. . . .	N	money
tabako	. . . .	N	tobacco; cigarette
matchi	. . . .	N	match

Drills

hirugohan	. . . .	N	lunch; noon meal
asagohan	. . . .	N	breakfast; morning meal

4.6 HIRAGANA PRACTICE

4.6.1 Recognize the difference or similarity between two *hiragana* in each of the following pairs:

に……に	は……け	た……た	さ……さ
に……は	は……ほ	た……に	さ……き
に……け	け……け	な……な	き……き
に……ほ	ほ……ほ	な……た	き……も
に……こ	ほ……ま	な……は	も……も
は……は	ま……ま	な……ほ	も……ま

4.6.2 Practice writing the following *hiragana*:

1. に [ni]
2. は [ha]
3. け [ke]
4. ほ [ho]
5. ま [ma]
6. た [ta]

7. な [na]

8. さ [sa]

9. き [ki]

10. も [mo]

4.7 DRILLS

4.7.1 Pronunciation Drill

Itoo san   depaato   kinoo   gakkoo   soosoo   Tookyoo   shokudoo   koohii   kyoo

ikimashoo   Arigatoo.   Soo desu.   Doo itashimashite.   Omachidoo sama.

4.7.2 Pattern Drill

1. Kono hen ni den'wa ga arimasu ka?

2. Asoko ni arimasu yo.

3. Ikimashoo ka?

4. Ee, ikimashoo.

5. Soko ni Yamada san ga imasu yo.

6. Kinoo eki de anata o mimashita yo.

7. Doko e ikimashita ka?

8. Shin'juku e ikimashita.

9. Depaato de kaimono o shimashita.

10. Depaato ni Keiko san to Kazuko san ga imashita yo.

11. Ima ohima ga arimasu ka?

12. Issho ni uchi de ban'gohan o tabemashoo.

4.7.3 Transformation Drill (statement ⟶ proposition)

1. Ban'gohan o *tabemasu*.   ⟶   Ban'gohan o *tabemashoo*.

2. Gakkoo e ikimasu.   ⟶   Gakkoo e ikimashoo.

3. Mizu o nomimasu.   ⟶   Mizu o nomimashoo.

4. Eiga o mimasu.   ⟶   Eiga o mimashoo.

5. Jisho o kaimasu.   ⟶   Jisho o kaimashoo.

6. Sugu kaerimasu.   ⟶   Sugu kaerimashoo.

7. Asoko e ikimasu.   ⟶   Asoko e ikimashoo.

8. Kaimono o shimasu.   ⟶   Kaimono o shimashoo.

9. Matchi o sagashimasu.   ⟶   Matchi o sagashimashoo.

10. Shokudoo de tabemasu.   ⟶   Shokudoo de tabemashoo.

11. Kazuko san o machimasu. ⟶ Kazuko san o machimashoo.

12. Tabako o kaimasu. ⟶ Tabako o kaimashoo.

4.7.4 Transformation Drill

1. Uchi e kaerimashoo. ⟶ Uchi e kaerimashoo *ka*?

2. Eki de machimashoo. ⟶ Eki de machimashoo ka?

3. Osake o nomimashoo. ⟶ Osake o nomimashoo ka?

4. Kaimono o shimashoo. ⟶ Kaimono o shimashoo ka?

5. Depaato de kaimashoo. ⟶ Depaato de kaimashoo ka?

6. Tegami o kakimashoo. ⟶ Tegami o kakimashoo ka?

7. Ashita kimashoo. ⟶ Ashita kimashoo ka?

8. Soko e ikimashoo. ⟶ Soko e ikimashoo ka?

9. Eiga o mimashoo. ⟶ Eiga o mimashoo ka?

10. Issho ni shimashoo. ⟶ Issho ni shimashoo ka?

11. Hirugohan o tabemashoo. ⟶ Hirugohan o tabemashoo ka?

4.7.5 Transformation Drill (imperfect ⟶ perfect)

1. *Ashita* Shin'juku e *ikimasu.* ⟶ *Kinoo* Shin'juku e *ikimashita.*

2. Ashita eiga o mimashoo. ⟶ Kinoo eiga o mimashita.

3. Ashita Amerika e kaerimasu. ⟶ Kinoo Amerika e kaerimashita.

4. Ashita osake o nomimasu. ⟶ Kinoo osake o nomimashita.

5. Ashita tegami o kakimasu. ⟶ Kinoo tegami o kakimashita.

6. Ashita uchi de machimasu. ⟶ Kinoo uchi de machimashita.

7. Ashita bifuteki o tabemasu. ⟶ Kinoo bifuteki o tabemashita.

8. Ashita hima ga arimasu. ⟶ Kinoo hima ga arimashita.

9. Ashita gakkoo e ikimasu. ⟶ Kinoo gakkoo e ikimashita.

10. Ashita taipuraitaa o kaimasu. ⟶ Kinoo taipuraitaa o kaimashita.

11. Ashita uchi ni imasu. ⟶ Kinoo uchi ni imashita.

12. Ashita kaimono o shimasu. ⟶ Kinoo kaimono o shimashita.

13. Ashita jisho o sagashimasu. ⟶ Kinoo jisho o sagashimashita.

54

4.7.6 Substitution Drill

Soko ni *depaato* ga arimasu ka?

1.	*shokudoo*	. . . .	Soko ni *shokudoo* ga arimasu ka?
2.	otearai	. . . .	Soko ni otearai ga arimasu ka?
3.	den'wa	. . . .	Soko ni den'wa ga arimasu ka?
4.	okane	. . . .	Soko ni okane ga arimasu ka?
5.	jisho	. . . .	Soko ni jisho ga arimasu ka?
6.	eki	. . . .	Soko ni eki ga arimasu ka?
7.	gakkoo	. . . .	Soko ni gakkoo ga arimasu ka?
8.	koohii	. . . .	Soko ni koohii ga arimasu ka?
9.	ocha	. . . .	Soko ni ocha ga arimasu ka?
10.	haizara	. . . .	Soko ni haizara ga arimasu ka?
11.	nani	. . . .	Soko ni nani ga arimasu ka?

4.7.7 Substitution Drill

Koko ni *Yamada san* ga imasu.

1.	*soko*	. . . .	*Soko* ni Yamada san ga imasu.
2.	*Keiko san*	. . . .	Soko ni *Keiko san* ga imasu.
3.	inu	. . . .	Soko ni inu ga imasu.
4.	eki	. . . .	Eki ni inu ga imasu.
5.	uchi	. . . .	Uchi ni inu ga imasu.
6.	tori	. . . .	Uchi ni tori ga imasu.
7.	Ishii san	. . . .	Uchi ni Ishii san ga imasu.
8.	shokudoo	. . . .	Shokudoo ni Ishii san ga imasu.
9.	asoko	. . . .	Asoko ni Ishii san ga imasu.
10.	Ueki san	. . . .	Asoko ni Ueki san ga imasu.

4.7.8 Substitution Drill

Depaato de *kaimono o shimashita*.

1.	*asoko*	. . . .	*Asoko* de kaimono o shimashita.
2.	*asagohan o tabemashoo*	. . . .	Asoko de *asagohan o tabemashoo*.
3.	shokudoo	. . . .	Shokudoo de asagohan o tabemashoo.

4.	koko	. . . .	Koko de asagohan o tabemashoo.
5.	Kazuko san o machimasu	. . . .	Koko de Kazuko san o machimasu.
6.	eki	. . . .	Eki de Kazuko san o machimasu.
7.	nani o kaimashita ka?	. . . .	Eki de nani o kaimashita ka?
8.	Hawai	. . . .	Hawai de nani o kaimashita .ka?
9.	Amerika	. . . .	Amerika de nani o kaimashita ka?
10.	Nihon	. . . .	Nihon de nani o kaimashita ka?
11.	nani o mimashoo ka?	. . . .	Nihon de nani o mimashoo ka?
12.	soko	. . . .	Soko de nani o mimashoo ka?
13.	terebi o mimashoo ka?	. . . .	Soko de terebi o mimashoo ka?
14.	doko	. . . .	Doko de terebi o mimashoo ka?

4.7.9 Substitution Drill

Hima ga arimasu ka?

1.	*okane*	. . . . . .	*Okane* ga arimasu ka?	7.	ohima	. . . . . .	Ohima ga arimasu ka?
2.	jisho	. . . . . .	Jisho ga arimasu ka?	8.	hon	. . . . . .	Hon ga arimasu ka?
3.	kamera	. . . . . .	Kamera ga arimasu ka?	9.	haizara	. . . . . .	Haizara ga arimasu ka?
4.	den'wa	. . . . . .	Den'wa ga arimasu ka?	10.	tabako	. . . . . .	Tabako ga arimasu ka?
5.	koohii	. . . . . .	Koohii ga arimasu ka?	11.	matchi	. . . . . .	Matchi ga arimasu ka?
6.	ocha	. . . . . .	Ocha ga arimasu ka?	12.	nani	. . . . . .	Nani ga arimasu ka?

4.7.10 Expansion Drill

1.	Kaimasu.	. . . .	Kaimasu.
	kamera o	. . . .	Kamera o kaimasu.
	Itoo san ga	. . . .	Itoo san ga kamera o kaimasu.
	depaato de	. . . .	Depaato de Itoo san ga kamera o kaimasu.
2.	Machimashita ka?	. . . .	Machimashita ka?
	Ueki san o	. . . .	Ueki san o machimashita ka?
	doko de	. . . .	Doko de Ueki san o machimashita ka?
	kinoo	. . . .	Kinoo doko de Ueki san o machimashita ka?
3.	Ikimashoo.	. . . .	Ikimashoo.
	gakkoo e	. . . .	Gakkoo e ikimashoo.

issho ni	....	Issho ni gakkoo e ikimashoo.
ashita	....	Ashita issho ni gakkoo e ikimashoo.

4.
Mimashoo ka?	....	Mimashoo ka?
eiga o	....	Eiga o mimashoo ka?
doko de	....	Doko de eiga o mimashoo ka?
kyoo	....	Kyoo doko de eiga o mimashoo ka?

5.
Kimasu.	....	Kimasu.
uchi e	....	Uchi e kimasu.
sugu	....	Sugu uchi e kimasu.
Suzuki san ga	....	Suzuki san ga sugu uchi e kimasu.

6.
Sagashimashita.	....	Sagashimashita.
anata o	....	Anata o sagashimashita.
gakkoo de	....	Gakkoo de anata o sagashimashita.
kinoo	....	Kinoo gakkoo de anata o sagashimashita.

4.7.11 Expansion Drill

1.
Imasu.	....	Imasu.
Yamada san ga	....	Yamada san ga imasu.
Yamada san to Ishii san ga	....	Yamada san to Ishii san ga imasu.
asoko ni	...	Asoko ni Yamada san to Ishii san ga imasu.

2.
Imashita.	....	Imashita.
inu ga	....	Inu ga imashita.
inu to tori ga	....	Inu to tori ga imashita.
kono hen ni	....	Kono hen ni inu to tori ga imashita.

3.
Arimasu.	....	Arimasu.
den'wa ga	....	Den'wa ga arimasu.
den'wa to taipuraitaa	....	Den'wa to taipuraitaa ga arimasu.
uchi ni	....	Uchi ni den'wa to taipuraitaa ga arimasu.

4.
Arimashita.	....	Arimashita.
depaato ga	....	Depaato ga arimashita.

| depaato to eki ga | .... | Depaato to eki ga arimashita. |
| soko ni | .... | Soko ni depaato to eki ga arimashita. |

4.7.12 Substitution Drill

Soko ni *Yamada san ga imasu.*
Soko ni *den'wa ga arimasu.*

1. *inu* ...... Soko ni *inu ga imasu.*
2. *shokudoo* ...... Soko ni *shokudoo ga arimasu.*
3. otearai ...... Soko ni otearai ga arimasu.
4. eki ...... Soko ni eki ga arimasu.
5. Keiko san ...... Soko ni Keiko san ga imasu.
6. depaato ...... Soko ni depaato ga arimasu.
7. tori ...... Soko ni tori ga imasu.
8. Ishii san ...... Soko ni Ishii san ga imasu.
9. jisho ...... Soko ni jisho ga arimasu.
10. tegami ...... Soko ni tegami ga arimasu.

4.7.13 Relational Checking Drill

Tookyoo

1. Ikimashita. .... Tookyoo *e* ikimashita.
2. Imasen. .... Tookyoo *ni* imasen.
3. Kaimono o shimashita ka? .... Tookyoo *de* kaimono o shimashita ka?
4. Imashita. .... Tookyoo *ni* imashita.
5. Kimasen. .... Tookyoo *e* kimasen.
6. Tabemashita. .... Tookyoo *de* tabemashita.
7. Sagashimashoo. .... Tookyoo *de* sagashimashoo.
8. Arimashita yo. .... Tookyoo *ni* arimashita yo.
9. Tegami o kakimasu. .... Tookyoo *de* tegami o kakimasu.
10. Kaimashoo. .... Tookyoo *de* kaimashoo.
11. Nomimasu. .... Tookyoo *de* nomimasu.
12. Machimashoo. .... Tookyoo *de* machimashoo.
13. Kaerimasu ka? .... Tookyoo *e* kaerimasu ka?
14. Mimashita. .... Tookyoo *de* mimashita.
15. Arimasu. .... Tookyoo *ni* arimasu.

4.7.14 Response Drill (short answer)

1. Kono hen ni' den'wa ga arimasu ka?
   ee ...... Ee, arimasu.

2. Ohima ga arimasu ka?
   iie ...... Iie, arimasen.

3. Doko de kamera o kaimashoo ka?
   soko ...... Soko de kaimashoo.

4. Doko ni Yamada san ga imashita ka?
   eki ...... Eki ni imashita.

5. Eiga o mimashoo ka?
   ee ...... Ee, mimashoo.

6. Nani ga arimashita ka?
   okane ...... Okane ga arimashita.

7. Ashita issho ni gakkoo e ikimashoo ka?
   ee ...... Ee, ikimashoo.

8. Kyoo kaimono o shimasu ka?
   iie ...... Iie, shimasen.

9. Nani o nomimashita ka?
   koohii to mizu ...... Koohii to mizu o nomimashita.

10. Doko de Ishii san o machimashita ka?
    shokudoo ...... Shokudoo de machimashita.

11. Asoko ni nani ga imasu ka?
    inu to tori ...... Inu to tori ga imasu.

12. Soko ni nani ga arimasu ka?
    haizara to tabako to matchi ...... Haizara to tabako to matchi ga arimasu.

4.7.15 E-J Expansion Drill

1. Imashita. ...... Imashita.

   in the department store ...... Depaato ni imashita.

   Keiko ...... Keiko san ga depaato ni imashita.

2. Shimasu. ...... Shimasu.

   shopping ...... Kaimono o shimasu.

   in Tōkyō ...... Tookyoo de kaimono o shimasu.

3. Tabemashoo. ...... Tabemashoo.

   lunch ...... Hirugohan o tabemashoo.

   at home ...... Uchi de hirugohan o tabemashoo.

4. Arimasu. ...... Arimasu.

 a dictionary ...... Jisho ga arimasu.

 here ...... Koko ni jisho ga arimasu.

5. Imasu ka? ...... Imasu ka?

 there ...... Soko ni imasu ka?

 a dog ...... Inu ga soko ni imasu ka?

6. Arimasu ka? ...... Arimasu ka?

 a telephone ...... Den'wa ga arimasu ka?

 where ...... Doko ni den'wa ga arimasu ka?

7. Mimashita. ...... Mimashita.

 a movie ...... Eiga o mimashita.

 in Ginza ...... Gin'za de eiga o mimashita.

8. Kaimashita ka? ...... Kaimashita ka?

 a television set ...... Terebi o kaimashita ka?

 where ...... Doko de terebi o kaimashita ka?

9. Sagashimashita. ...... Sagashimashita.

 Mr. Itō ...... Itoo san o sagashimashita.

 at the station ...... Eki de Itoo san o sagashimashita.

4.8 EXERCISES

4.8.1 Apply as many Predicates as possible out of Group B to each of the Group A Predicate Modifiers.

A	B
Shin'juku e	arimashita ka ?
Soko de	imasu.
Yamada san o	tabemasu ka ?
Nani o	ikimashoo.
Nani ga	arimasen.
Depaato de	kakimasu.
Doko ni	kaimashita ka ?
Inu to tori ga	imasu ka ?

Tegami o	machimashoo.
Osake ga	kimashita.
Kazuko san ga	nomimasen.
Ocha o	mimashita.
Ban'gohan o	

4.8.2 Insert appropriate words in the blanks; each pair consists of a question and an answer to the question.

1. a. Soko ni shokudoo ga (   ) ka?

    b. Iie, (   ).

2. a. (   ) o kaimashita ka?

    b. Jisho (   ) hon (   ) kaimashita.

3. a. Uchi (   ) nani o nomimashita ka?

    b. Koohii (   ) mizu o nomimashita.

4. a. (   ) e ikimashoo ka?

    b. Shokudoo e (   ).

5. a. Nani o shimashita (   )?

    b. Eiga o (   ).

6. a. Asoko (   ) Itoo san ga (   ) ka?

    b. (   ), Suzuki san ga imashita.

4.8.3 What would you say when:

1. you want to thank someone?

2. someone thanks you?

3. you kept someone waiting?

4. someone apologizes to you for his having kept you waiting?

5. you greet someone in the afternoon?

6. you want to excuse yourself for a while?

7. you want to ask if something or someone is "so"?

4.8.4 Answer the following questions in Japanese:

1. Kinoo nani o shimashita ka?

2. Ashita doko e ikimashoo ka?

3. Soko ni nani ga arimasu ka?

4. Koko ni inu ga imasu ka?

5. Mainichi doko de hirugohan o tabemasu ka?

6. Ima ohima ga arimasu ka?

7. Issho ni uchi e kaerimashoo ka?

8. Doko ni tabako ga arimasu ka?

LESSON 5

5.1 USEFUL EXPRESSIONS

Hajimemashite.	"How do you do?" This expression literally means "It is the first time."
Doozo yoroshiku	This expression is usually used as a reply to *Hajimemashite,* but can be used together with, or can be used by itself. Literally, this means "Please extend a special favor to me," and may be used in various cases other than introductions.
Sorosoro shitsurei shimasu.	"I'd better be leaving now." This means literally "I am going to commit the rudeness of leaving now."
Mata irasshai.	"Come again." This expression should not be used to a superior; *Mata irashite kudasai* is preferred.

5.2 DIALOG

— In front of Professor Nakamura's office —

Miss Koyama : Nakamura sen'sei*¹, kono kata*² wa*³ Sumisu san desu.*⁴

Sumisu san wa mae Meriiran'do Daigaku*⁵ no*⁶ gakusei deshita.*⁷

Mr. Smith : Hajimemashite.

Prof. Nakamura : Doozo yoroshiku

Mr. Smith : Kore*⁸ wa sen'sei*⁹ no heya desu ka /

Prof. Nakamura : Ee, soo desu.

Mr. Smith : Are mo*¹⁰ sen'sei no heya desu ka /

Prof. Nakamura : Iie, chigaimasu. Are wa Katoo sen'sei no heya desu.

Mr. Smith : Katoo sen'sei no heya desu ka. Watakushi no nihon'go*¹¹ no

sen'sei wa Katoo sen'sei deshita.

Prof. Nakamura : Doori de, anata wa nihon'go ga joozu*¹²*¹³ desu nee.*¹⁴

Mr. Smith : Iie, mada heta desu. Demo, watakushi wa gaikokugo no ben'kyoo

⌐ga suki desu.   Doitsugo mo*10 koko de naraimashita.

Prof. Nakamura :   Sen'sei wa donata*15 deshita ka /

Mr. Smith :   Namae wa*3 wasuremashita.   (Looking at his watch)   A, ohiru desu ne*16/   Sorosoro shitsurei shimasu.

Prof. Nakamura :   Soo desu ka /   Jaa, mata irasshai.

Mr. Smith :   Hai, mata kimasu.

5.3 PATTERN SENTENCES

5.3.1

N	R
Are	mo

→

NM		N	C
N	R		
sen'sei	no	heya	desu

"That is also the teacher's room."

5.3.2

N	R
Sumisu san	wa

→

N	C
gakusei	deshita

"Mr. Smith was a student."

5.3.3

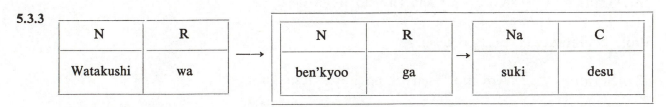

N	R
Watakushi	wa

→

N	R
ben'kyoo	ga

→

Na	C
suki	desu

"I like studying."

5.4 NOTES

5.4.1 *Sen'sei* means "teacher." When referring to a person who is a teacher, *sen'sei* may be used instead of *-san*. Physicians, lawyers, etc. may also be called *sen'sei*.

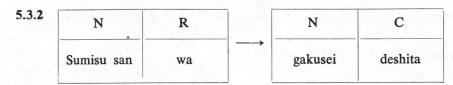

Nakamura sen'sei   "Prof., Dr., or Mr. Nakamura"

5.4.2 *Kono kata* means "this person." *-Kata* is a dependent Nominative meaning "person," and is a polite equivalent for *hito*. However, *-kata* is always preceded by a word while *hito* can be used by itself. The *kono* will be studied in the following lesson.

Kono kata wa Sumisu san desu.	"This person is Mr. Smith."
Kono kata wa donata desu ka?	"Who is this person?" (polite)
Koko ni hito ga imasu.	"Here are [some] people."

5.4.3 The Relational *wa* following a Nominative functions to turn the Nominative into the topic (often the one already under discussion) of what is about to be mentioned or described in the following part of the sentence. The Relational *wa* may take the place of the subject Relational *ga* or the object Relational *o*:

Nominative (subject) + *ga* + Predicate ⟶ Nominative (subject) + *wa* + Predicate

Nominative (object) + *o* + Verb ⟶ Nominative (object) + *wa* + Verb

Watakushi *ga* Yamada desu.	⟶	Watakushi *wa* Yamada desu.
Osake *o* nomimasu ka?	⟶	Osake *wa* nomimasu ka?

As explained in Note 4.4.3, the subject Relational *ga* is equally emphasized as the following Predicate. Therefore, when a sentence has the subject followed by *ga*, the sentence is mainly meant to explain "WHO does, or WHAT happens," or "WHO or WHAT is so," etc.

Watakushi ga shimashita.	"*I* did [it]." (an emphasis on "I")
Eki ga arimasu.	"There is *a station*." (an emphasis on "a station")

On the other hand, when *ga* is replaced by *wa*, the subject is no longer emphatic, and the Predicate or some other part of the sentence instead forms the main body of the sentence content. The Relational *wa* is used in the place of *ga* when the sentence is meant to describe "how or what something or someone is or does," rather than "WHAT or WHO is so or does."

Watakushi wa shimashita.	"I *did* [it]."
Eki wa arimasu.	"*There is* a station."

Often the above differences are made in English by stressing a certain word.

When the subject of a question is an interrogative Nominative, such as *donata* "who?" *nani* "what?" *dore* "which?" the main body of the question and that of the answer to it lies in the subject, and naturally the subject should be emphasized by using the subject Relational *ga*. *Wa* is never to be used after an interrogative Nominative.

Predicate + *ka*? ⟶ interrogative Nominative (subject) + *ga* + Predicate + *ka*?

Donata ga kimashita ka?	"Who came (here)?"
Nani ga arimasu ka?	"What is there?"
Dore ga jisho desu ka?	"Which is the dictionary?"

5.4.4 The *desu* is the Copula representing the normal imperfect tense. In this lesson, the Copula occurs only after a Nominative, and is used in the meaning of "A is B," or "A=B" in which B is a Nominative. The subject of this pattern can be either animate or inanimate.

Nominative (subject) + $\begin{Bmatrix} wa \\ ga \end{Bmatrix}$ + Nominative + *desu*

watakushi
anata
Sumisu san + $\begin{Bmatrix} wa \\ ga \end{Bmatrix}$ + $\begin{Bmatrix} gakusei \\ sen'sei \\ tomodachi \end{Bmatrix}$ + desu
kono kata

"I am
"you are + $\begin{Bmatrix} a\ student" \\ a\ teacher" \\ a\ friend" \end{Bmatrix}$
"Mr. Smith is
"this person is

kore
sore + $\begin{Bmatrix} wa \\ ga \end{Bmatrix}$ + $\begin{Bmatrix} kyooshitsu \\ heya \\ Hawai\ Daigaku \end{Bmatrix}$ + desu

"this is
"that is + $\begin{Bmatrix} a\ classroom" \\ a\ room" \\ the\ University\ of\ Hawaii" \end{Bmatrix}$

Anata wa gakusei desu ka?   "Are you a student?"

Kore wa kamera desu.   "This is a camera."

Although both *desu* and *arimasu* may be translated "is" in English equivalents, *desu* cannot replace *arimasu* in the sentence *Kamera wa heya ni arimasu* "The camera is in the room." When an interrogative Nominative occurs before the Copula, the subject of the Predicate is never followed by *ga*, but is always followed by *wa*.

Nominative (subject) + *wa* + interrogative Nominative + *desu ka*?

Koko wa doko desu ka?   "What place is this?" (Sometimes this means "Where am I now?")

Anata wa donata desu ka?   "Who are you?" "What is your name?"

To say "What is this?" *nan*, the contracted form of *nani* "what," will occur before *desu*.

Kore wa nan desu ka?   "What is this?"

Anata no namae wa nan desu ka?   "What is your name?"

Nan occurring before the Relational *no* will be introduced in Note 5.4.6. The adjectival Nominative, such as *joozu*, which occurs before the Copula *desu* will be explained in Note 5.4.12.

5.4.5 Names of organizations, such as universities, corporations, etc., are always used without *no* "of" as follows:

Meriiran'do Daigaku   "University of Maryland"

Hawai Daigaku   "University of Hawaii"

Kariforunia Daigaku   "University of California"

Tookyoo Gin'koo   "Bank of Tōkyō"

Shin'juku Eki   "Shinjuku Station"

5.4.6 The Relational *no* occurs between Nominatives. The Nominative followed by *no* forms a Nominative Modifier and describes the following Nominative. Note that it sometimes corresponds to "of," but not always. The meaning of N₁ *no* N₂ will be "N₂ belonging to N₁," "N₂ related to N₁," "N₂ located in N₁," etc.

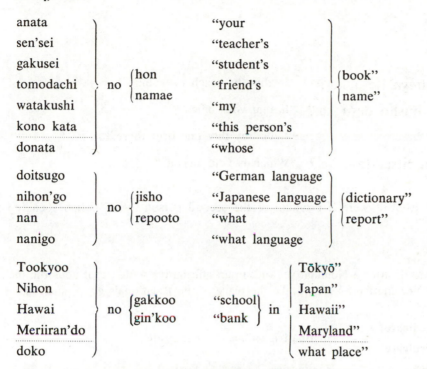

When two or more Nominative Modifiers, Nominative plus *no*, occur, the first Nominative Modifier may modify directly the following Nominative or both the Modifiers may modify another following Nominative. The context usually explains which is the case.

$$\text{N1 } no \text{ + N2 } no \text{ + N3} \longrightarrow \begin{cases} \left.\begin{array}{l}\text{N1 } no \\ \text{N2 } no\end{array}\right\} \longrightarrow \text{N3} \\ \text{or} \\ \text{(N1 } no \text{ + N2) } no \longrightarrow \text{N3} \end{cases}$$

$$\left.\begin{array}{l}\text{watakushi no} \\ \text{nihon'go \quad no}\end{array}\right\} \text{sen'sei} \longrightarrow \text{watakushi no nihon'go no sen'sei} \quad \text{"my Japanese language teacher"}$$

(watakushi no tomodachi) no sen'sei ⟶ watakushi no tomodachi no sen'sei   "my friend's teacher"

When one of the two or more Nominative Modfiers indicates possession, that Modifier of possession usually precedes.

5.4.7 *Deshita* is the TA form or the perfect tense form of the Copula *desu*. *Deshita* may be used to mean "A was B."

$$\text{Nominative} \atop \text{(subject)} + \begin{Bmatrix} ga \\ wa \end{Bmatrix} + \text{Nominative} + desu \longrightarrow {\text{Nominative} \atop \text{(subject)}} + \begin{Bmatrix} ga \\ wa \end{Bmatrix} + \text{Nominative} + deshita$$

Sumisu san wa mae gakusei deshita.   "Mr. Smith was a student before."

Kinoo deshita ka ?   "Was [it] yesterday?"

68

5.4.8 *Kore* is a Nominative meaning "this" as in "This is my room." Here is this series of words:

kore "this"
sore "that"
are "that over there"
dore "which?"

Kore wa sen'sei no heya desu ka ? "Is this the teacher's room?"

Sore wa anata no jimusho desu ka ? "Is that your office?"

Are o kaimashoo. "Let's buy that one over there."

Dore ga anata no en'pitsu desu ka ? "Which is your pencil?"

5.4.9 *Sen'sei* can also be used as if it were a pronoun of the second person "you," when speaking to a teacher, a doctor, etc.

5.4.10 The Relational *mo* may occur after a Nominative, and, in an affirmative sentence, it adds the meaning of "also" or "too" to the Nominative. *Mo* can take the place of the Relationals *ga, o,* and *wa.*

Nominative + *ga* + Predicate
Nominative + *wa* + Predicate ⟶ **Nominative + *mo* + Predicate**
Nominative + *o* + Verb ⟶ **Nominative + *mo* + Verb**

Are mo sen'sei no heya desu ka ? "Is that one over there the teacher's room, too?"

Watakushi wa nihon'go o naraimashita. "I studied Japanese."

Watakushi *mo* nihon'go o naraimashita. "I studied Japanese, too." (as well as someone else did)

Watakushi wa nihon'go *mo* naraimashita. "I studied Japanese also." (as well as some other language)

5.4.11 *Nihon'go* is a Nominative meaning "the Japanese language." The name of a language is normally formed by adding *-go* to a country's name. *Gaikokugo* "foreign language" is a combination of *gaikoku* "foreign country" and *-go* "language."

Nihon "Japan" ...... nihon'go "the Japanese language"
Doitsu "Germany" ...... doitsugo "the German language"
Furan'su "France" ...... furan'sugo "the French language"
Roshia "Russia" ...... roshiago "the Russian language"
Chuugoku "China" ...... chuugokugo "the Chinese language"

Exception: Amerika "U.S.A."
Igirisu "England" .... eigo "the English language"

Nanigo is used to ask a name of a specific language or "what language?"

Anata wa nanigo o hanashimasu ka ?   "What language do you speak?"

5.4.12 *Joozu* "skillful," *heta* "unskillful," *suki* "fondness," and *kirai* "dislike" are called adjectival Nominatives. These adjectival Nominatives may occur before the Copula *desu, deshita,* etc., and usually describe "how something is," or "how someone is," as an Adjective does. In most cases, adjectival Nominatives correspond to English adjectives, but since they are Nominatives, their behavior is not that of Adjectives; an adjectival Nominative does not inflect and the Copula following it does. The subject of the Predicate, which is described by the adjectival Nominatives, may be human, animate or inanimate, and is followed by *ga*.

$$\text{Nominative (subject)} + \textit{ga} + \textbf{adjectival Nominative} + \begin{cases} \textit{desu} \\ \textit{deshita} \end{cases}$$

Nihon'go ga joozu desu.   "[His] Japanese is good."

Eigo ga heta desu.   "[His] English is bad."

Mae kirai deshita.   "[It] was disliked [by him] before."

Osake ga suki desu ka ?   "Is *sake* liked [by you]?"

5.4.13 When it is necessary to identify "about WHOM that description is said," *wa* usually occurs after the person or animate Nominative, and "WHAT is such and such" is followed by the Relational *ga*.

In order to express the following ideas:

	(a)	(b)
Someone	is good	at something.
	is poor	at something.
	likes	something or someone else.
	dislikes	something or someone else.

(a) is followed by the Relational *wa*, and (b) by the Relational *ga*. When a sentence includes both of the Relationals *wa* and *ga*, *wa* normally precedes *ga*. This may be called "absolute sequence" in contrast with "relative sequence" that has been introduced in Note 4.4.14.

Thus:

Anata wa nihon'go ga joozu desu nee.   "You speak Japanese very well."

Watakushi wa doitsugo ga heta desu.   "My German is poor."

Yamada san wa Ueki san ga suki desu.   "Mr. Yamada likes Mr. Ueki."

Kazuko san wa ben'kyoo ga kirai desu.   "Kazuko dislikes studying."

Note that such adjectival Nominatives as are introduced in this lesson require both *wa* and *ga*, but ordinary adjectival Nominatives require only *ga*.

5.4.14 *Nee* is a Sentence Particle that stands at the end of a sentence like *ka* and *yo,* and is used to express "admiration," "surprise," or other similar exclamations, usually expecting the hearer's concurrence. *Nee* follows, among others, Predicates of description, such as adjectival Nominative or Adjective.

Joozu desu nee.   "How proficient [you] are!"

5.4.15 *Donata* is an interrogative Nominative meaning "who?" *Donata* is a polite equivalent of *dare*. *Anata wa dare desu ka?* conveys the meaning "Who are you?" *Anata wa donata desu ka?* is similar to "May I have your name?"

Sen'sei wa donata deshita ka?   "Who was [your] teacher?"

Donata ga sen'sei desu ka?   "Who is [your] teacher?"

Dare ga kimasu ka?   "Who is coming?"

5.4.16 *Ne* said with a rising intonation is a Sentence Particle, and means the strong expectation of the hearer's agreement to what the speaker has mentioned. It often corresponds to "isn't it?" "aren't you?" "don't you think?" etc. Do not confuse it with the *nee* introduced in Note 5.4.14.

Ohiru desu ne?   "It's noon, isn't it?"

Anata wa gakusei desu ne?   "You are a student, aren't you?"

When the *ne* is said lightly, it merely functions to add softness or friendliness to speech. This is common practice in informal speech, particularly of women.

5.5 VOCABULARY

Dialog

Koyama	. . . .	N	family name
Nakamura	. . . .	N	family name
sen'sei	. . . .	N	teacher
-kata	. . . .	Nd	person (see 5.4.2)
wa	. . . .	R	(see 5.4.3)
Sumisu	. . . .	N	Smith
desu	. . . .	C	(see 5.4.4)
mae	. . . .	N	before (see 9.4.1)
Meriiran'do	. . . .	N	Maryland
daigaku	. . . .	N	university; college
no	. . . .	R	(see 5.4.6)
gakusei	. . . .	N	student
deshita	. . . .	C	TA form of *desu* (see 5.4.7)

kore	....	N	this one (see 5.4.8)
heya	....	N	room
are	....	N	that one over there (see 5.4.8)
mo	....	R	also; too (see 5.4.10)
chigaimasu	....	V	differ; is different
Katoo	....	N	family name
watakushi	....	N	I (the contracted form *watashi* may also be used)
nihon'go	....	N	Japanese language
doori de	....	SI	no wonder!; indeed!
joozu	....	Na	skillful; proficient; good (at) (see 5.4.12)
nee	....	SP	(see 5.4.14)
mada	....	Adv.	still
heta	....	Na	unskillful; poor (at) (see 5.4.12)
demo	....	SI	but; however
gaikokugo	....	N	foreign language
ben'kyoo	....	N	study
suki	....	Na	like; fond of (see 5.4.12)
doitsugo	....	N	German language
naraimashita	....	V	studied; took lessons; was taught; learned (Note that *naraimasu* is not always equivalent to "learn.")
donata	....	Ni	who? (polite equivalent of *dare*) (see 5.4.15)
namae	....	N	name
wasuremashita	....	V	forgot (TA form of *wasuremasu* ⟵ *wasureru*)
(o)hiru	....	N	noon (It sometimes means "lunch.")
ne	....	SP	(see 5.4.16)
mata	....	Adv.	again

Notes

hito	....	N	person
dore	....	Ni	which one? (see 5.4.3)
tomodachi	....	N	friend
kyooshitsu	....	N	classroom
nan	....	Ni	what? (see 5.4.4)
Kariforunia*	....	N	California (*Keeping the original sound.)
gin'koo	....	N	bank
repooto	....	N	term paper; report
sore	....	N	that one (see 5.4.8)
jimusho	....	N	office

en'pitsu	. . . .	N	pencil
-go	. . . .	Nd	language (see 5.4.11)
Doitsu	. . . .	N	Germany
Furan'su	. . . .	N	France
furan'sugo	. . . .	N	French language
Roshia	. . . .	N	Russia
roshiago	. . . .	N	Russian language
Chuugoku	. . . .	N	China
chuugokugo	. . . .	N	Chinese language
Igirisu	. . . .	N	England
eigo	. . . .	N	English language
nanigo	. . . .	Ni	what language?
hanashimasu	. . . .	V	speak; talk (normal form of *hanasu*)
kirai	. . . .	Na	dislike (see 5.4.12)
dare	. . . .	Ni	who? (see 5.4.15)

5.6 HIRAGANA PRACTICE

5.6.1 Recognize the difference or similarity between two *hiragana* in each of the following pairs:

ら・・・・・ら	え・・・・・え	ろ・・・・・る	む・・・・・む
ら・・・・・う	え・・・・・そ	そ・・・・・そ	む・・・・・す
ら・・・・・え	ち・・・・・ち	そ・・・・・る	よ・・・・・よ
ら・・・・・ち	ち・・・・・ろ	る・・・・・る	よ・・・・・む
う・・・・・う	ろ・・・・・ろ	る・・・・・ら	よ・・・・・ま
う・・・・・ち	ろ・・・・・ら	す・・・・・す	
う・・・・・ろ	ろ・・・・・そ	す・・・・・よ	

5.6.2 Practice writing the following *hiragana*:

1. う [u] う う う
2. ら [ra] ら ら ら ら
3. え [e] え え え え

4.	そ	[so]			
5.	ち	[chi]			
6.	ろ	[ro]			
7.	る	[ru]			
8.	す	[su]			
9.	よ	[yo]			
10.	む	[mu]			

5.6.3 Read and write the following:

ほん   えき   うち   なまえ

さけ   にほん   いま

5.7 DRILLS

5.7.1 Pronunciation Drill

deshita   watakushi   naraimashita   kyooshitsu   shitsurei   Roshia   wasuremashita

hanashimashita   en'pitsu   Doitsu   heta desu   suki desu   chigaimasu   furan'sugo

Igirisu   Sumisu

5.7.2 Pattern Drill

1. Kono kata wa Sumisu san desu.

2. Sumisu san wa mae Meriiran'do Daigaku no gakusei deshita.

3. Kore wa sen'sei no heya desu ka?

4. Are mo sen'sei no heya desu ka?

5. Watakushi no nihon'go no sen'sei wa Katoo sen'sei deshita.

6. Anata wa nihon'go ga joozu desu nee.

7. Watakushi wa gaikokugo no ben'kyoo ga suki desu.

8. Mada heta desu.

9. Doitsugo mo koko de naraimashita.

10. Sen'sei wa donata deshita ka?

11. Namae wa wasuremashita.

5.7.3 Substitution Drill

Kore wa *kyooshitsu* desu ka?

1.	*are*	....	*Are* wa kyooshitsu desu ka?
2.	*gin'koo*	....	Are wa *gin'koo* desu ka?
3.	jimusho	....	Are wa jimusho desu ka?
4.	Shin'juku Eki	....	Are wa Shin'juku Eki desu ka?
5.	sore	....	Sore wa Shin'juku Eki desu ka?
6.	en'pitsu	....	Sore wa en'pitsu desu ka?
7.	inu	....	Sore wa inu desu ka?
8.	otearai	....	Sore wa otearai desu ka?
9.	tori	....	Sore wa tori desu ka?
10.	kore	....	Kore wa tori desu ka?
11.	nan	....	Kore wa nan desu ka?
12.	sore	....	Sore wa nan desu ka?
13.	are	....	Are wa nan desu ka?

5.7.4 Substitution Drill

Anata wa *sen'sei* desu ka?

1.	gakusei	....	Anata wa gakusei desu ka?
2.	donata	....	Anata wa donata desu ka?
3.	kono kata	....	Kono kata wa donata desu ka?
4.	tomodachi	....	Kono kata wa tomodachi desu ka?
5.	nan no sen'sei	....	Kono kata wa nan no sen'sei desu ka?
6.	anata	....	Anata wa nan no sen'sei desu ka?
7.	Katoo sen'sei	....	Anata wa Katoo sen'sei desu ka?

5.7.5 Transformation Drill

1. *Ima* watakushi wa gakusei *desu*. ——→ *Mae* watakushi wa gakusei *deshita*.

2. Ima kono kata wa sen'sei desu. ——→ Mae kono kata wa sen'sei deshita.

3. Ima koko wa gin'koo desu. ——→ Mae koko wa gin'koo deshita.

4. Ima nihon'go ga heta desu. ——→ Mae nihon'go ga heta deshita.

5. Ima eigo ga joozu desu. ——→ Mae eigo ga joozu deshita.

6. Ima ben'kyoo ga kirai desu. ——→ Mae ben'kyoo ga kirai deshita.

7. Ima eiga ga suki desu. ——→ Mae eiga ga suki deshita.

8. Ima soo desu ka? ——→ Mae soo deshita ka?

5.7.6 Transformation Drill (*ga* ——→ *wa*)

1. Suzuki san *ga* imasu. ——→ Suzuki san *wa* imasu.

2. Are ga kyooshitsu desu. ——→ Are wa kyooshitsu desu.

3. Nakamura san ga kimashita. ——→ Nakamura san wa kimashita.

4. Chuugokugo ga joozu desu. ——→ Chuugokugo wa joozu desu.

5. Watakushi ga Sumisu desu. ——→ Watakushi wa Sumisu desu.

6. Hon ga koko ni arimasu. ——→ Hon wa koko ni arimasu.

7. Kono kata ga watakushi no sen'sei desu. ——→ Kono kata wa watakushi no sen'sei desu.

8. Sen'sei no namae ga chigaimasu. ——→ Sen'sei no namae wa chigaimasu.

9. Ten'pura ga kirai desu. ——→ Ten'pura wa kirai desu.

10. Den'wa ga arimasu. ——→ Den'wa wa arimasu.

11. Sore ga daigaku desu. ——→ Sore wa daigaku desu.

12. Tabako ga suki desu. ——→ Tabako wa suki desu.

5.7.7 Response Drill (*o* ——→ *wa*)

1. Namae *o* wasuremashita ka? . . . . Hai, namae *wa* wasuremashita.

2. Eigo o naraimashita ka? . . . . Hai, eigo wa naraimashita.

3. En'pitsu o kaimashita ka? . . . . Hai, en'pitsu wa kaimashita.

4. Asagohan o tabemashita ka? . . . . Hai, asagohan wa tabemashita.

5. Kaimono o shimashita ka? . . . . Hai, kaimono wa shimashita.

6. Mizu o nomimashita ka? . . . . Hai, mizu wa nomimashita.

7. Repooto o kakimashita ka? . . . . Hai, repooto wa kakimashita.

76

5.7.8 Transformation Drill (*wa, ga, o* —→ *mo*)

1. Nihon'go *o* hanashimasu.   —→ Nihon'go *mo* hanashimasu.

2. Anata wa gakusei desu ka?   —→ Anata mo gakusei desu ka?

3. Ben'kyoo ga suki desu.   —→ Ben'kyoo mo suki desu.

4. Sore wa kyooshitsu desu ka? —→ Sore mo kyooshitsu desu ka?

5. Repooto o kakimashita.   —→ Repooto mo kakimashita.

6. Kono kata wa Furan'su e kaerimasu. —→ Kono kata mo Furan'su e kaerimasu.

7. Kore wa jisho desu.   —→ Kore mo jisho desu.

8. Shin'juku de eiga o mimashita. —→ Shin'juku de eiga mo mimashita.

9. Sumisu san wa tomodachi desu. —→ Sumisu san mo tomodachi desu.

10. Inu ga imasu.   —→ Inu mo imasu.

11. Chuugokugo o naraimashoo. —→ Chuugokugo mo naraimashoo.

12. Namae o wasuremashita. —→ Namae mo wasuremashita.

5.7.9 Expansion Drill

1. Kore wa hon desu.
   watakushi no   .... Kore wa watakushi no hon desu.

2. Jisho o kaimashita.
   nihon'go no   .... Nihon'go no jisho o kaimashita.

3. Watakushi wa gakusei desu.
   Hawai Daigaku no   .... Watakushi wa Hawai Daigaku no gakusei desu.

4. Eiga o mimashoo.
   Igirisu no   .... Igirisu no eiga o mimashoo.

5. Namae wa nan desu ka?
   anata no   .... Anata no namae wa nan desu ka?

6. Kono kata wa sen'sei desu ka?
   nan no   .... Kono kata wa nan no sen'sei desu ka?

7. Are wa heya desu ka?
   donata no   .... Are wa donata no heya desu ka?

8. Anata wa gakusei desu ka?
   doko no   .... Anata wa doko no gakusei desu ka?

9. Sore wa gin'koo desu.
   Nihon no   ,... Sore wa Nihon no gin'koo desu.

10. Depaato de kaimono o shimashita.   .... Gin'za no depaato de kaimono o shimashita.
    Gin'za no

11. Itoo san wa tomodachi desu.   .... Itoo san wa Sumisu san no tomodachi desu.
    Sumisu san no

12. Tabako to sake ga suki desu.   .... Nihon no tabako to sake ga suki desu.
    Nihon no

5.7.10 Expansion Drill

1. Kore wa watakushi no hon desu.   .... Kore wa watakushi no nihon'go no hon desu.
   Kore wa nihon'go no hon desu.

2. Anata no jisho o mimashoo.   .... Anata no eigo no jisho o mimashoo.
   Eigo no jisho o mimashoo.

3. Katoo sen'sei no kyooshitsu e ikimashoo. .... Katoo sen'sei no nihon'go no kyooshitsu e ikimashoo.
   Nihon'go no kyooshitsu e ikimashoo.

4. Watakushi no sen'sei wa Sumisu sen'sei deshita. Watakushi no roshiago no sen'sei wa Sumisu sen'sei
   Roshiago no sen'sei wa Sumisu sen'sei deshita.   deshita.

5. Kono kata wa Kariforunia Daigaku no   Kono kata wa Kariforunia Daigaku no furan'sugo no
      gakusei desu.   ....   gakusei desu.
   Kono kata wa furan'sugo no gakusei desu.

6. Sore wa donata no hon desu ka?   .... Sore wa donata no gaikokugo no hon desu ka?
   Sore wa gaikokugo no hon desu ka?

7. Are wa daigaku no jisho desu.   .... Are wa daigaku no nihon'go no jisho desu.
   Are wa nihon'go no jisho desu.

5.7.11 Expansion Drill

1. Heta deshita.   .... Heta deshita.

   furan'sugo ga   .... Furan'sugo ga heta deshita.

   Kazuko san wa   .... Kazuko san wa furan'sugo ga heta deshita.

2. Joozu desu nee.   .... Joozu desu nee.

   roshiago ga   .... Roshiago ga joozu desu nee.

   anata wa   .... Anata wa roshiago ga joozu desu nee.

3. Suki desu.   .... Suki desu.

   ben'kyoo ga   .... Ben'kyoo ga suki desu.

   gaikokugo no   .... Gaikokugo no ben'kyoo ga suki desu.

   watakushi wa   .... Watakushi wa gaikokugo no ben'kyoo ga suki desu.

4. Kirai desu. .... Kirai desu.

   sake ga .... Sake ga kirai desu.

   Nihon no .... Nihon no sake ga kirai desu.

   Sumisu san wa .... Sumisu san wa Nihon no sake ga kirai desu.

5.7.12 Response Drill

1. Anata wa sen'sei desu ka?
   iie, gakusei .... Iie, gakusei desu.

2. Nanigo o naraimashita ka?
   eigo .... Eigo o naraimashita.

3. Kono kata wa donata desu ka?
   Katoo sen'sei .... (Kono kata wa) Katoo sen'sei desu.

4. Dore ga anata no heya desu ka?
   sore .... Sore ga watakushi no heya desu.

5. Anata wa mae Meriiran'do Daigaku no
     gakusei deshita ka?   Hai, (watakushi wa mae) Meriiran'do Daigaku no
   hai ....   gakusei deshita.

6. Anata wa furan'sugo o hanashimasu ka?
   iie, chuugokugo .... Iie, chuugokugo o hanashimasu.

7. Kore wa nan desu ka?
   Nihon no kamera .... (Sore wa) Nihon no kamera desu.

8. Anata wa koohii ga suki desu ka?
   iie, ocha .... Iie, (watakushi wa) ocha ga suki desu.

9. Dore ga anata no en'pitsu desu ka?
   kore to sore .... Kore to sore ga watakushi no en'pitsu desu.

5.7.13 E-J Expansion Drill

1. Gakusei desu. .... Gakusei desu.

   of the Japanese language .... Nihon'go no gakusei desu.

   of the University of Maryland .... Meriiran'do Daigaku no nihon'go no gakusei desu.

   I am .... Watakushi wa Meriiran'do Daigaku no nihon'go no
     gakusei desu.

2. Naraimashita. .... Naraimashita.

   what language? .... Nanigo o naraimashita ka?

   at the University of California .... Kariforunia Daigaku de nanigo o naraimashita ka?

   Mr. Smith .... Sumisu san wa Kariforunia Daigaku de nanigo o
     naraimashita ka?

3. Suki deshita.   .... Suki deshita.

   the study   .... Ben'kyoo ga suki deshita.

   the study of foreign languages   .... Gaikokugo no ben'kyoo ga suki deshita.

   before   .... Mae gaikokugo no ben'kyoo ga suki deshita.

   Miss Itō   .... Itoo san wa mae gaikokugo no ben'kyoo ga suki deshita.

4. Joozu desu ka?   .... Joozu desu ka?

   Russian too   .... Roshiago mo joozu desu ka?

   you   .... Anata wa roshiago mo joozu desu ka?

   now   .... Ima anata wa roshiago mo joozu desu ka?

5. Ikimasu ka?   .... Ikimasu ka?

   to a university   .... Daigaku e ikimasu ka?

   university in France   .... Furan'su no daigaku e ikimasu ka?

   who?   .... Dare ga Furan'su no daigaku e ikimasu ka?

6. Mimasu.   .... Mimasu.

   movie   .... Eiga o mimasu.

   American movie   .... Amerika no eiga o mimasu.

   again   .... Mata Amerika no eiga o mimasu.

   tomorrow   .... Ashita mata Amerika no eiga o mimasu.

7. Kirai desu.   .... Kirai desu.

   dog   .... Inu ga kirai desu.

   friend too   .... Tomodachi mo inu ga kirai desu.

   friend of mine   .... Watakushi no tomodachi mo inu ga kirai desu.

8. Kaimashita ka?   .... Kaimashita ka?

   dictionary   .... Jisho o kaimashita ka?

   of what?   .... Nan no jisho o kaimashita ka?

   yesterday   .... Kinoo nan no jisho o kaimashita ka?

9. Heta deshita.   .... Heta deshita.

   French   .... Furan'sugo ga heta deshita.

   before   .... Mae furan'sugo ga heta deshita.

   I   .... Watakushi wa mae furan'sugo ga heta deshita.

10. Wasuremashita.   .... Wasuremashita.

    name too   .... Namae mo wasuremashita.

    the teacher's name   .... Sen'sei no namae mo wasuremashita.

    teacher of German   .... Doitsugo no sen'sei no namae mo wasuremashita.

5.7.14 E-J Response Drill (Review)

1. Dore o kaimashoo ka?
    that one over there   .... Are o kaimashoo.

2. Heya ni nani ga arimasu ka?
    books and pencils   .... Hon to en'pitsu ga arimasu.

3. Doko e ikimashoo ka?
    to the office   .... Jimusho e ikimashoo.

4. Jisho wa doko ni arimasu ka?   ....
    in the classroom   .... Kyooshitsu ni arimasu.

5. Doko de kono kata o mimashita ka?
    at the bank   .... Gin'koo de mimashita.

6. Shokudoo ni dare ga imasu ka?
    teacher   .... Sen'sei ga imasu.

7. Nani o naraimashoo ka?
    foreign languages   .... Gaikokugo o naraimashoo.

8. Donata o machimashita ka?
    Mr. Nakamura's friend   .... Nakamura san no tomodachi o machimashita.

9. Doitsu e ikimashoo ka?
    no, to the States   .... Iie, Amerika e ikimashoo.

10. Nanigo o hanashimasu ka?
    Chinese   .... Chuugokugo o hanashimasu.

5.8 EXERCISES

5.8.1 What would you say when:

1. you are introduced to someone?

2. you are about to leave the place you have visited?

3. you agree with what someone says?

4. you want to deny what someone says?

5. you want to tell someone to come again?

5.8.2 Choose one of the following Relationals, referring to the given English sentence:

1. Kore (wa, ga) watakushi no heya desu.   "This is my room." (no emphasis on "this")

2. Dore (wa, ga) anata no hon desu ka?   "Which is your book?"

3. Kono kata (wa, ga) Yamada san desu.   "This person is Mr. Yamada." (emphasis on "this person")

4. Anata (wa, ga) kaimono (wa, ga) kirai desu ka?   "Do you dislike shopping?"

5. Kono kata (wa, ga) Yamada san desu.   "This person is Mr. Yamada." (no emphasis on "this person")

6. Anata (wa, ga) doko de naraimashita ka?   "Where did you take lessons?"

7. Anata (wa, mo) doitsugo (o, mo) naraimashita ka?   "Did you study German (in addition to other languages)?"

8. Anata (wa, mo) nihon'go (ga, mo) joozu desu nee.   "Your Japanese is good (like other people)."

9. Donata (wa, ga) anata no sen'sei desu ka?   "Who is your teacher?"

10. Anata no sen'sei (wa, ga) donata desu ka?   "Who is your teacher?"

11. Nanigo (wa, ga) suki desu ka?   "What language do you like?"

12. Sore (wa, ga) nan desu ka?   "What is that?"

13. Nani (ga, o) chigaimasu ka?   "What is different?"

5.8.3 Rearrange each group of the following words into a good Japanese sentence:

1. ka   ohima   ima   desu
   (   )

2. donata   wa   are   en'pitsu   desu   no   ka
   (   )

3. Sumisu san   ga   nihon'go   nee   joozu   wa   desu
   (   )

4. ka   sen'sei   deshita   donata   wa
   (   )

5. soko   mo   tomodachi   o   nihon'go   naraimashita   de
   (   )

6. wa   Hawai Daigaku   deshita   gakusei   mae   watakushi   no
   (   )

7. ka   desu   gakkoo   nan   no   namae   wa
   (   )

82

5.8.4 Carry on dialogs according to the following English:

1. Mr. Smith greets Mr. Yamada to whom he has just been introduced.

   Mr. Yamada greets him back.

   Mr. Smith asks Mr. Yamada if he is a student.

   Mr. Yamada answers that he is a student of Tōkyō University.

   Mr. Smith asks if Mr. Yamada studied French at the university.

   Mr. Yamada answers that he studied German.

   Mr. Smith says that he also studied German, and that he speaks French, too.

2. "Whose book is this?"

   "That is Professor Smith's book."

   "What book is this?"

   "That's a book of the French language. Professor Smith is a teacher of French."

   "Is he? Is that one over there a book of French too?"

   "No, that is different. That is a book of Japanese. I studied Japanese at the University of Maryland."

   "No wonder your Japanese is good."

   "No, it isn't. But I liked the study of Japanese."

LESSON 6

— Review —

6.1 PATTERN

6.1.1 Place Nominative + *e* + motion Verb

a.   (2)

koko
soko
asoko
kono hen

gin'koo
jimusho
eki
resutoran
shokudoo
(o)tearai
heya
daigaku
gakkoo
kyooshitsu
Yamada san no uchi
Tookyoo no depaato

		(1)		
	e	ikimasu	ka ?	
		kimasu	yo	
		kaerimasu	ne	

Igirisu
Chuugoku
Roshia
Furan'su
Doitsu
Amerika
Nihon
Gin'za
Kan'da
Shin'juku
Hawai Daigaku
Kariforunia Daigaku
Meriiran'do Daigaku
Tookyoo Gin'koo

     ↓
   (2)

doko
donata no uchi
dare no heya
doko no resutoran
nan no gakkoo

		(1)	
	e	....	ka ?
		....	
		....	

b.

(3)	wa (ga) (mo)	(2)	e	(1)	ka? yo ne
watakushi		soko			
watashi		asoko			
anata					
kono kata				ikimasu	ka?
Sumisu san		kyooshitsu		kimasu	yo
tomodachi		uchi		kaerimasu	ne
sen'sei		Igirisu			
gakusei		Hawai Daigaku			
kono hito					
inu		uchi			

↓

(3)	ga	(2)	e	(1)	ka?
donata		....		....	
dare		....		....	ka?
nani		....		....	

6.1.2 Nominative + *o* + transitive Verb

a.

(2)	o (wa) (mo)	(1)	ka? yo ne
ocha			
(o)sake			
koohii			
gyuunyuu		nomimasu	
biiru			
mizu			
kore			
gohan			
asagohan			
hirugohan			
ban'gohan			
pan		tabemasu	ka?
bifuteki			yo
ten'pura			ne
sore			
repooto			
tegami			
namae		kakimasu	
furan'sugo			
hon			
are			
chuugokugo			
roshiago		naraimasu	
furan'sugo			
doitsugo			

nihon'go gaikokugo		hanashimasu		
en'pitsu jisho hon taipuraitaa kamera tabako matchi		kaimasu		
eiga terebi kore sore are	o (wa) (mo)	mimasu	ka ? yo ne	
namae eigo		wasuremasu		
Kazuko san tomodachi sen'sei anata tegami den'wa		machimasu		
haizara hon Keiko san		sagashimasu		
kaimono		shimasu		

↓

(2)	(1)	
nani dore	nomimasu	
nani dore	tabemasu	
nani dore	kakimasu	
nani dore nanigo	naraimasu hanashimasu	ka ?
nani dore	kaimasu	
nani dore	mimasu	
nani dore nanigo	wasuremasu	

nani / dore / donata / dare		machimasu	
nani / dore / donata / dare	o	sagashimasu	ka ?
nani		shimasu	

b.

(3)		(2)		(1)	
watakushi		mizu		nomimasu	
watashi		gohan		tabemasu	
anata		tegami		kakimasu	
kono kata	wa	gaikokugo		naraimasu	
tomodachi	(ga)	jisho	o	hanashimasu	ka ?
sen'sei	(mo)	eiga		kaimasu	yo
gakusei		namae		mimasu	ne
Sumisu san		Ishii san		wasuremasu	
Keiko san		sen'sei		machimasu	
		kaimono		sagashimasu	
				shimasu	

↓

(3)		(2)		(1)	
donata / dare	ga	....	o	....	ka ?

6.1.3 Place Nominative + *de* + Nominative + *o* + transitive Verb

a.

(3)		(2)		(1)	
resutoran / shokudoo / koko		mizu / ocha / are		nomimasu	
uchi / Gin'za / soko	de	asagohan / bifuteki	o / mo	tabemasu	ka ? / yo / ne
kyooshitsu / heya / jimusho		repooto / tegami		kakimasu	
gakkoo / daigaku / Nihon		nihon'go		naraimasu / hanashimasu	

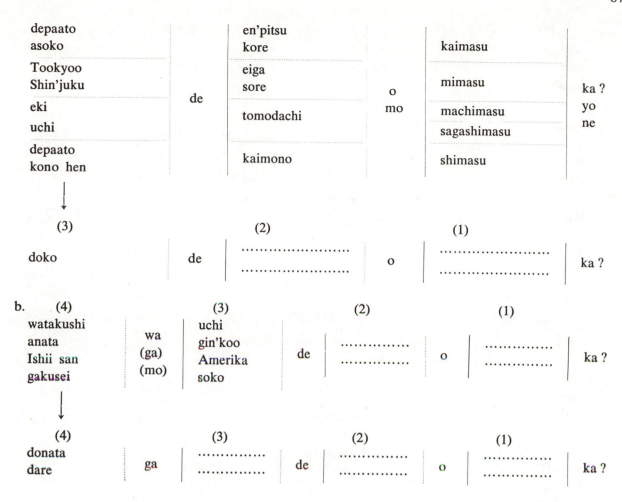

```
depaato              en'pitsu
asoko                kore              kaimasu
                                                          ka ?
Tookyoo              eiga
Shin'juku            sore              mimasu             yo
                de            o                            ne
eki                               mo   machimasu
                     tomodachi
uchi                                    sagashimasu

depaato
kono hen             kaimono           shimasu
```

(3)   (2)   (1)

```
doko         de   ..................   o   ..................   ka ?
                  ..................       ..................
```

b.   (4)   (3)   (2)   (1)

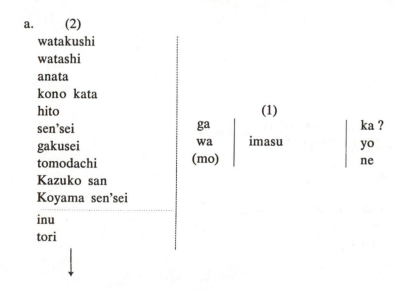

```
watakushi        uchi
anata       wa   gin'koo
Ishii san   (ga) Amerika   de  ........  o  ........  ka ?
gakusei     (mo) soko          ........     ........
```

(4)   (3)   (2)   (1)

```
donata      ga   ........   de   ........   o   ........   ka ?
dare             ........        ........       ........
```

6.1.4 Place Nominative + *ni* + {animate Nominative + *ga* + *imasu* / inanimate Nominative + *ga* + *arimasu*}

a.   (2)

```
watakushi
watashi
anata
kono kata
hito                      (1)
sen'sei          ga              ka ?
gakusei          wa    imasu     yo
tomodachi        (mo)            ne
Kazuko san
Koyama sen'sei

inu
tori
```

88

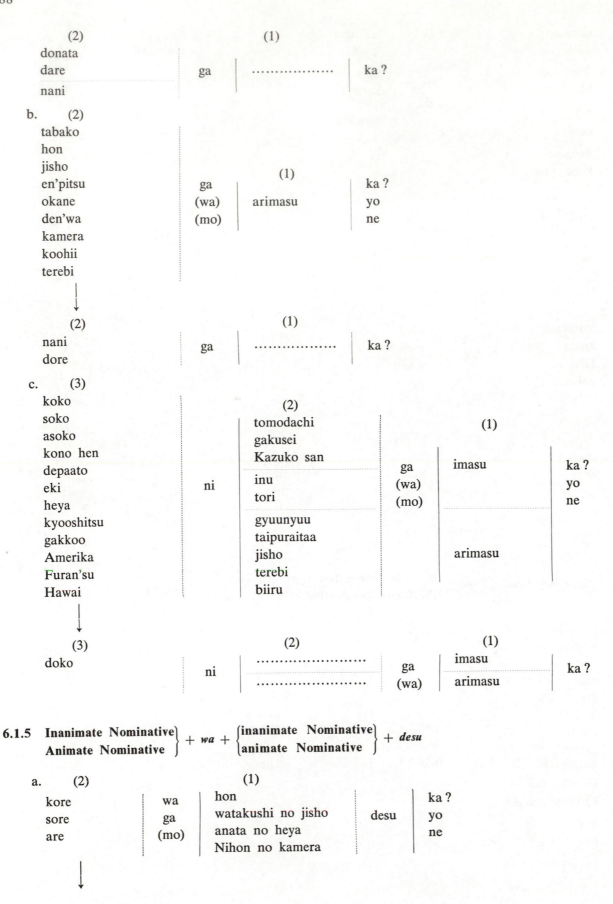

	(2)		(1)		
donata					
dare		ga	....	ka ?	
nani					

b.　(2)

tabako				
hon				
jisho			(1)	
en'pitsu	ga		ka ?	
okane	(wa)	arimasu	yo	
den'wa	(mo)		ne	
kamera				
koohii				
terebi				

↓

	(2)		(1)	
nani	ga	....	ka ?	
dore				

c.　(3)

koko			(2)			(1)		
soko		tomodachi					
asoko		gakusei					
kono hen		Kazuko san		ga	imasu	ka ?	
depaato	ni	inu		(wa)		yo	
eki		tori		(mo)		ne	
heya							
kyooshitsu		gyuunyuu					
gakkoo		taipuraitaa					
Amerika		jisho			arimasu		
Furan'su		terebi					
Hawai		biiru					

↓

	(3)		(2)		(1)	
doko	ni	....	ga	imasu	ka ?	
		....	(wa)	arimasu		

6.1.5 Inanimate Nominative ⎫
Animate Nominative ⎬ + *wa* + {**inanimate Nominative**} + *desu*
⎭ {**animate Nominative**}

a.　(2)　　　　　　　　(1)

kore	wa	hon	desu	ka ?
sore	ga	watakushi no jisho		yo
are	(mo)	anata no heya		ne
		Nihon no kamera		

↓

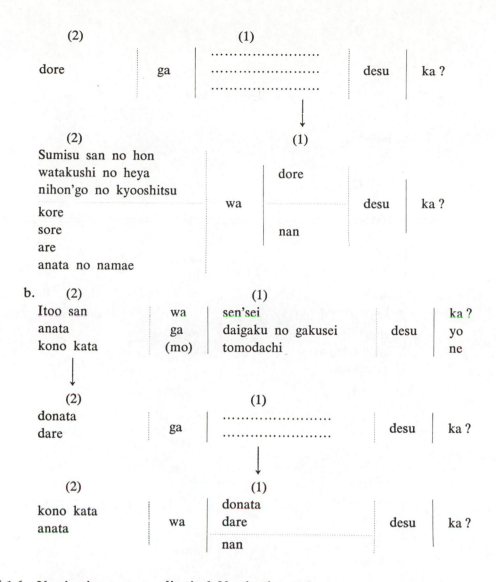

```
        (2)                    (1)
    dore       ga    ......................    desu   ka ?
                     ......................
                     ......................
                              |
                              ↓

        (2)                         (1)
    Sumisu san no hon
    watakushi no heya                dore
    nihon'go no kyooshitsu    wa              desu   ka ?
    kore
    sore                             nan
    are
    anata no namae
```

b.
```
        (2)                    (1)
    Itoo san    wa     sen'sei                       ka ?
    anata       ga     daigaku no gakusei    desu    yo
    kono kata   (mo)   tomodachi                     ne
       |
       ↓
        (2)                    (1)
    donata      ga    ......................    desu   ka ?
    dare              ......................
                              |
                              ↓
        (2)                    (1)
    kono kata                  donata
    anata       wa    dare                     desu   ka ?
                               nan
```

6.1.6 Nominative + *ga* + adjectival Nominative + *desu*

a.
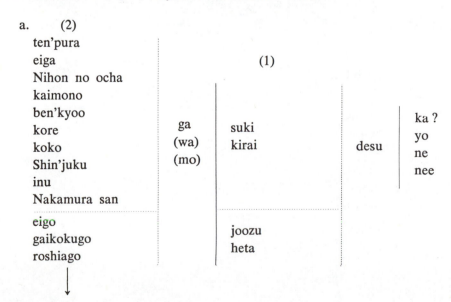

```
        (2)
    ten'pura
    eiga                         (1)
    Nihon no ocha
    kaimono
    ben'kyoo
    kore          ga    suki              ka ?
    koko          (wa)  kirai     desu    yo
    Shin'juku     (mo)                    ne
    inu                                   nee
    Nakamura san

    eigo                joozu
    gaikokugo           heta
    roshiago
       |
       ↓
```

	(2)		(1)		
	dore				
	nani		suki		
	doko		kirai		
	donata	ga		desu	ka ?
	dare				
	nani		joozu		
	nanigo		heta		

b.

	(3)		(2)		(1)		
	watakushi		tabako				ka ?
	anata		bifuteki				yo
	kono kata		sake		suki	desu	ne
	Sumisu san	wa	sore		kirai		nee
	tomodachi		Furan'su	ga			
	sen'sei		inu				
	gakusei		Kazuko san		joozu		
			eigo		heta		
			chuugokugo				
			gaikokugo				

↓

	(3)		(2)		(1)		
	....		nani				
			dore		suki		
			doko		kirai		
	....	wa	donata	ga		desu	ka ?
			dare				
	....		nani		joozu		
			dore		heta		
			nanigo				

6.1.7 Nominative + *no* + Nominative

a.

	(2)		(1)
	watakushi		tomodachi
	anata		inu
	kono kata		namae
	sen'sei		hon
	gakusei	no	heya
	Suzuki san		tegami
			jisho
	gakkoo		jimusho
	Meriiran'do Daigaku		gakusei
	koko		sen'sei

↓

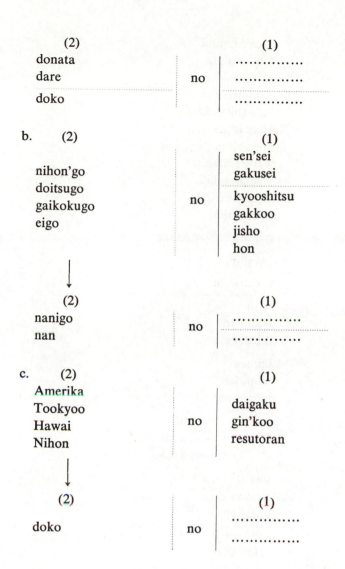

	(2)			(1)
	donata		no	....
	dare		no	....
	doko			....

b.

	(2)			(1)
	nihon'go			sen'sei
	doitsugo			gakusei
	gaikokugo		no	kyooshitsu
	eigo			gakkoo
				jisho
				hon

	(2)			(1)
	nanigo		no	....
	nan			....

c.

	(2)			(1)
	Amerika			daigaku
	Tookyoo		no	gin'koo
	Hawai			resutoran
	Nihon			

	(2)			(1)
	doko		no	....
				....

6.2 CONJUGATION

6.2.1 Verb

a.

ikimasu
ikimasen
ikimashita
ikimashoo

b.

		ikimashita
kinoo		ikimashita
mae	uchi e	kimashita
kyoo		kaerimashita

kinoo mae kyoo	sore o	nomimashita tabemashita kakimashita naraimashita hanashimashita kaimashita mimashita wasuremashita machimashita sagashimashita shimashita
	koko de	(~ o)　~-mashita
	eki ni	imashita arimashita
ima kyoo ashita mainichi	soko e	ikimasu ikimasen ikimashoo
	sore o	mimasu mimasen mimashoo
	soko de	(~ o)　~-masu ~-masen ~-mashoo
	eki ni	imasu imasen imashoo arimasu arimasen

6.2.2 Copula

a.   Nominative + *desu*
      Nominative + *deshita*

b.

ima	gakusei tomodachi	desu
mae	joozu heta suki kirai	deshita

6.3 AURAL COMPREHENSION

Listen to the following narration read by the instructor:

わたくしは　<u>すみす</u>です。　まえ、<u>あめりかの</u>　だいがくで

にほんごを　ならいました。　でも、まだ　へたです。

　わたくしは　きのう、にほんへ　きました。　いま、とうきょうに

います。　わたくしは　にほんごの　べんきょうが　すきです。

にほんの　がっこうで　また　にほんごを　ならいます。

94

LESSON 7

7.1 USEFUL EXPRESSIONS

Doozo.

"Please." "Here you are." "Please go ahead." This expression is used alone to mean offering or invitation.

7.2 DIALOG

— Books, magazines, and newspapers —

Bill : Suujii san, itsumo*1 dono*2 hon'ya*3 de hon o kaimasu ka /

Susie : Taitei*1 Maruzen de kaimasu. Chotto*1 tooi*4 desu ga,*5 totemo ii desu yo.

Anata wa /

Bill : Boku*6 wa taitei gakkoo no toshokan de karimasu. Sono hon wa zuibun*1

ookii desu nee. Takakatta*7 n*8 desu ka /

Susie : Iie, yasukatta n desu.

Bill : Moo*1 yomimashita ka /

Susie : Ee, yomimashita.

Bill : Doo*9 deshita ka /

Susie : Totemo omoshirokatta desu. Anata mo yomimasen ka*10/

Bill : Doomo arigatoo.

Susie : Doozo. (Looking at a magazine in Bill's hand) Sore wa Nihon no zasshi desu ne /

Nihon'go no zasshi wa yasashii desu ka, muzukashii desu ka*11/

Bill : Yasashii desu. Dakara, boku wa tokidoki Nihon no zasshi to shin'bun o

yomimasu.

Susie : Erai desu nee.

7.3 PATTERN SENTENCES

7.3.1

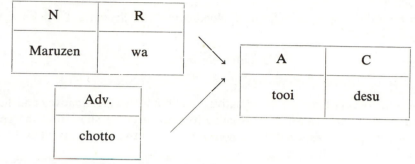

"Maruzen is a little far."

7.3.2

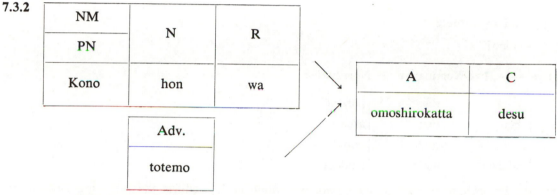

"This book was very interesting."

7.4 NOTES

7.4.1 *Itsumo* "always" (Note: *itsumo* often means "usually" in Japanese), *taitei* "generally," *totemo* "very," *tokidoki* "sometimes," *chotto* "a little," *zuibun* "extremely," and *moo* "already" are Adverbs. They usually occur immediately before Predicates or in any other place except after Predicates, and form Predicate Modifiers.

Predicate ⟶ Adverb + Predicate

Itsumo dono hon'ya de hon o kaimasu ka ?	"At which book store do [you] usually buy books?"
Totemo ii desu.	"[It] is very good."
Zuibun joozu desu nee.	"How skillful!"
Chotto takai desu.	"[It] is a little expensive."
Nihon no gakusei wa taitei koohii ga suki desu.	"Japanese students generally like coffee."
Watakushi wa itsumo uchi de hirugohan o tabemasu.	"I always have lunch at home."

Tokidoki depaato e ikimasu.	"[I] sometimes go to department stores."
Moo jisho o kaimashita ka?	"Did [you] already buy a dictionary?"

When *zuibun* is used with an Adjective or an adjectival Nominative, the Sentence Particles *nee, ne,* and *yo* are used.

Zuibun ookii desu nee.	"It's extremely big!"

7.4.2 *Dono* is a Pre-Nominative that occurs before a Nominative, modifying the Nominative, and has the meaning of "which," as in "which book store?" Pre-Nominatives are used to show that the speaker is referring to specific things or people as English demonstrative adjectives such as "this," "that," and "which?" do. Here are words of this series:

kono	"this"
sono	"that"
ano	"that over there"
dono	"which?"

Nominative ——→ Pre-Nominative + Nominative

kono	-kata	"this"	person"
sono	-hen	"that"	area"
ano	hon	"that"	book"
dono	gakusei	"which"	student"

Note that the Pre-Nominative *kono, sono, ano,* and *dono* each modifies the following Nominative; and that *kore, sore, are,* and *dore* are Nominatives.

Kore wa yasui desu ka?	"Is this inexpensive?"
Kono hon wa yasui desu ka?	"Is this book inexpensive?"
Ano kata wa donata desu ka?	"Who is that person?"
Sono hen de kaimashoo.	"Let's buy it around there."
Dono gin'koo e ikimasu ka?	"Which bank are [you] going to?"

7.4.3 *Hon'ya* is a combination of *hon* "book" and *-ya* "-store" or "-shop," and means "bookstore." In the same manner, the words for most of the stores or shops where a certain product is sold, or for the dealers in the product, are formed:

hon'ya	"bookstore or book dealer"
kameraya	"camera shop or camera dealer"
shin'bun'ya	"newsstand or news dealer"
tabakoya	"tobacco shop or tobacco dealer"
pan'ya	"bakery or baker"

Women often refer to stores or dealers with *-san,* and others often use *-san* when they are thinking specifically of the dealer.

kameraya san   shin'bun'ya san   pan'ya san   tabakoya san

7.4.4 *Tooi* is the imperfect tense form of an Adjective meaning "is far." The imperfect tense form of any Adjective has one of these endings: *-ai, -ii, -ui,* or *-oi,* and the final *-i* is the inflected part of the Adjective. In the normal spoken style of Japanese, Adjectives are followed by the Copula *desu* when they are in the position of the final Predicate.

tooi desu	"is far"	......	chikai desu	"is near"
ii desu* (yoi desu)	"is good"	......	warui desu	"is bad"
takai desu	"is expensive"	......	yasui desu	"is inexpensive"
ookii desu	"is big"	......	chiisai desu	"is small"
omoshiroi desu	"is interesting"	......	tsumaranai desu	"is uninteresting"
muzukashii desu	"is difficult"	......	yasashii desu	"is easy"
erai desu	"is great"			

* Note that *ii* is the colloquial alternative of *yoi* meaning "good," and all the inflected forms of the Adjective meaning "good" are based on *yoi*. (See Note 7.4.7.)

The normal pattern of an Adjectival Predicate will be:

Adjective + *desu* ⟶ Nominative (subject) + { *ga* / *wa* or *mo* } + (Adverb) + Adjective + *desu*

Kono eiga wa totemo omoshiroi desu.	"This movie is very interesting."
Anata no uchi wa tooi desu ka?	"Is your house far?"
Dore ga muzukashii desu ka?	"Which is difficult?"
Bifuteki mo takai desu.	"Beefsteak is also expensive."
Ano byooin wa totemo ii desu.	"That hospital is very good."

7.4.5 *Ga* that occurs at the end of a non-final clause, or before a comma, is the clause Relational corresponding to "but," "although," etc. The Relational *ga* is used to connect two sentences, like a conjunction in English.

Sentence 1 / Sentence 2 } ⟶ Sentence 1 + *ga,* + Sentence 2

Tooi desu. / Ii desu. } ⟶ Tooi desu ga, ii desu.   "[It] is far, but [it] is good."

Ookii desu. / Yasui desu. } ⟶ Ookii desu ga, yasui desu.   "[The house] is large, but [it] is inexpensive."

In Japanese *ga* sometimes may be used less strictly than "but" in English. In that case, *ga* may be used merely to connect two sentences as if it were "and" in English.

98

Watakushi mo sono eiga o   "I saw that movie too, and it was interesting."
  mimashita ga, omoshirokatta desu.

7.4.6 *Boku* is an informal equivalent of *watakushi* "I," and is used only by men. *Atashi* is used by women. Neither *boku* nor *atashi* may be used on formal occasions.

7.4.7 *Takakatta* is the TA form or the perfect tense form of the Adjective *takai* and means "was expensive." As explained in Note 7.4.4, Adjectives inflect in Japanese. The plain perfect tense form — the TA form — of an Adjective is formulated by inflecting the *-i* ending of the imperfect tense form into *-katta*. The Copula *desu* will also follow this form in the normal spoken style.

Adjective(-*i*) + *desu* ⟶ Adjective(-*katta*) + *desu*

tooi desu	⟶ tookatta desu	"was far"
chikai desu	⟶ chikakatta desu	"was near"
ii desu* (yoi desu)	⟶ yokatta desu	"was good"
warui desu	⟶ warukatta desu	"was bad"
takai desu	⟶ takakatta desu	"was expensive"
yasui desu	⟶ yasukatta desu	"was inexpensive"
ookii desu	⟶ ookikatta desu	"was big"
chiisai desu	⟶ chiisakatta desu	"was small"
omoshiroi desu	⟶ omoshirokatta desu	"was interesting"
tsumaranai desu	⟶ tsumaranakatta desu	"was dull"
muzukashii desu	⟶ muzukashikatta desu	"was difficult"
yasashii desu	⟶ yasashikatta desu	"was easy"
erai desu	⟶ erakatta desu	"was great"

* The perfect tense form of *ii desu* is *yokatta desu*.

This text does not consider *takai deshita* as good usage, but prefers *takakatta desu*.

7.4.8 The *n* sometimes occurs between an Adjective and the Copula *desu*: *takai n desu*. In this case, *n* is called the Pre-Copula. The difference between *desu* and *n desu* is slight, but it may be said that *n desu* is a little more emphatic, colloquial, and elucidative.

Heya ga ookii n desu.   "The room is big, you know."

Eiga wa tsumaranakatta n desu ka? "Was the movie dull?"

7.4.9 *Doo* is an interrogative Nominative meaning "how?" Here are the Nominatives of this series:

koo "this way"
soo "that way" or "so"
aa "that way"
doo "what way?" or "how?"

Doo desu ka ?		"How is [it]?"

When these words are used before Predicates, they are classified as Adverbs.

Koo shimashoo ka ?   "Shall we do [it] this way?"

7.4.10 The negative imperfect tense form of a Verb plus the interrogative Sentence Particle *ka* can mean "Won't you (do)?"

Verb(*-masu*) + *ka* ? ⟶ Verb(*-masen*) + *ka* ?

Anata mo yomimasen ka ?   "Won't you read [it], too?"

Issho ni ikimasen ka ?   "Won't you go with me?"

Koohii o nomimasen ka ?   "Won't you have coffee?"

7.4.11 *Nihon'go no zasshi wa yasashii desu ka, muzukashii desu ka?* is called an alternate question, meaning "Are Japanese magazines easy or difficult?" An alternate question is one in which the listener is given two or more choices for an answer. When the original sentences share one or more Predicate Modifiers (abbr. PM), the Predicate Modifier may be deleted except in the first choice. Predicates in an alternate question may be identical or different.

PM_1 + PM_2 + Predicate1 + *ka?*
PM_1 + PM_3 + Predicate2 + *ka?*
⟶ PM_1 + PM_2 + Predicate1 + *ka*, PM_3 + Predicate2 + *ka?*

Kono jisho wa ii desu ka, warui desu ka ?   "Is this dictionary good, or bad?"

Kore wa anata no heya desu ka, Nakamura san no heya desu ka ?   "Is this your room, or Mr. Nakamura's room?"

Anata wa itsumo Asahi Shin'bun o yomimasu ka, Yomiuri Shin'bun o yomimasu ka, Mainichi Shin'bun o yomimasu ka ?   "Do you always read the Asahi newspaper, or the Yomiuri newspaper, or the Mainichi newspaper?"

7.5 VOCABULARY

Dialog

Suujii	....	N	Susie
itsumo	....	Adv.	always; usually (see 7.4.1)
dono	....	PN	which? (see 7.4.2)
hon'ya	....	N	book store (see 7.4.3)
taitei	....	Adv.	generally; in most cases
Maruzen	....	N	Maruzen Book Store
chotto	....	Adv.	a little

tooi	.... A	is far (see 7.4.4)
ga	.... Rc	but; although (see 7.4.5)
totemo	.... Adv.	very (see 7.4.1)
ii	.... A	is good (see 7.4.4)
boku	.... N	I (used by men) (see 7.4.6)
toshokan	.... N	(school or public) library
karimasu	 V	borrow (normal form of *kariru*)
sono	.... PN	that (see 7.4.2)
zuibun	.... Adv.	extremely; quite (see 7.4.1)
ookii	.... A	is big; is large
takakatta	.... A	was expensive (TA form of *takai*)
n (desu)	.. .. PC	(see 7.4.8)
yasukatta	. .. ... A	was inexpensive (TA form of *yasui*)
moo	.. .... Adv.	already (see 7.4.1)
yomimashita	 V	read (TA form of *yomimasu* ⟵ *yomu*⟩
doo	.... N	how? (see 7.4.9)
omoshirokatta	.... A	was interesting (TA form of *omoshiroi*)
zasshi	.... N	magazine
yasashii	.... A	is easy
muzukashii	.... A	is difficult
dakara	.. .. SI	so; therefore
tokidoki	.... Adv.	sometimes; once in a while
shin'bun	.... N	newspaper
erai	.... A	is great; is remarkable

Notes

takai	.... A	is expensive
kono	.... PN	this (see 7.4.2)
ano	.... PN	that over there (see 7.4.2)
yasui	.... A	is inexpensive
-ya	...... Nd	-store; -dealer (see 7.4.3)
kameraya	.... N	camera shop; camera dealer
shin'bun'ya	.... N	newsstand; newsdealer
tabakoya	.... N	tobacco shop
pan'ya	.... N	bakery
chikai	.... A	is near
yoi	,....... A	is good (see 7.4.4)

warui	....	A	is bad
chiisai	....	A	is small; is little (in size)
omoshiroi	....	A	is interesting
tsumaranai	....	A	is uninteresting; is dull; is unimportant
byooin	....	N	hospital
atashi	....	N	I (used by women) (see 7.4.6)
tookatta	....	A	was far (TA form of *tooi*)
chikakatta	....	A	was near (TA form of *chikai*)
yokatta	....	A	was good (TA form of *yoi*)
warukatta	....	A	was bad (TA form of *warui*)
ookikatta	....	A	was big; was large (TA form of *ookii*)
chiisakatta	....	A	was small; was little (in size) (TA form of *chiisai*)
tsumaranakatta	....	A	was uninteresting; was dull; was unimportant (TA form of *tsumaranai*)
muzukashikatta	....	A	was difficult (TA form of *muzukashii*)
yasashikatta	....	A	was easy (TA form of *yasashii*)
erakatta	....	A	was great (TA form of *erai*)
koo	....	N	in this way
soo	....	N	in that way; so
aa	....	N	in that way
Asahi Shin'bun	....	N	Asahi Newspaper (one of the big three newspapers in Japan)
Yomiuri Shin'bun	......	N	Yomiuri Newspaper (")
Mainichi Shin'bun	......	N	Mainichi Newspaper (")

7.6 HIRAGANA PRACTICE

7.6.1 Recognize the difference or similarity between two *hiragana* in each of the following pairs:

あ……あ	の……の	ね……ぬ	わ……れ
あ……め	の……お	ぬ……ぬ	れ……れ
あ……の	の……つ	ぬ……め	れ……ね
め……め	お……お	ぬ……わ	
め……の	お……あ	わ……わ	
め……ぬ	ね……ね	わ……ね	

102

7.6.2 Practice writing the following *hiragana:*

1. あ [a] あ あ あ あ あ
2. め [me] め め め め
3. の [no] の の の
4. ぬ [nu] ぬ ぬ ぬ ぬ ぬ
5. お [o] お お お お
6. ね [ne] ね ね ね ね ね
7. わ [wa] わ わ わ わ わ
8. れ [re] れ れ れ れ

7.6.3 Read and write the following:

これ　　それ　　あれ　　わるい　　おてあらい

おもしろい　　あの　いぬ　　あさくさ　　わたくし

おおきい　　この　ほん　　あなたも　わすれましたね。

7.7 DRILLS

7.7.1 Pronunciation Drill

ookikatta desu	yasashikatta desu	yokatta desu	warukatta n desu
muzukashikatta n desu	chiisakatta n desu	omoshirokatta desu	takakatta desu
tsumaranakatta desu	chikakatta desu	yasukatta desu	tookatta n desu

7.7.2 Pattern Drill

1. Itsumo dono hon'ya de hon o kaimasu ka?

2. Taitei Maruzen de kaimasu.

3. Chotto tooi desu ga, totemo ii desu yo.

4. Sono hon wa buibun ookii desu nee.

5. Takakatta n desu ka?

6. Iie, yasukatta n desu.

7. Moo yomimashita ka?

8. Totemo omoshirokatta desu.

9. Anata mo yomimasen ka?

10. Nihon'go no zasshi wa yasashii desu ka, muzukashii desu ka?

11. Boku wa tokidoki Nihon no zasshi to shin'bun o yomimasu.

7.7.3 Transformation Drill

1. Kono hon wa taka*i* desu. ⟶ Kono hon wa taka*katta* desu.

2. Eiga wa tsumaranai desu. ⟶ Eiga wa tsumaranakatta desu.

3. Ano kata wa erai desu. ⟶ Ano kata wa erakatta desu.

4. Boku no inu wa ookii desu. ⟶ Boku no inu wa ookikatta desu.

5. Kono zasshi wa omoshiroi desu. ⟶ Kono zasshi wa omoshirokatta desu.

6. Ano hon'ya wa chiisai desu. ⟶ Ano hon'ya wa chiisakatta desu.

7. Kono hon wa ii desu. ⟶ Kono hon wa yokatta desu.

8. Sen'sei no namae wa muzukashii desu. ⟶ Sen'sei no namae wa muzukashikatta desu.

9. Tomodachi no uchi wa chikai desu. ⟶ Tomodachi no uchi wa chikakatta desu.

10. Kono jisho wa yasui desu. ⟶ Kono jisho wa yasukatta desu.

11. Nihon'go no shin'bun wa yasashii desu. ⟶ Nihon'go no shin'bun wa yasashikatta desu.

12. Sono gakusei wa warui desu. ⟶ Sono gakusei wa warukatta desu.

13. Tabakoya wa tooi desu. ⟶ Tabakoya wa tookatta desu.

7.7.4 Substitution Drill

A. Kono zasshi wa *omoshiroi* desu.

1. *yokatta* ...... Kono zasshi wa *yokatta* desu.

2. yasashii ...... Kono zasshi wa yasashii desu.

3. yasukatta ...... Kono zasshi wa yasukatta desu.

4. omoshirokatta ...... Kono zasshi wa omoshirokatta desu.

5. muzukashii ...... Kono zasshi wa muzukashii desu.

6. tsumaranai ...... Kono zasshi wa tsumaranai desu.

104

B. Suujii san no uchi wa *chiisai* desu.

1. tooi ...... Suujii san no uchi wa *tooi* desu.

2. ookii ...... Suujii san no uchi wa ookii desu.

3. chikakatta ...... Suujii san no uchi wa chikakatta desu.

4. takai ...... Suujii san no uchi wa takai desu.

5. chiisakatta ...... Suujii san no uchi wa chiisakatta desu.

7.7.5 Expansion Drill

A. 1. Gakkoo no toshokan wa ookii desu.
totemo ...... Gakkoo no toshokan wa totemo ookii desu.

2. Kono shin'bun wa tsumaranai desu.
chotto ...... Kono shin'bun wa chotto tsumaranai desu.

3. Roshiago wa muzukashii desu nee.
zuibun ...... Roshiago wa zuibun muzukashii desu nee.

4. Ano heya wa chiisakatta desu.
chotto ...... Ano heya wa chotto chiisakatta desu.

5. Kono zasshi wa omoshiroi desu.
itsumo ...... Kono zasshi wa itsumo omoshiroi desu.

6. Pan'ya wa tookatta desu.
totemo ...... Pan'ya wa totemo tookatta desu.

B. 1. Toshokan de hon o karimasu.
taitei ...... *Taitei* toshokan de hon o karimasu.

2. Asahi Shin'bun o yomimasu.
itsumo ...... Itsumo Asahi Shin'bun o yomimasu.

3. Eiga o mimasu.
tokidoki ...... Tokidoki eiga o mimasu.

4. Uchi e kaerimashoo.
sugu ...... Sugu uchi e kaerimashoo.

5. Yomimashita ka?
moo ...... Moo yomimashita ka?

6. Toshokan e ikimashoo.
mata ...... Mata toshokan e ikimashoo.

7. Shimasen ka?
koo ...... Koo shimasen ka?

7.7.6 Substitution Drill (Pre-Nominative)

1. *Kore* wa omoshiroi desu nee.
hon ...... *Kono hon* wa omoshiroi desu nee.

2. Sore wa yasukatta desu.
kamera ...... Sono kamera wa yasukatta desu.

3. Are wa watakushi no heya desu.
   heya ...... Ano heya wa watakushi no heya desu.

4. Sore wa Asahi Shin'bun desu.
   shin'bun ...... Sono shin'bun wa Asahi Shin'bun desu.

5. Kore wa yasashii desu.
   zasshi ...... Kono zasshi wa yasashii desu.

6. Dore ga muzukashikatta desu ka?
   gaikokugo ...... Dono gaikokugo ga muzukashikatta desu ka?

7. Are wa totemo chiisai desu.
   hon'ya ...... Ano hon'ya wa totemo chiisai desu.

8. Sore o moo yomimashita ka?
   shin'bun ...... Sono shin'bun o moo yomimashita ka?

9. Kore wa ii desu.
   byooin ...... Kono byooin wa ii desu.

10. Dore o mimashita ka?
    eiga ...... Dono eiga o mimashita ka?

7.7.7 Combination Drill

1. Zasshi wa yasui desu.
   Hon wa takai desu. ⟶ Zasshi wa yasui desu ga, hon wa takai desu.

2. Chotto tooi desu.
   Totemo ii desu. ⟶ Chotto tooi desu ga, totemo ii desu.

3. Boku wa gakusei desu.
   Boku no tomodachi wa sen'sei desu. ⟶ Boku wa gakusei desu ga, boku no tomodachi wa sen'sei desu.

4. Kono jisho wa chiisai desu.
   Kono jisho wa takakatta desu. ⟶ Kono jisho wa chiisai desu ga, takakatta desu.

5. Eiga wa yasashii desu.
   Furan'sugo wa muzukashii desu. ⟶ Eigo wa yasashii desu ga, furan'sugo wa muzukashii desu.

6. Tokidoki hon o kaimasu.
   Taitei toshokan de karimasu. ⟶ Tokidoki hon o kaimasu ga, taitei toshokan de karimasu.

7. Gin'koo wa chikai desu.
   Eki wa chotto tooi desu. ⟶ Gin'koo wa chikai desu ga, eki wa chotto tooi desu.

8. Mae chuugokugo o naraimashita.
   Moo wasuremashita. ⟶ Mae chuugokugo o naraimashita ga, moo wasuremashita.

7.7.8 Transformation Drill (alternate question)

A. 1. Nihon'go wa yasashii desu.
      Nihon'go wa muzukashii desu. ⟶ Nihon'go wa yasashii desu ka, muzukashii desu ka?

   2. Anata no uchi wa tooi desu.
      Anata no uchi wa chikai desu. ⟶ Anata no uchi wa tooi desu ka, chikai desu ka?

3. Eiga wa omoshirokatta desu.
   Eiga wa tsumaranakatta desu. $\left.\right\}\longrightarrow$ Eiga wa omoshirokatta desu ka, tsumaranakatta desu ka?

4. Ano heya wa yokatta desu.
   Ano heya wa warukatta desu. $\left.\right\}\longrightarrow$ Ano heya wa yokatta desu ka, warukatta desu ka?

5. Anata wa kaimono ga suki desu.
   Anata wa kaimono ga kirai desu. $\left.\right\}\longrightarrow$ Anata wa kaimono ga suki desu ka, kirai desu ka?

6. Sumisu san wa nihon'go ga joozu desu.
   Sumisu san wa nihon'go ga heta desu. $\left.\right\}\longrightarrow$ Sumisu san wa nihon'go ga joozu desu ka, heta desu ka?

B. 1. Asahi Shin'bun o yomimasu.
   Yomiuri Shin'bun o yomimasu. $\left.\right\}\longrightarrow$ Asahi Shin'bun o yomimasu ka, Yomiuri Shin'bun o yomimasu ka?

2. Hon wa toshokan de karimasu.
   Hon wa hon'ya de kaimasu. $\left.\right\}\longrightarrow$ Hon wa toshokan de karimasu ka, hon'ya de kaimasu ka?

3. Ano kata wa doitsugo o naraimashita.
   Ano kata wa furan'sugo o naraimashita. $\left.\right\}\longrightarrow$ Ano kata wa doitsugo o naraimashita ka, furan'sugo o naraimashita ka?

4. Uchi e kaerimashoo.
   Kaimono o shimashoo. $\left.\right\}\longrightarrow$ Uchi e kaerimashoo ka, kaimono o shimashoo ka?

5. Ocha o nomimasu.
   Koohii o nomimasu. $\left.\right\}\longrightarrow$ Ocha o nomimasu ka, koohii o nomimasu ka?

6. Kono zasshi o yomimashita.
   Sono shin'bun o yomimashita. $\left.\right\}\longrightarrow$ Kono zasshi o yomimashita ka, sono shin'bun o yomimashita ka?

7. Ashita eiga o mimashoo.
   Ashita uchi ni imashoo. $\left.\right\}\longrightarrow$ Ashita eiga o mimashoo ka, uchi ni imashoo ka?

7.7.9 Response Drill (antonym response)

1. Byooin wa *chikai* desu ka? $\longrightarrow$ *Iie,* (byooin wa) *tooi* desu.

2. Sono eiga wa tsumaranakatta desu ka? $\longrightarrow$ Iie, (sono eiga wa) omoshirokatta desu.

3. Gakkoo no toshokan wa chiisai desu ka? $\longrightarrow$ Iie, (gakkoo no toshokan wa) ookii desu.

4. Roshiago no ben'kyoo wa yasashikatta desu ka? $\longrightarrow$ Iie, (Roshiago no ben'kyoo wa) muzukashikatta desu.

5. Ano taipuraitaa wa warui desu ka? $\longrightarrow$ Iie, (ano taipuraitaa wa) ii desu.

6. Kono hon wa yasukatta desu ka? $\longrightarrow$ Iie, (kono hon wa) takakatta desu.

7. Kyooshitsu wa ookikatta desu ka? $\longrightarrow$ Iie, (kyooshitsu wa) chiisakatta desu.

8. Nihon'go no shin'bun wa muzukashii desu ka? $\longrightarrow$ Iie, (nihon'go no shin'bun wa) yasashii desu.

9. Tookyoo Eki wa tookatta desu ka? $\longrightarrow$ Iie, (Tookyoo Eki wa) chikakatta desu.

10. Nihon no kamera wa takai desu ka? $\longrightarrow$ Iie, (Nihon no kamera wa) yasui desu.

11. Kono zasshi wa omoshiroi desu ka? $\longrightarrow$ Iie, (kono zasshi wa) tsumaranai desu.

7.7.10 Transformation Drill

1. Issho ni *ikimasu.*   ⟶ Issho ni *ikimasen ka?*

2. Kono hon o yomimasu. ⟶ Kono hon o yomimasen ka?

3. Hirugohan o tabemasu. ⟶ Hirugohan o tabemasen ka?

4. Doitsugo o naraimasu. ⟶ Doitsugo o naraimasen ka?

5. Kamera to hon o kaimasu. ⟶ Kamera to hon o kaimasen ka?

6. Resutoran o sagashimasu. ⟶ Resutoran o sagashimasen ka?

7. Eki de machimasu. ⟶ Eki de machimasen ka?

8. Uchi e kaerimasu. ⟶ Uchi e kaerimasen ka?

7.8 EXERCISES

7.8.1 Fill in each blank with an appropriate word to match the idea expressed in English:

1. (   ) sono shin'bun o yomimashita ka?   "Have you already read that newspaper?"

2. Kono zasshi wa (   ) omoshiroi desu.   "This magazine is very interesting."

3. Ano jisho wa (   ) takakatta n desu.   "That dictionary was a little expensive."

4. Anata wa nihon'go ga (   ) joozu desu nee.   "Your Japanese is extremely good!"

5. Watakushi wa (   ) Asahi Shin'bun o yomimasu.   "I always read the Asahi newspaper."

6. (   ) kaerimasu.   "I'll come back soon."

7. Hon wa (   ) toshokan de karimasu (   ), (   ) Maruzen de kaimasu.

    "I generally borrow books at the library, but I sometimes buy them at Maruzen."

8. (   ) deshita ka?   "How was it?"

9. (   ) kimasu.   "I'll come again."

7.8.2 Transform the following into the perfect tense form:

1. Ano eigo no hon wa muzukashii desu.   4. Totemo chiisai desu.

2. Doo desu ka?   5. Kono en'pitsu wa ii desu yo.

3. Shin'bun o yomimasu ka?   6. Byooin wa chikai desu ka?

7.8.3 Choose the right word:

1. (   ) ga anata no zasshi desu ka?   3. (   ) wa boku no heya desu.
   dore, dono   *kore, kono*

2. (   ) kamera wa takakatta desu ka?   4. (   ) hon'ya e ikimashoo.
   sore, sono   *are, ano*

LESSON 8

8.1 USEFUL EXPRESSIONS

Ogen'ki desu ka /

This expression is the most common equivalent for "How are you?" Literally this means "Are you in good spirits?" *Gen'ki desu ka?* may also be used in less formal or polite speech.

Okagesama de.

This expression, which is used in various situations, is often used in reply to the above expression, and means "(Fine), thank you." The literal meaning is "Thanks to you, to God, etc." The informal expression, *(Ee), gen'ki desu* can also be used.

8.2 DIALOG

— Going to a coffee shop —

Yamamoto : Watanabe san ja arimasen*1 ka /

Watanabe : A! Yamamoto san Ogen'ki desu ka /

Yamamoto : Okagesama de. Anata wa /

Watanabe : Watakushi mo gen'ki desu.

Yamamoto : Ima isogashii desu ka /

Watanabe : Iie, amari*2 isogashiku arimasen.*3

Yamamoto : Chotto*4 sono hen de ocha o nomimasen ka /

Watanabe : Ee. Ano kissaten e hairimashoo ka /

Yamamoto : Ano mise no koohii wa chittomo*2 oishiku arimasen. Sore ni, on'gaku

mo*5 yoku arimasen yo. Den'en e ikimashoo.

Watanabe : Den'en wa tooi desu ka /

Yamamoto : Iie, tooku arimasen. Chikai n desu.

Watanabe : Jaa, soko e ikimashoo.

Yamamoto : Den'en wa amari kirei ja arimasen ga, shizuka desu. Sore ni, rekoodo ga totemo ii n desu. Anata mo on'gaku ga suki desu ka /

Watanabe :   Ee, kurashikku ga daisuki desu. Demo, jazu to popyuraa wa*6 amari

kikimasen.

Yamamoto : Watashi mo*5 jazu wa*6 suki ja arimasen. Saa, koko desu. Hairimashoo.

8.3 PATTERN SENTENCES

8.3.1

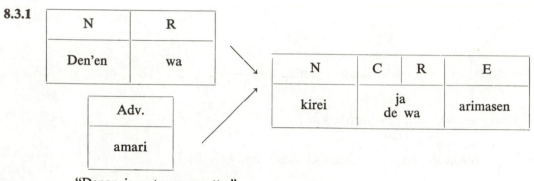

"Denen is not very pretty."

8.3.2

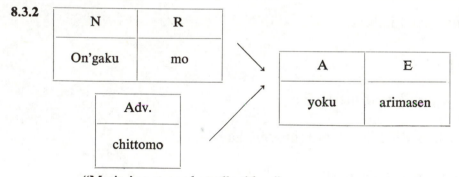

"Music is not good at all, either."

8.4 NOTES

8.4.1   *Watanabe san ja arimasen* is the negative of *Watanabe san desu*. The negative of a Nominative plus *desu* is formulated by transforming *desu* into *ja arimasen*. The *ja arimasen* is the contracted form of *de wa arimasen*. The original form *de wa arimasen* is common in formal speech.

$$\text{Nominative} + desu \longrightarrow \text{Nominative} + \left\{ \begin{matrix} ja \\ de\ wa \end{matrix} \right\} arimasen$$

Ano kata wa Yamada san desu.   "That person is Mr. Yamada."

Ano kata wa Yamada san ja arimasen.	"That person is not Mr. Yamada."
Ano kata wa Yamada san de wa arimasen.	"That person is not Mr. Yamada."

Do not confuse a Nominative plus *ja arimasen* "(A) is not (B)" with a Nominative plus *ga arimasen* "there is not."

Hon ja arimasen.	"[It] is not a book."
Hon ga arimasen.	"There is no book."

Nominatives that occur before *desu* can also be adjectival Nominatives, such as *suki* "is fond of," *shizuka* "quiet," *kirei* "pretty" or "clean," *joozu* "proficient," *daikirai* "dislike very much," etc. Therefore, the negative of these adjectival Nominatives plus *desu* will be adjectival Nominative plus *ja arimasen*. Do not confuse this with the negative of an Adjective which will be introduced in Note 8.4.3.

adjectival Nominative + *desu* ⟶ adjectival Nominative + $\begin{Bmatrix} ja \\ de\ wa \end{Bmatrix}$ *arimasen*

kirei desu	⟶	kirei ja arimasen	"is not pretty"
joozu desu	⟶	joozu ja arimasen	"is not proficient"
heta desu	⟶	heta ja arimasen	"is not poor (at it)"
suki desu	⟶	suki ja arimasen	"do not like"
kirai desu	⟶	kirai ja arimasen	"do not dislike"
daisuki desu	⟶	daisuki ja arimasen	"is not crazy (about it)"
daikirai desu	⟶	daikirai ja arimasen	"do not dislike much"
gen'ki desu	⟶	gen'ki ja arimasen	"is not healthy"
shizuka desu	⟶	shizuka ja arimasen	"is not quiet"
hima desu	⟶	hima ja arimasen	"is not free"
dame desu	⟶	dame ja arimasen	"is not 'no good' "

8.4.2   There are some Adverbs, such as *amari* "(not) very," *chittomo* "(not) at all," that are used with negative Predicates. Since these Adverbs are used mainly in negation, when they are used alone, they may also carry a negative connotation.

$\begin{Bmatrix} amari \\ chittomo \end{Bmatrix}$ + negative Predicate

Suki desu ka?	"Do [you] like [it]?"
Iie, amari (suki ja arimasen).	"No, [I] don't like [it] very much."
Joozu desu ka?	"Is [he] good at [it]?"
Chittomo (joozu ja arimasen).	"[He is] not [good] at all."

Piano o hikimasu ka?   "Do [you] play the piano?"

Hai, hikimasu ga, amari joozu de   "Yes, I do, but I'm not very good at it."
   wa arimasen.

8.4.3   *Isogashiku arimasen* is the negative of *isogashii desu* "is busy." The normal negative imperfect tense
form of an Adjective is formed by the KU form of the Adjective and *arimasen*. The KU form is
formed by changing the *-i* ending of an Adjective into *-ku*.

Adjective(*-i*) + *desu* ⟶ Adjective(*-ku*) + (*wa*) + *arimasen*

isogashii desu	⟶	isogashiku arimasen	"is not busy"
oishii desu	⟶	oishiku arimasen	"is not tasty"
mazui desu	⟶	mazuku arimasen	"is not tasteless"
yoi desu (ii desu)	⟶	yoku arimasen	"is not good"
takai desu	⟶	takaku arimasen	"is not expensive"
omoshiroi desu	⟶	omoshiroku arimasen	"is not interesting"
muzukashii desu	⟶	muzukashiku arimasen	"is not difficult"
tooi desu	⟶	tooku arimasen	"is not far"
kitanai desu	⟶	kitanaku arimasen	"is not dirty"
urusai desu	⟶	urusaku arimasen	"is not noisy"

Sometimes the Relational *wa* may be injected between the KU form and *arimasen*. In this case,
takaku wa arimasen, for example, will be close to the idea "as to 'expensive,' it is not so," and
this may be used in a response to a question asking if something is expensive.

Takai desu ka?   "Is [it] expensive?"

Iie, takaku wa arimasen.   "No, [it] is not."

8.4.4   The Adverb *chotto* "for a while" is often used in sentences of request, proposition, or invitation, to
make them sound casual.

Chotto sono hen de ocha o   "Won't you stop for a while and have some tea in
   nomimasen ka?   this area?"

Chotto uchi e kimasen ka?   "Won't you drop in at my house?"

Chotto machimashoo.   "Let's wait (for him) for a while."

8.4.5   The Relational *mo,* when used in a negative sentence, means "either" in the negative sense.

On'gaku mo yoku arimasen.   "The music is not good either."

Watakushi mo ikimasu.   "I am going, too."

Watakushi mo ikimasen.	"I am not going, either."
Jazu mo kikimasu.	"I will listen to jazz, too."
Jazu mo kikimasen.	"I will not listen to jazz, either."

8.4.6 In a negative answer, the Relational *wa* often takes the place of the Relational *ga* or *o*. As the negation is the answer to the question, the Relational *wa* is often used in order to give prominence to the negative Predicate.

Jazu o kikimasu ka?	"Do [you] listen to jazz?"
Iie, jazu wa kikimasen.	"No, [I] don't listen to jazz."
On'gaku ga suki desu ka?	"Do [you] like music?"
Iie, on'gaku wa suki ja arimasen.	"No, [I] do not like music."

When stressing "WHAT or WHO," the Relational *wa* cannot replace the *ga* and *o* following "WHAT or WHO" even in negation.

Nani ga oishiku arimasen ka?	"What is not tasty?"
Koocha ga oishiku arimasen.	"It is the black tea that is not tasty."
Dare ga kimasen ka?	"Who is not coming?"
Suujii san ga kimasen.	"It is Susie who is not coming."

8.5 VOCABULARY

Dialog

Yamamoto	....	N	family name
Watanabe	....	N	family name
ja arimasen	....	C	negative of *desu* (see 8.4.1)
(o)gen'ki	....	Na	healthy; in good spirits
isogashii	....	A	is busy
amari	....	Adv.	(not) very much; (not) very often (see 8.4.2)
isogashiku	....	A	KU form of *isogashii* – is busy (see 8.4.3)
arimasen	....	E	(see 8.4.1 & 8.4.3)
kissaten	....	N	coffee shop
hairimashoo	....	V	let us go in (OO form of *hairimasu* ⟵ *hairu*)
mise	....	N	shop; store
chittomo	....	Adv.	(not) at all (see 8.4.2)

114

oishiku	.... A	KU form of *oishii* – is tasty; is good
sore ni	.... SI	besides; moreover
on'gaku	.... N	music
mo	.... R	(not) either (see 8.4.5)
yoku	.... A	KU form of *yoi* – is good
Den'en	.... N	name of a coffee shop
tooku	.... A	KU form of *tooi* – is far
kirei	.... Na	pretty; clean (*Kirei* is not an Adjective but an adjectival Nominative. Adjectives never end in *-ei*.)
shizuka	.... Na	quiet
rekoodo	.... N	record
kurashikku	.... N	classical music
daisuki	.... Na	like very much
jazu	.... N	jazz
popyuraa	.... N	popular music
wa	.... R	(see 8.4.6)
kikimasen	 V	do not listen to; do not hear (negative of *kikimasu* ⟵ *kiku*) (*Kikimasu* is a transitive Verb: the Relational *o* occurs with this Verb to show a direct object. *Jazu o kikimasu*.)
saa	.... SI	now!

Notes

de wa arimasen	 C	formal equivalent of *ja arimasen* (see 8.4.1)
daikirai	.... Na	dislike very much
dame	.... Na	no good
piano	.... N	piano
hikimasu	 V	play (musical instruments, such as piano, organ, violin, guitar, etc.) (normal form of *hiku*)
oishii	.... A	is tasty
mazui	.... A	is tasteless; does not taste good
mazuku	.... A	KU form of *mazui* – is tasteless; does not taste good
takaku	.... A	KU form of *takai* – is expensive
omoshiroku	.... A	KU form of *omoshiroi* – is interesting
muzukashiku	.... A	KU form of *muzukashii* – is difficult

kitanai	. . . .	A	is dirty; is unclean; is messy
kitanaku	. . . .	A	KU form of *kitanai* – is dirty; is unclean; is messy
urusai	. . . .	A	is noisy; is annoying
urusaku	. . . .	A	KU form of *urusai* – is noisy; is annoying
koocha	. . . .	N	black tea

Drills

| gitaa | . . . . | N | guitar |
| baiorin | . . . . | N | violin |

8.6 HIRAGANA PRACTICE

8.6.1 Recognize the difference or similarity between two *hiragana* in each of the following pairs:

ふ……ふ	や……や	ゆ……ゆ	を……を
か……か	や……み	ゆ……め	と……を
せ……せ	み……み	ひ……ひ	
せ……や	み……や	と……と	

8.6.2 Practice writing the following *hiragana*:

1. ふ [fu]
2. か [ka]
3. せ [se]
4. や [ya]
5. み [mi]
6. ゆ [yu]
7. ひ [hi]

8. と [to] と と と と

9. を [o] を を を を を

8.6.3 Read and write the following:

ほんや　　のみます　　ゆき　　ふね　　おかね

やまもとさんも　みせに　いました。

あの　ひとを　みましたよ。

8.7 DRILLS

8.7.1 Pronunciation Drill

kissaten	issho	zasshi	chotto
kurashikku	gakkoo	chittomo	
Itte kudasai.	Matte kudasai.	Mata irasshai.	

8.7.2 Pattern Drill

1. Watanabe san ja arimasen ka?

2. Amari isogashiku arimasen.

3. Ano mise no koohii wa chittomo oishiku arimasen.

4. Sore ni, on'gaku mo yoku arimasen yo.

5. Tooku arimasen.

6. Den'en wa amari kirei ja arimasen.

7. Demo, jazu to popyuraa wa amari kikimasen.

8. Watashi mo jazu wa suki ja arimasen.

8.7.3 Transformation Drill

A. 1. Ano kata wa *Watanabe san desu.* ⟶ Ano kata wa *Watanabe san ja arimasen.*
    (de wa arimasen)

2. Are wa Nihon no shin'bun desu. ⟶ Are wa Nihon no shin'bun ja arimasen.

3. Watakushi wa gakusei desu. ⟶ Watakushi wa gakusei ja arimasen.

4. Ano mise wa tabakoya desu. ⟶ Ano mise wa tabakoya ja arimasen.

5. Kore wa kurashikku no rekoodo desu. → Kore wa kurashikku no rekoodo ja arimasen.

6. Sore wa daigaku no jimusho desu. ⟶ Sore wa daigaku no jimusho ja arimasen.

B. 1. Jazu wa *suki desu*. $\longrightarrow$ Jazu wa *suki ja arimasen*.
                                                    (*de wa arimasen*)

2. Kono kissaten wa kirei desu. $\longrightarrow$ Kono kissaten wa kirei ja arimasen.

3. Gen'ki desu. $\longrightarrow$ Gen'ki ja arimasen.

4. Kono hen wa shizuka desu. $\longrightarrow$ Kono hen wa shizuka ja arimasen.

5. Watanabe san wa eigo ga joozu desu. $\rightarrow$ Watanabe san wa eigo ga joozu ja arimasen.

6. Ima hima desu. $\longrightarrow$ Ima hima ja arimasen.

7. Dame desu. $\longrightarrow$ Dame ja arimasen.

8. Eiga wa kirai desu. $\longrightarrow$ Eiga wa kirai ja arimasen.

9. Sono gakusei wa nihon'go ga
    heta desu. $\longrightarrow$ Sono gakusei wa nihon'go ga heta ja arimasen.

8.7.4 Transformation Drill

1. Watakushi no uchi wa *tooi desu*. $\longrightarrow$ Watakushi no uchi wa *tooku arimasen*.

2. Kono hon wa ii desu. $\longrightarrow$ Kono hon wa yoku arimasen.

3. Kono heya wa kitanai desu. $\longrightarrow$ Kono heya wa kitanaku arimasen.

4. Kono hen wa urusai desu. $\longrightarrow$ Kono hen wa urusaku arimasen.

5. Nihon'go no kyooshitsu wa ookii desu. $\longrightarrow$ Nihon'go no kyooshitsu wa ookiku arimasen.

6. Hon wa takai desu. $\longrightarrow$ Hon wa takaku arimasen.

7. Kono gitaa wa yasui desu. $\longrightarrow$ Kono gitaa wa yasuku arimasen.

8. Ano gakusei wa erai desu. $\longrightarrow$ Ano gakusei wa eraku arimasen.

9. Watakushi wa ima isogashii desu. $\longrightarrow$ Watakushi wa ima isogashiku arimasen.

10. Kono mise no koohii wa oishii desu. $\longrightarrow$ Kono mise no koohii wa oishiku arimasen.

11. Ano eiga wa omoshiroi desu. $\longrightarrow$ Ano eiga wa omoshiroku arimasen.

12. Kono mise no bifuteki wa mazui desu. $\longrightarrow$ Kono mise no bifuteki wa mazuku arimasen.

8.7.5 Response Drill

1. Nihon'go wa muzukashii desu ka?
    chittomo ...... Iie, chittomo muzukashiku arimasen.

2. Ano mise wa kirei desu ka?
    amari ...... Iie, amari kirei ja arimasen.

3. Sono koocha wa oishii desu ka?
    chittomo ...... Iie, chittomo oishiku arimasen.

4. Anata no heya wa chiisai desu ka?
    amari ...... Iie, amari chiisaku arimasen.

5. Toshokan wa shizuka desu ka?
   amari ...... Iie, amari shizuka ja arimasen.

6. Kono hon wa yasashii desu ka?
   chittomo ...... Iie, chittomo yasashiku arimasen.

7. Anata wa doitsugo ga joozu desu ka?
   amari ...... Iie, amari joozu ja arimasen.

8. Kazuko san wa popyuraa on'gaku ga
   kirai desu ka?
   amari ...... Iie, amari kirai ja arimasen.

9. Kyoo sen'sei wa isogashii desu ka?
   chittomo ...... Iie, chittomo isogashiku arimasen.

8.7.6 Mixed Response Drill (negative and antonym)

1. Sono kissaten wa tooi desu ka? ...... *Iie,* tooku arimasen. Chikai desu.

2. Kamera wa yasui desu ka? ...... Iie, yasuku arimasen. Takai desu.

3. Gakkoo no toshokan wa ookii desu ka? .... Iie, ookiku arimasen. Chiisai desu.

4. Kono byooin wa shizuka desu ka? ...... Iie, shizuka ja arimasen. Urusai desu.

5. Inu ga suki desu ka? ...... Iie, suki ja arimasen. Kirai desu.

6. Sono rekoodo wa warui desu ka? ...... Iie, waruku arimasen. Ii desu.

7. Ano eiga wa omoshiroi desu ka? ...... Iie, omoshiroku arimasen. Tsumaranai desu.

8. Kono heya wa kirei desu ka? ...... Iie, kirei ja arimasen. Kitanai desu.

9. Ashita isogashii desu ka? ...... Iie, isogashiku arimasen. Hima desu.

10. Chuugokugo wa muzukashii desu ka? ...... Iie, muzukashiku arimasen. Yasashii desu.

11. Anata wa furan'sugo ga joozu desu ka? .... Iie, joozu ja arimasen. Heta desu.

12. Bifuteki wa mazui desu ka? ...... Iie, mazuku arimasen. Oishii desu.

13. Piano ga heta desu ka? ...... Iie, heta ja arimasen. Joozu desu.

8.7.7 Response Drill (*o,* and *ga* ⟶ *wa* in negation)

1. Koocha *o* nomimasu ka?
   koohii ...... Iie, koocha *wa* nomimasen. Koohii o nomimasu.

2. Kurashikku o kikimasu ka?
   jazu ...... Iie, kurashikku wa kikimasen. Jazu o kikimasu.

3. Toshokan de zasshi o karimasu ka?
   hon ...... Iie, zasshi wa karimasen. Hon o karimasu.

4. Asahi Shin'bun o yomimasu ka?
   Yomiuri Shin'bun ...... Iie, Asahi Shin'bun wa yomimasen. Yomiuri Shin'bun o yomimasu.

5. Amerika no eiga o mimasu ka?
   Nihon no eiga ...... Iie, Amerika no eiga wa mimasen. Nihon no eiga o mimasu.

6. Jisho o kaimasu ka? ...... Iie, jisho wa kaimasen. Zasshi o kaimasu.
   zasshi

7. Piano o hikimasu ka? ...... Iie, piano wa hikimasen. Gitaa o hikimasu.
   gitaa

8. Jazu ga suki desu ka? ...... Iie, jazu wa suki ja arimasen. Kurashikku ga
   kurashikku   suki desu.

9. Kono hen ni shin'bun'ya ga arimasu ka? .... Iie, shin'bun'ya wa arimasen. Hon'ya ga arimasu.
   hon'ya

10. Tori ga kirai desu ka? ...... Iie, tori wa kirai ja arimasen. Inu ga kirai desu.
    inu

11. Baiorin ga joozu desu ka? ...... Iie, baiorin wa joozu ja arimasen. Piano ga
    piano   joozu desu.

8.7.8 Transformation Drill (*o, ga, wa* ⟶ *mo; sore ni* insertion)

1. Watakushi wa gen'ki ja arimasen.
   Watanabe san *wa* gen'ki ja arimasen. ⟶ Watakushi wa gen'ki ja arimasen. *Sore ni,* Watanabe san *mo* gen'ki ja arimasen.

2. Koohii wa nomimasen.
   Koocha wa nomimasen. ⟶ Koohii wa nomimasen. Sore ni, koocha mo nomimasen.

3. Rekoodo ga yoku arimasen.
   Koohii ga oishiku arimasen. ⟶ Rekoodo ga yoku arimasen. Sore ni, koohii mo oishiku arimasen.

4. Koko wa shizuka ja arimasen.
   Soko wa shizuka ja arimasen. ⟶ Koko wa shizuka ja arimasen. Sore ni, soko mo shizuka ja arimasen.

5. Watakushi wa isogashiku arimasen.
   Tomodachi wa isogashiku arimasen. ⟶ Watakushi wa isogashiku arimasen. Sore ni, tomodachi mo isogashiku arimasen.

6. Popyuraa on'gaku wa kikimasen.
   Jazu wa kikimasen. ⟶ Popyuraa on'gaku wa kikimasen. Sore ni, jazu mo kikimasen.

7. Kono kyooshitsu wa kirei ja arimasen.
   Ano kyooshitsu wa kirei ja arimasen. ⟶ Kono kyooshitsu wa kirei ja arimasen. Sore ni, ano kyooshitsu mo kirei ja arimasen.

8. Watakushi wa ten'pura o tabemasen.
   Watakushi wa ocha o nomimasen. ⟶ Watakushi wa ten'pura o tabemasen. Sore ni, ocha mo nomimasen.

8.7.9 E-J Review Response Drill (Adverbs)

1. On'gaku wa yokatta desu ka?
   very   ...... Hai, (on'gaku wa) *totemo* yokatta desu.

2. Ima isogashii desu ka?
   not at all   ...... Iie, (ima) chittomo isogashiku arimasen.

3. Eiga wa omoshirokatta desu ka?
   a little   ...... Ee, (eiga wa) chotto omoshirokatta desu.

4. Sono kissaten wa kirei desu ka?
   not very . . . . . . Iie, (sono kissaten wa) amari kirei ja arimasen.

5. Nihon no kamera wa takai desu ka?
   not at all . . . . . . Iie, (Nihon no kamera wa) chittomo takaku arimasen.

6. Ano mise wa ookii desu ka?
   not very . . . . . . Iie, (ano mise wa) amari ookiku arimasen.

7. Sumisu san wa nihon'go ga joozu desu ka?
   very . . . . . . Hai, (Sumisu san wa nihon'go ga) totemo joozu desu.

8. Furan'sugo wa muzukashii desu ka?
   a little . . . . . . Hai, (furan'sugo wa) chotto muzukashii desu.

8.8 EXERCISES

8.8.1 Compose short sentences in Japanese by using the words given below, and then give the English equivalents for them:

1. totemo   2. amari   3. chittomo   4. chotto

8.8.2 Correct errors, if any.

1. Watakushi wa on'gaku o daisuki desu.

2. Koko wa kireku arimasen nee.

3. Ima amari isogashiku ja arimasen.

4. Koko no koohii wa chittomo oishii desu.

5. Sore mo iku arimasen.

6. Soko wa amari tooiku arimasen.

7. Ano kissaten de hairimashoo ka?

8. Tokidoki on'gaku ni kikimasu.

9. Uchi de piano ga hikimashoo.

8.8.3 Ask questions that will lead to the following answers:

1. Okagesama de (gen'ki desu).

2. Iie, kono koocha wa chittomo oishiku arimasen.

3. Kissaten e hairimashita.

4. Ee, totemo chikai n desu.

5. Iie, amari yasashiku arimasen.

6. Iie, dame desu.

8.8.4   Connect antonymous expressions with a line:

1. Kirai desu.   Isogashii desu.

2. Kirei desu.   Chiisai desu.

3. Omoshiroi desu.   Chikai desu.

4. Takai desu.   Yoi desu.

5. Hima desu.   Yasashii desu.

6. Ookii desu.   Tsumaranai desu.

7. Heta desu.   Shizuka desu.

8. Muzukashii desu.   Daikirai desu.

9. Tooi desu.   Kitanai desu.

10. Urusai desu.   Ii desu.

11. Daisuki desu.   Joozu desu.

12. Warui desu.   Suki desu.

13. Dame desu.   Yasui desu.

LESSON 9

123

9.1 USEFUL EXPRESSIONS

(Dooshite) gozon'ji desu ka /   "(How) do you happen to know [it]?" *Gozon'ji desu ka?* is a polite equivalent for *Shitte imasu ka?*

Sore wa sumimasen deshita.   "I am sorry for what I have done." This expression is used to apologize for what you have done or the trouble that you have caused. *Sore wa* can be omitted.

Sore wa zan'nen deshita ne.   This expression is used to express "regret," "pity," "disappointment," etc. This will correspond to "What a pity (that you could not enjoy much)," or "That was too bad (that you could not enjoy much because of the bad weather)." The opposite expression would be (*Sore wa*) *yokatta desu ne* "How lucky you were!" or "I am glad to hear (that you have enjoyed)," etc.

9.2 DIALOG

— Going sightseeing —

Mr. Sumino: Kinoo*1 anata wa uchi ni imasen deshita*2 ne /

Miss Brown: Ee,*3 imasen deshita. Demo, dooshite*4 gozon'ji desu ka /

Mr. Sumino: Asa to yoru*1 den'wa*5 o shimashita ga, hen'ji ga arimasen deshita yo /

Miss Brown: Sore wa sumimasen deshita. Kinoo wa*1 Nikkoo ni imashita.

Mr. Sumino: Soo deshita ka. Itsu*1 dekakemashita ka /

Miss Brown: Kinoo no asa*1 dekakemashita. Soshite, kesa kaerimashita.

Mr. Sumino: Jidoosha de*6 ikimashita ka /

Miss Brown: Iie, Asakusa kara*7 den'sha de ikimashita.

Mr. Sumino: Anata wa otera ya*8 jin'ja ga suki desu ka /

Miss Brown: Ee, mae wa*9 toku ni suki ja arimasen deshita*10 ga, ima wa daisuki desu.

Mr. Sumino: Chuuzen'jiko e mo*11 ikimashita ka /

Miss Brown : Ee, ikimashita. Demo, ten'ki ga yoku arimasen deshita.*12 Dakara,

amari tanoshiku arimasen deshita.

Mr. Sumino : Sore wa zan'nen deshita ne. Watashi wa sen'getsu*13 Kyooto e

ryokoo*5 shimashita.

Miss Brown : Jaa, Ryooan'ji o ken'butsu shimashita ka / Asoko no ishi no niwa wa

subarashii desu ne /

Mr. Sumino : Ryooan'ji e wa*11 ikimasen deshita. Demo, kon'getsu*13 ka*14 raigetsu

mata Kyooto e ikimasu.

Miss Brown : Ii desu nee.

9.3 PATTERN SENTENCES

9.3.1

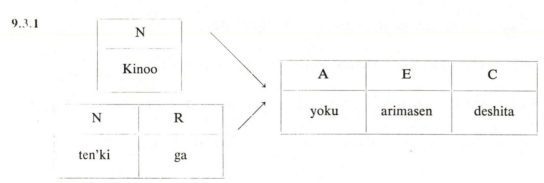

"The weather was not good yesterday."

9.3.2

N	R			V	C
Ryooan'ji	e	wa	⟶	ikimasen	deshita

"[I] did not go to Ryōanji Temple."

9.3.3

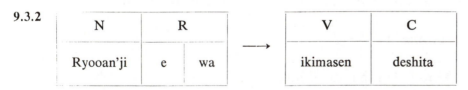

N	(R)			N	C	R	E	C
Mae	wa		⟶	suki	ja de wa		arimasen	deshita

"[I] did not like [it] before."

9.4 NOTES

9.4.1 The time Nominatives, such as *kinoo* "yesterday," *ima* "now," *mainichi* "every day," etc., may be used adverbially without any Relational following. Usually a time word phrase precedes another Predicate Modifier.

Kinoo Nikkoo e ikimashita.	"[He] went to Nikkō yesterday."
Ashita no asa uchi ni imasu.	"[I] will be at home tomorrow morning."

Here are more time expressions:

ashita	kyoo	kinoo
"tomorrow"	"today"	"yesterday"
ashita no asa	kesa	kinoo no asa
"tomorrow morning"	"this morning"	"yesterday morning"
ashita no hiru	kyoo no hiru	kinoo no hiru
"tomorrow noon"	"this noon"	"yesterday noon"
ashita no yoru	kyoo no yoru	kinoo no yoru
ashita no ban	kon'ban	kinoo no ban
"tomorrow night"	"tonight"	"last night"

The interrogative time Nominative to ask "when?" is *itsu.*

Itsu dekakemashita ka ?	"When did [he] go out?"

The Relational of topic *wa* or the Relational *mo* "also, or (not) either" may occasionally be placed after these time Nominatives. Their function is the same as that of substituting *ga* or *o*.

Kinoo Nikkoo e ikimashita.	"[I] went to Nikkō yesterday."
Kinoo wa Nikkoo e ikimashita.	"As for yesterday, [I] went to Nikkō."
Kinoo mo Nikkoo e ikimashita.	"[I] went to Nikkō yesterday too."
Kinoo mo Nikkoo e ikimasen deshita.	"[I] did not go to Nikkō yesterday either."
Maishuu kyookai e ikimasu ka ?	"Do you go to church every week?"

The *mai-* as in *mainichi* "every day" may be attached to *asa, ban, -shuu* "week," *-getsu* "month," *-nen* "year," and the combination means "every ~."

maiasa	"every morning"	mainichi	"every day"	maigetsu	"every month"
maiban	"every night"	maishuu	"every week"	mainen	"every year"

9.4.2 *Imasen deshita* is the perfect tense form of *imasen* "(someone) is not (there)," or the perfect negative form of *imasu* "(someone) is (there)." The negative perfect tense form of a Verb is formulated by adding *deshita,* the perfect tense form of the Copula *desu,* to the negative imperfect tense form of the Verb.

Verb(-*masen*) ——→ Verb(-*masen*) + *deshita*	
imasu	"(someone) is (there)"
imasen	"(someone) is not (there)"
imashita	"(someone) was (there)"
imasen deshita	"(someone) was not (there)"
Kesa shin'bun o yomimashita ka?	"Did [you] read a newspaper this morning?"
Iie, yomimasen deshita.	"No, [I] didn't."

9.4.3 The Sentence Interjective *hai* or *ee* may occur with the negative response, and *iie* with the affirmative response. In Japanese, *hai* or *ee* is used when the answerer agrees to the questioner's thought or expectation. Therefore, if the negative question *Ikimasen ne?* that expects a negative answer is made and the answerer agrees to the questioner's expectation, the answerer expresses his agreement first by *hai* or *ee*, and then gives the negative response, *ikimasen*. When the answerer does not agree with the questioner as to what has been asked, he will say *iie* as a sign of disagreement and then will go on with his own statement such as *ikimasu*.

Uchi ni imasen deshita ne?	"[You] were not home, were [you]?"
Ee, imasen deshita.	"That's right. [I] wasn't."
Kono hon wa omoshiroku arimasen ne?	"This book is not interesting, is it?"
Iie, omoshiroi desu.	"(You are wrong.) It is interesting."
Ee, omoshiroku arimasen.	"(You are right.) It is not interesting."
Kinoo kimasen deshita ne?	"[you] didn't come yesterday, did [you]?"
Iie, kimashita yo.	"(You are wrong.) [I] did come."
Hai, kimasen deshita.	"(You are right.) [I] did not come."

9.4.4 *Dooshite* is an interrogative Adverb meaning "why?" or "how?" The connotation of a sentence usually determines which is the case.

Dooshite gozon'ji desu ka?	"How do you happen to know it?"
Dooshite kimasen deshita ka?	"Why didn't [you] come?"

9.4.5 Some Nominatives, such as *ryokoo* "traveling," *kaimono* "shopping," *ben'kyoo* "study," can form their verbal expressions by adding the Verb *shimasu* ←—— *suru* "do" to the Nominatives. These combinations may be treated as single Verbs, but sometimes the Relational *o* may be inserted between the Nominative and *shimasu*.

ryokoo (o) shimasu	"travel"
den'wa (o) shimasu	"make a phone call"

ken'butsu (o) shimasu	"sightsee" or "go sightseeing"
kaimono (o) shimasu	"go shopping"
ben'kyoo (o) shimasu	"study"
kekkon (o) shimasu	"marry"

No difference in meaning occurs when the Relational *o* is inserted. When there is *o*, however, *ryokoo* or *kaimono* is the object of the Verb *shimasu*, while *ryokoo* or *kaimono* is part of the Verb when *o* is not used.

9.4.6 The *de* in *Jidoosha de ikimashita* means "by (car.)" The Relational *de*, used after a Nominative that represents "a tool," means "using," "by means of," "with (a tool)," etc.

jidoosha, den'sha, hikooki, fune } de { ikimasu "go", kimasu "come", kaerimasu "go back", ryokoo shimasu "travel", dekakemasu "go out" } by { car, train, plane, boat }

en'pitsu, hiragana } de kakimasu "write" { with a pen, in *hiragana* }

nihon'go, den'wa } de hanashimasu "talk" { in Japanese, by phone }

hashi, naifu to fooku, supuun } de tabemasu "eat" { with chopsticks, with a knife and a fork, with a spoon }

den'wa de kikimasu — "hear on the phone"

Nan de is used to ask "by what (means)?" "with what?" etc.

Nan de Nikkoo e ikimashita ka? "How (by what) did [you] go to Nikkō?"

Jidoosha de ikimashita. "[I] went by car."

Fune de ryokoo shimasu ka, hikooki de ryokoo shimasu ka? "Are [you] going to travel by boat or by plane?"

9.4.7 *Kara* that occurs after a place Nominative is a Relational meaning "from." This Relational occurs, like *e*, with motion Verbs.

motion Verb { ikimasu, kimasu, kaerimasu } ⟶ place Nominative + *kara* + motion Verb { ikimasu, kimasu, kaerimasu }

Asakusa kara den'sha de ikimashita. "[I] went by train from Asakusa."

Kesa Nikkoo kara kaerimashita. "[I] came back from Nikkō this morning."

Itsu gakkoo kara kaerimasu ka?	"When are [you] coming back from school?"
Doko kara kimashita ka?	"Where did [you] come from?"

When you say "(Someone) came from the States to Japan," *Amerika kara* usually precedes *Nihon e*: *Amerika kara Nihon e kimashita.*

9.4.8 The *ya* between Nominatives is a Relational, and is used like the Relational *to* "and," which has been introduced in Note 4.4.11. Both *to* and *ya* may correspond to "and" in English, but *ya* is used merely to pick up some of the things in a group and mention them, while *to* functions to list all the things to be mentioned.

Otera ya jin'ja ga suki desu ka?	"Do [you] like temples, shrines, and the like?"
Kyooto to Nara e ikimashita.	"[I] went to Kyōto and Nara."
Kyooto ya Nara e ikimashita.	"[I] went to Kyōto, Nara, and some other place(s)."

9.4.9 The Relational *wa* has another function to contrast one with the other(s).

Mae wa suki ja arimasen deshita ga, *ima* wa daisuki desu.	"[I] didn't like [it] before, but [I] like [it] very much now."
Boku wa ikimasen ga, *Sumino san* wa ikimasu.	"I am not going, but Mr. Sumino is going."

Sometimes only the first part of the above sentence occurs, and the second may not be expressed. But, even in that case, the Relational *wa* is that of contrast.

Buraun san to Sumino san ga imashita ka?	"Were Mr. Brown and Mr. Sumino [there]?"
Sumino san wa imashita.	"Mr. Sumino was [there]." (implies "Mr. Brown wasn't.")

9.4.10 *Suki ja arimasen deshita* is the perfect tense form of *suki ja arimasen* "do not like," or the negative perfect tense form of *suki desu* "like." The negative perfect tense form of a Nominative plus *desu* is formed by adding *deshita* to the negative imperfect tense form of a Nominative plus *ja arimasen* or *de wa arimasen*.

$$\text{Nominative} + \left\{ \begin{matrix} ja \\ de\ wa \end{matrix} \right\} arimasen \longrightarrow \text{Nominative} + \left\{ \begin{matrix} ja \\ de\ wa \end{matrix} \right\} arimasen + deshita$$

suki desu	"like"
suki ja arimasen	"do not like"
suki deshita	"liked"
suki ja arimasen deshita	"did not like"

Amari kirei ja arimasen deshita.	"[It] was not very pretty."
Amari kirei de wa arimasen deshita.	

9.4.11 *Chuuzen'jiko e mo* means "also to Lake Chūzenji." Some Relationals, such as *wa, mo,* can take the places of the Relationals *ga* and *o,* as introduced in Note 5.4.3, 5.4.10, 8.4.5, and 8.4.6. With other Relationals, such as *de, ni, e, kara,* the *wa* or *mo* occurs immediately after another Relational. This combination of Relationals will be called "multiple Relationals." The function of *wa* and *mo* in multiple Relationals is the same as that of *wa* and *mo* substituting for *ga* and *o.*

~ e		~ e wa	~ e mo
~ kara		~ kara wa	~ kara mo
~ ni	→	~ ni wa	~ ni mo
~ de		~ de wa	~ de mo

or

Kyooto e ryokoo shimashita.	"[I] traveled to Kyōto."
Kyooto e wa ryokoo shimasen deshita.	"[I] did not travel to Kyōto."
Kyooto e mo ryokoo shimashita.	"[I] traveled to Kyōto, too."

9.4.12 *Yoku arimasen deshita* is the perfect tense form of *yoku arimasen* "is not good," or the negative perfect tense form of *yoi desu* "is good." The negative perfect tense form of an Adjective is formulated by the negative imperfect — the KU form of the Adjective plus *arimasen,* — plus *deshita.*

Adjective(-*ku*) + *arimasen* ⟶ **Adjective(-*ku*)** + *arimasen* + *deshita*

yoi desu	"[it] is good"
yoku arimasen	"[it] is not good"
yokatta desu	"[it] was good"
yoku arimasen deshita	"[it] was not good"
Eiga wa omoshirokatta desu ka?	"Was the movie interesting?"
Iie, chittomo omoshiroku arimasen deshita.	"No, it wasn't interesting at all."

9.4.13 *Kon'getsu* is the Nominative meaning "this month," and occurs in a sentence like other time Nominatives introduced in Note 9.4.1.

raigetsu "next month"   kon'getsu "this month"   sen'getsu "last month"

Kon'getsu mata Kyooto e ikimasu.	"[I] am going to Kyōto this month again."
Raigetsu kekkon shimasu.	"[I] am going to marry next month."

Kon- refers to "this," *rai-* to "next," *sen-* to "last," and *-getsu* means "month."

9.4.14 *Ka* between Nominatives is a Relational, and is used like the Relationals *to* and *ya. Ka,* however, is used as an equivalent of "or" as in "A or B."

Kon'getsu ka raigetsu ikimasu.	"[I] will go [there] this month or next month."
Hon ka zasshi o kaimasu.	"[I] will buy a book or a magazine."
Buraun san wa kissaten ka shokudoo ni imashita yo.	"Mr. Brown was in a coffee shop or an eating place."

130

9.5 VOCABULARY

Dialog

Sumino	N	family name	
imasen deshita	V	was not (in a place) (negative perfect tense form of *imasu* ⟵ *iru*) (see 9.4.2)	
dooshite	Adv.	how?; why? (see 9.4.4)	
gozon'ji	N	know	
asa	N	morning (see 9.4.1)	
yoru	N	night (see 9.4.1)	
den'wa (o) shimashita	V	made a phone call (TA form of *den'wa shimasu* ⟵ *den'wa suru*) (see 9.4.5)	
hen'ji	N	reply	
arimasen deshita	V	(there) was not (see 9.4.2)	
Nikkoo	N	city in Tochigi Prefecture (famous for the Tōshōgū Shrine)	
itsu	Ni	when? (see 9.4.1)	
dekakemashita	V	went out; set out (TA form of *dekakemasu* ⟵ *dekakeru*)	
kesa	N	this morning	
jidoosha	N	automobile	
de	R	by means of (see 9.4.6)	
Asakusa	N	a place in downtown Tōkyō	
kara	R	from (a place) (see 9.4.7)	
den'sha	N	electric train; streetcar	
(o)tera	N	Buddhist temple	
ya	R	and (selective) (see 9.4.8)	
jin'ja	N	*Shintō* shrine	
toku ni	PM	particularly	
ja arimasen deshita	C	was not (negative perfect tense form of *desu*) (see 9.4.10)	
Chuuzen'jiko	N	Lake Chūzenji in Nikkō	
ten'ki	N	weather	
yoku arimasen deshita	A	was not good (negative perfect tense form of *yoi*)	
tanoshiku	A	KU form of *tanoshii* – is pleasant	
zan'nen	Na	regrettable; disappointing	
sen'getsu	N	last month (see 9.4.13)	
Kyooto	N	old capital of Japan; Kyōto Prefecture	
ryokoo (o) shimashita	V	traveled; took a trip (see 9.4.5)	
Ryooan'ji	N	Ryōanji Temple in Kyōto (famous for its stone garden)	
ken'butsu (o) shimashita	V	saw the sights of; visited (transitive Verb) (see 9.4.5)	

ishi	....	N	stone
niwa	....	N	garden
subarashii	....	A	is wonderful
ikimasen deshita	......	V	did not go (negative perfect tense form of *ikimasu* ←— *iku*)
kon'getsu	....	N	this month
ka	....	R	or (see 9.4.14)
raigetsu	....	N	next month

Notes

ban	....	N	evening; night
kon'ban	....	N	tonight
maiasa	....	N	every morning
maiban	....	N	every night
maishuu	....	N	every week
-shuu	....	Nd	week
maigetsu	....	N	every month
-getsu	....	Nd	month
mainen	....	N	every year
-nen	....	Nd	year
kyookai	....	N	church
ben'kyoo (o) shimasu	...	V	study (normal form of *ben'kyoo* (*o*) *suru*)
kekkon (o) shimasu	....	V	marry (normal form of *kekkon* (*o*) *suru*)
hikooki	....	N	airplane
fune	....	N	boat; ship
hiragana	....	N	the Japanese cursive syllabary
hashi	....	N	chopsticks
naifu	....	N	knife
fooku	....	N	fork
supuun	....	N	spoon
Nara	....	N	old capital of Japan; Nara Prefecture
Buraun	....	N	Brown
de wa arimasen deshita	..	C	formal equivalent of *ja arimasen deshita* (see 9.4.10)

Drills

gaikoku	....	N	foreign country; abroad
Yooroppa	....	N	Europe

132

9.6 HIRAGANA PRACTICE

9.6.1 Recognize the difference or similarity between two *hiragana* in each of the following pairs:

か……が	す……ず	と……ど	ひ……ぴ
き……ぎ	せ……ぜ	は……ば	ふ……ぷ
く……ぐ	そ……ぞ	ひ……び	へ……ぺ
け……げ	た……だ	ふ……ぶ	ほ……ぽ
こ……ご	ち……ぢ	へ……べ	
さ……ざ	つ……づ	ほ……ぼ	
し……じ	て……で	は……ば	

9.6.2 Read and write the following:

がいこく　　　ぼく　　　　ぎんざ　　　　すばらしい

しんぶん　　　らいげつ　　えんぴつ

わたなべさんが　います。

ごぞんじですか。

まいばん　てんぷらを　たべました。

ざんねんですね。

へんじが　ありませんでした。

9.7　DRILLS

9.7.1　Pronunciation Drill

gozon'ji	ten'ki	ken'butsu	hen'ji	den'sha	sen'getsu	kon'ban
Ryooan'ji	den'wa	ben'kyoo	kon'getsu	jin'ja	Chuuzen'jiko	zan'nen

9.7.2　Pattern Drill

1. Kinoo anata wa uchi ni imasen deshita ne?

2. Ee, imasen deshita.

3. Asa to yoru den'wa o shimashita ga, hen'ji ga arimasen deshita yo.

4. Kinoo wa Nikkoo ni imashita.

5. Itsu dekakemashita ka?

6. Kinoo no asa dekakemashita.

7. Asakusa kara den'sha de ikimashita.

8. Mae wa toku ni suki ja arimasen deshita ga, ima wa daisuki desu.

9. Chuuzen'jiko e mo ikimashita ka?

10. Ten'ki ga yoku arimasen deshita.

11. Dakara, amari tanoshiku arimasen deshita.

12. Ryooan'ji e wa ikimasen deshita.

9.7.3 Transformation Drill

A. 1. *Ashita* uchi ni *imasen*. ⟶ *Kinoo* uchi ni *imasen deshita*.

2. Ashita ben'kyoo shimasen. ⟶ Kinoo ben'kyoo shimasen deshita.

3. Ashita Kyooto o ken'butsu shimasen. ⟶ Kinoo Kyooto o ken'butsu shimasen deshita.

4. Ashita dekakemasen. ⟶ Kinoo dekakemasen deshita.

5. Ashita uchi e kimasen. ⟶ Kinoo uchi e kimasen deshita.

6. Ima wa amari gen'ki ja arimasen. ⟶ Kinoo den'wa shimasen deshita.

7. Ashita eiga o mimasu. ⟶ Kinoo eiga o mimasen deshita.

8. Ashita otera e ikimasen. ⟶ Kinoo otera e ikimasen deshita.

9. Ashita ryokoo shimasen. ⟶ Kinoo ryokoo shimasen deshita.

B. 1. *Ima* wa otera ya jin'ja ga suki *ja arimasen*. ⟶ *Mae wa* otera ya jin'ja ga suki *ja arimasen deshita*.

2. Ima wa hima ja arimasen. ⟶ Mae wa hima ja arimasen deshita.

3. Ima wa Itoo san wa tomodachi ja arimasen. ⟶ Mae wa Itoo san wa tomodachi ja arimasen deshita.

4. Ima wa shizuka ja arimasen. ⟶ Mae wa shizuka ja arimasen deshita.

5. Ima wa sen'sei ja arimasen. ⟶ Mae wa sen'sei ja arimasen deshita.

6. Ima wa amari gen'ki ja arimasen. ⟶ Mae wa amari gen'ki ja arimasen deshita.

7. Ima wa kirei ja arimasen. ⟶ Mae wa kirei ja arimasen deshita.

9.7.4 Transformation Drill

1. Kyoo ten'ki ga *yoku arimasen*. ⟶ Kyoo ten'ki ga *yoku arimasen deshita*.

2. Ryokoo wa tanoshiku arimasen. ⟶ Ryokoo wa tanoshiku arimasen deshita.

3. Heya wa kitanaku arimasen. ⟶ Heya wa kitanaku arimasen deshita.

4. Gin'koo wa tooku arimasen. ⟶ Gin'koo wa tooku arimasen deshita.

5. Sono tera wa ookiku arimasen. ⟶ Sono tera wa ookiku arimasen deshita.

6. Rekoodo wa yasuku arimasen. ⟶ Rekoodo wa yasuku arimasen deshita.

7. Kyoo no hirugohan wa oishiku arimasen. ⟶ Kyoo no hirugohan wa oishiku arimasen deshita.

9.7.5 Response Drill (negative)

1. Ten'ki wa yokatta desu ka? ...... Iie, (ten'ki wa) yoku arimasen deshita.

2. Hashi de tabemashita ka? ...... Iie, hashi de tabemasen deshita.

3. Soko wa kirei deshita ka? ...... Iie, (soko wa) kirei ja arimasen deshita.

4. Gaikoku e ryokoo shimashita ka? ...... Iie, (gaikoku e) ryokoo shimasen deshita.

5. Hen'ji ga arimashita ka? ...... Iie, (hen'ji ga) arimasen deshita.

6. Nikkoo wa kitanakatta desu ka? ...... Iie, (Nikkoo wa) kitanaku arimasen deshita.

7. Sono kissaten wa shizuka deshita ka? ...... Iie, (sono kissaten wa) shizuka ja arimasen deshita.

8. Ryokoo wa tanoshikatta desu ka? ...... Iie, (ryokoo wa) tanoshiku arimasen deshita.

9. Mae popyuraa on'gaku ga suki deshita ka? .. Iie, (mae popyuraa on'gaku ga) suki ja arimasen deshita.

10. Maiban isogashikatta desu ka? ...... Iie, (maiban) isogashiku arimasen deshita.

11. Buraun san wa nihon'go ga joozu deshita ka?. Iie, (Buraun san wa nihon'go ga) joozu ja arimasen deshita.

12. Maiasa koohii o nomimashita ka? ...... Iie, (maiasa koohii o) nomimasen deshita.

9.7.6 Expansion & Substitution Drill

1. Ten'ki ga yoku arimasen deshita. ...... Ten'ki ga yoku arimasen deshita.

   kinoo ...... Kinoo ten'ki ga yoku arimasen deshita.

   kinoo no asa ...... Kinoo no asa ten'ki ga yoku arimasen deshita.

   kinoo no asa wa ...... Kinoo no asa wa ten'ki ga yoku arimasen deshita.

   kinoo no asa mo ...... Kinoo no asa mo ten'ki ga yoku arimasen deshita.

2. Nihon'go o ben'kyoo shimasu. ...... Nihon'go o ben'kyoo shimasu.

   kon'ban ...... Kon'ban nihon'go o ben'kyoo shimasu.

   kon'ban wa ...... Kon'ban wa nihon'go o ben'kyoo shimasu.

   kon'ban mo ...... Kon'ban mo nihon'go o ben'kyoo shimasu.

3. Yooroppa e ryokoo shimasu. ...... Yooroppa e ryokoo shimasu.

raigetsu	. . . . .	Raigetsu Yooroppa e ryokoo shimasu.
raigetsu wa	. . . . .	Raigetsu wa Yooroppa e ryokoo shimasu.
raigetsu mo	. . . . .	Raigetsu mo Yooroppa e ryokoo shimasu.

4. Ten'ki ga subarashikatta desu.   . . . . .   Ten'ki ga subarashikatta desu.

   kesa   . . . . .   Kesa ten'ki ga subarashikatta desu.

   kesa wa   . . . . .   Kesa wa ten'ki ga subarashikatta desu.

   kesa mo   . . . . .   Kesa mo ten'ki ga subarashikatta desu.

5. Uchi ni imasu.   . . . . .   Uchi ni imasu.

   ashita no ban   . . . . .   Ashita no ban uchi ni imasu.

   ashita no ban wa   . . . . .   Ashita no ban wa uchi ni imasu.

   ashita no ban mo   . . . . .   Ashita no ban mo uchi ni imasu.

9.7.7 Transformation Drill (multiple Relationals)

1. Hawai Daigaku de ben'kyoo shimashita. ⟶ Hawai Daigaku de *mo* ben'kyoo shimashita.
2. Sono hen ni otearai ga arimasu. ⟶ Sono hen ni mo otearai ga arimasu.
3. Doitsu kara kimashita. ⟶ Doitsu kara mo kimashita.
4. Gin'za de kaimono shimashoo. ⟶ Gin'za de mo kaimono shimashoo.
5. Jidoosha de ryokoo shimashita. ⟶ Jidoosha de mo ryokoo shimashita.
6. Kyooto e ryokoo shimasen ka? ⟶ Kyooto e mo ryokoo shimasen ka?
7. Kissaten e hairimashoo. ⟶ Kissaten e mo hairimashoo.
8. Toshokan de hon o karimasu. ⟶ Toshokan de mo hon o karimasu.
9. Amerika kara kaerimasu. ⟶ Amerika kara mo kaerimasu.
10. Ano mise e ikimashoo. ⟶ Ano mise e mo ikimashoo.

9.7.8 Response Drill (multiple Relationals)

1. Kinoo gakkoo e ikimashita ka? ⟶ *Iie*, (kinoo) gakkoo *e wa* ikimasen deshita.
2. Uchi de rekoodo o kikimasu ka? ⟶ Iie, uchi de wa (rekoodo o) kikimasen.
3. Kyooshitsu ni sen'sei ga imashita ka? ⟶ Iie, kyooshitsu ni wa (sen'sei ga) imasen deshita.
4. Yooroppa kara kimashita ka? ⟶ Iie, Yooroppa kara wa kimasen deshita.
5. Shin'juku de eiga o mimasu ka? ⟶ Iie, Shin'juku de wa (eiga o) mimasen.
6. Den'sha de ikimashita ka? ⟶ Iie, den'sha de wa ikimasen deshita.
7. Hon'ya ni shin'bun ga arimasu ka? ⟶ Iie, hon'ya ni wa (shin'bun ga) arimasen.
8. Sen'getsu Nara e ryokoo shimashita ka? ⟶ Iie, (sen'getsu) Nara e wa ryokoo shimasen deshita.

9.7.9 Substitution Drill

Jidoosha de ikimasu *ka?*

1.	den'sha	. . . .	Den'sha de ikimasu ka?
2.	kaerimashita ka?	. . . .	Den'sha de kaerimashita ka?
3.	nan	. . . .	Nan de kaerimashita ka?
4.	hanashimasu ka?	. . . .	Nan de hanashimasu ka?
5.	den'wa	. . . .	Den'wa de hanashimasu ka?
6.	nihon'go	. . . .	Nihon'go de hanashimasu ka?
7.	kakimasu ka?	. . . .	Nihon'go de kakimasu ka?
8.	nan	. . . .	Nan de kakimasu ka?
9.	ryokoo shimasu ka?	. . . .	Nan de ryokoo shimasu ka?
10.	fune	. . . .	Fune de ryokoo shimasu ka?
11.	hikooki	. . . .	Hikooki de ryokoo shimasu ka?
12.	nan	. . . .	Nan de ryokoo shimasu ka?
13.	tabemasu ka?	. . . .	Nan de tabemasu ka?
14.	hashi	. . . .	Hashi de tabemasu ka?
15.	fooku	. . . .	Fooku de tabemasu ka?

9.7.10 E-J Response Drill

1. Itsu otera ya jin'ja o ken'butsu shimashita ka?

last month	. . . .	Sen'getsu ken'butsu shimashita.
last night	. . . .	Kinoo no ban (yoru) ken'butsu shimashita.
yesterday morning	. . . .	Kinoo no asa ken'butsu shimashita.
this morning	. . . .	Kesa ken'butsu shimashita.
yesterday noon	. . . .	Kinoo no hiru ken'butsu shimashita.

2. Itsu eiga e ikimashoo ka?

tonight	. . . .	Kon'ban (eiga e) ikimashoo.
this month	. . . .	Kon'getsu (eiga e) ikimashoo.
tomorrow evening	. . . .	Ashita no ban (eiga e) ikimashoo.
every evening	. . . .	Maiban (eiga e) ikimashoo.
tomorrow morning	. . . .	Ashita no asa (eiga e) ikimashoo.
every week	. . . .	Maishuu (eiga e) ikimashoo.

| *next month* | . . . . | Raigetsu (eiga e) ikimashoo. |
| *every month* | . . . . | Maigetsu (eiga e) ikimashoo. |

9.7.11 Response Drill (short answer with *ee* or *iie*)

1. Kinoo no yoru anata wa uchi ni imasen deshita ne?
   imasen deshita .... *Ee,* imasen deshita.

2. Anata wa jin'ja ga suki ja arimasen ka?
   suki desu .... Iie, suki desu.

3. Sen'getsu Nikkoo e ikimashita ka?
   ikimashita .... Ee, ikimashita.

4. Kesa den'wa shimasen deshita ne?
   shimashita .... Iie, shimashita.

5. Kesa Tookyoo e ikimashita ka?
   ikimasen deshita .... Iie, ikimasen deshita.

6. Kon'getsu ryokoo shimashita ne?
   shimasen deshita. ... ... Iie, shimasen deshita.

7. Tanoshiku arimasen deshita ka?
   tanoshiku arimasen deshita .... Ee, tanoshiku arimasen deshita.

8. Soko wa shizuka ja arimasen deshita ka?
   shizuka deshita .... Iie, shizuka deshita.

9.7.12 E-J Response Drill (*to, ya,* and *ka*)

1. Itsu Gin'za de kaimono o shimashita ka?
   yesterday and today ...... Kinoo *to* kyoo (Gin'za de) kaimono o shimashita.

2. Doko o ken'butsu shimashoo ka?
   Kyōto or Nara ...... Kyooto *ka* Nara o ken'butsu shimashoo.

3. Nani o nomimashita ka?
   coffee, tea, etc. ...... Koohii *ya* ocha o nomimashita.

4. Sumino san wa itsu kekkon shimashita ka?
   last month or this month ...... Sen'getsu *ka* kon'getsu kekkon shimashita.

5. Dare ga jimusho ni imasu ka?
   Mr. Brown and (his) friend ...... Buraun san *to* tomodachi ga jimusho ni imasu.

6. Raigetsu doko e ryokoo shimasu ka?
   to the States, France, etc. ...... (Raigetsu) Amerika *ya* Furan'su e ryokoo shimasu.

7. Itsu gakkoo kara kaerimasu ka?
   at noon or at night ...... Hiru *ka* yoru (gakkoo kara) kaerimasu.

9.7.13 Response Drill

1. Kon'ban *mo* ten'ki ga warui desu ka?
   hai ...... *Hai,* kon'ban *mo* (ten'ki ga) warui desu.

2. Suujii san mo kekkon shimashita ka?
   hai
   ...... Hai, Suujii san mo kekkon shimashita.

3. Kinoo no yoru eiga mo mimashita ka?
   iie
   ...... Iie, (kinoo no yoru) eiga *wa* mimasen deshita.

4. Kinoo *mo* gakkoo e kimashita ka?
   iie
   ...... Iie, kinoo wa (gakkoo e) kimasen deshita.

5. Nikkoo *e mo* ikimashita ka?
   iie
   ...... Iie, Nikkoo *e wa* ikimasen deshita.

6. Tookyoo ni mo otera ga arimasu ka?
   ee
   ...... Ee, Tookyoo ni mo (otera ga) arimasu.

7. Meriiran'do Daigaku de mo ben'kyoo shimashita ka?
   hai
   ...... Hai, Meriiran'do Daigaku de mo ben'kyoo shimashita.

9.8   EXERCISES

9.8.1   Insert a Relational in each blank and give an English equivalent for each sentence:

1. Mae (　　) amari suki ja arimasen deshita (　　), ima (　　) daisuki desu.
2. Buraun san wa Igirisu kara hikooki (　　) kimashita.
3. Sono otera (　　) (　　) ikimasen deshita.
4. Jin'ja (　　) tera (　　) suki desu.
5. Kinoo (　　) yoru dekakemashita.
6. Amerika (　　) (　　) otera ga arimasen ne?
7. Ryooan'ji (　　) ken'butsu shimashita ka?
8. Sen'getsu Kyooto (　　) ryokoo shimashita. Soshite, Nikkoo (　　) (　　) ikimashita
9. Itsu gaikoku (　　) kaerimasu ka?
10. Itsumo hashi (　　) tabemasu ka, fooku (　　) supuun (　　) tabemasu ka?

9.8.2   Ask appropriate questions that fit the following answers:

1. Kesa dekakemashita.
2. Iie, uchi e wa kaerimasen deshita.
3. Hai, Nikkoo e mo ikimasen deshita.
4. Iie, den'wa o shimashita yo.
5. Ee, ryokoo wa tanoshiku arimasen deshita.
6. Iie, ten'ki wa amari yoku arimasen deshita.
7. Iie, maiasa jidoosha de ikimashita.

9.8.3   Transform the following into the negative perfect tense form:

1. Subarashii desu. ⟶

2. Maishuu on'gaku o kikimasu. ⟶

3. Sen'sei wa Nakamura sen'sei deshita. ⟶

4. Kono hon wa muzukashiku arimasen. ⟶

5. Maiasa eki de tomodachi o machimashita. ⟶

6. Gozon'ji desu ka? ⟶

9.8.4 Carry on the following dialog in Japanese:

— The weather wasn't good yesterday, was it?

— No, it wasn't good. Were you home yesterday?

— No, I came back from Kyōto yesterday evening.

— Oh, is that right? How was the trip?

— It was wonderful. I visited temples, shrines, and the like in Kyōto.

— Did you visit Ryōanji Temple, too?

— No, I did not visit Ryōanji Temple. Therefore, I am going there next month again.

— That sounds great.

LESSON 10

— Review —

10.1 CONJUGATION

10.1.1 Adjective

chiisa*i*
ooki*i*
too*i*
chika*i*
yasu*i*
taka*i*
yo*i*
waru*i*
yasashi*i*
muzukashi*i*
oishi*i*　　　　　*desu*　⟶　~　*-ku*　　*arimasen*
mazu*i*
omoshiro*i*
tsumarana*i*
tanoshi*i*
kitana*i*
urusa*i*
era*i*
subarashi*i*
isogashi*i*

~　*-katta*　　*desu*　⟶　~　*-ku*　　*arimasen deshita*

10.1.2 Verb

nomi*masu*
tabe*masu*
kaki*masu*
narai*masu*
hanashi*masu*
kai*masu*
mi*masu*　　　　⟶　~　*-masen*
wasure*masu*
machi*masu*
sagashi*masu*
shi*masu*
yomi*masu*
kiki*masu*

hikimasu
karimasu
ben'kyoo (o) shimasu
ken'butsu (o) shimasu

den'wa (o) shimasu
kekkon (o) shimasu

kimasu
ikimasu
kaerimasu   ⟶   ~   -masen
hairimasu
dekakemasu
ryokoo (o) shimasu

arimasu
imasu

~   -mashita   ⟶   ~   -masen deshita

10.1.3 Adjectival Nominative ⎱ + Copula
Nominative ⎰

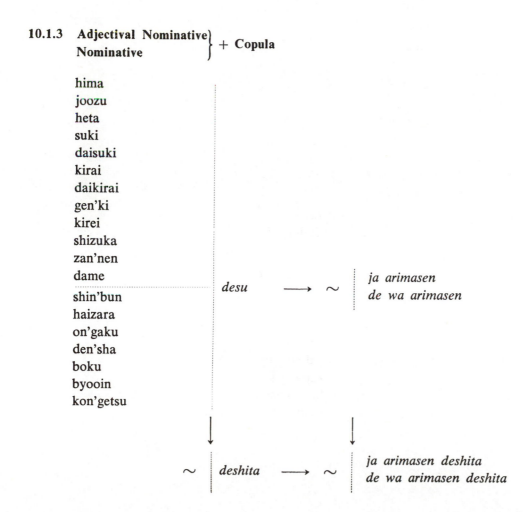

hima
joozu
heta
suki
daisuki
kirai
daikirai
gen'ki
kirei
shizuka
zan'nen
dame   desu   ⟶   ~   ja arimasen
                                            de wa arimasen
shin'bun
haizara
on'gaku
den'sha
boku
byooin
kon'getsu

~   deshita   ⟶   ~   ja arimasen deshita
                              de wa arimasen deshita

10.2 PATTERN

10.2.1 Nominative + $\left\{ \begin{array}{c} wa \\ mo \\ ga \end{array} \right\}$ + Adjective + *desu*

(2)		(1)	
		chiisa	
kissaten		ooki	
pan'ya		too	
niwa		chika	
kyookai		kitana	
		urusa	
zasshi		yasu	
rekoodo		taka	
jidoosha	wa	yo	-i desu
ten'ki	(mo)	waru	-katta desu
nihon'go	(ga)	yasashi	-ku arimasen
furan'sugo		muzukashi	-ku arimasen deshita
koocha		oishi	
ten'pura		mazu	
		omoshiro	
hon		tsumarana	
eiga		tanoshi	
		subarashi	
tomodachi		era	
ano hito		isogashi	

$\downarrow$

(2)		(1)		
....				
....				
....	wa	doo	desu	ka ?
....			deshita	
....				

$\downarrow$

(2)		(1)		
doko				
nani		....		
dore		....	-i desu	
dono ～	ga	....	-katta desu	ka ?
		....	-ku arimasen	
donata		....	-ku arimasen deshita	
dare				

10.2.2 Relational *kara* "from"

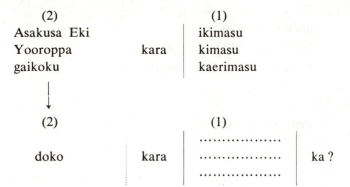

(2)		(1)
Asakusa Eki		ikimasu
Yooroppa	kara	kimasu
gaikoku		kaerimasu

↓

(2)		(1)	
		....	
doko	kara	....	ka ?
		....	

10.2.3 Relational *de* "by means of"

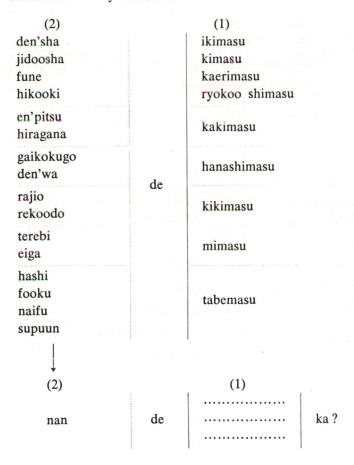

(2)		(1)
den'sha		ikimasu
jidoosha		kimasu
fune		kaerimasu
hikooki		ryokoo shimasu
en'pitsu		
hiragana		kakimasu
gaikokugo		
den'wa	de	hanashimasu
rajio		
rekoodo		kikimasu
terebi		
eiga		mimasu
hashi		
fooku		tabemasu
naifu		
supuun		

↓

(2)		(1)	
		....	
nan	de	....	ka ?
		....	

10.2.4 Multiple Relationals

kameraya			dekakemasu/∼-masen
hon'ya	e		kimasu
jin'ja	kara		kaerimasu
byooin		wa	
otera		mo	
Kyooto	ni		imasu/∼-masen
Yooroppa			arimasu

niwa kyookai	ni		
shokudoo			nomimasu/∼-masen tabemasu/∼-masen
toshokan			ben'kyoo shimasu/∼-masen
hon'ya tabakoya pan'ya gaikoku	de	wa mo	kaimasu/∼-masen
kissaten mise byooin			machimasu/∼-masen
jidoosha hikooki	de		ikimasu/∼-masen ryokoo shimasu
en'pitsu			kakimasu/∼-masen
gaikokugo			hanashimasu/∼-masen

10.2.5 Relationals *ka, ya, to*

Buraun san anata sen'sei		Suujii san Yamamoto san gakusei	ga	imasu ben'kyoo shimasu den'wa shimasu
hashi		fooku		sagashimasu
zasshi		shin'bun		yomimasu
jazu		popyuraa	o	kikimasu
hon		zasshi		karimasu
nihon'go	ka	chuugokugo		ben'kyoo shimasu
piano	ya	baiorin		hikimasu
Nikkoo	to	Nara	e	ryokoo shimasu
Asakusa		Shin'juku		dekakemasu
kissaten		resutoran	kara	kimasu
toshokan		uchi		yomimasu
shokudoo		resutoran	de	kikimasu
gakkoo		toshokan		karimasu ben'kyoo shimasu
Furan'su		Doitsu	ni	imasu arimasu
fune den'sha		hikooki jidoosha	de	kimasu kaerimasu
hashi		fooku		tabemasu

10.2.6 Time Nominative

a.

ashita		gaikoku kara kaerimasu
ashita no asa		
ashita no hiru	(wa)	totemo isogashii desu
ashita no ban	(mo)	
ashita no yoru		watakushi wa hima desu
raigetsu		

↓

itsu	....	ka ?
	....	

		den'sha de ikimasu
kyoo		eiga o mimashita
kesa		
kyoo no hiru	(wa)	ten'ki ga ii desu
kon'ban	(mo)	tsugoo ga warukatta n desu
kyoo no yoru		gen'ki desu
kon'getsu		shizuka deshita

↓

itsu	....	ka ?
	....	

kinoo		
kinoo no asa		toshokan ni imashita
kinoo no hiru	(wa)	
kinoo no ban	(mo)	tanoshikatta desu
kinoo no yoru		hima deshita
sen'getsu		

↓

itsu	....	ka ?
	....	

b.

mainichi	dekakemashita
maiasa	ben'kyoo shimashita
maiban	piano o hikimasu
maishuu	isogashii desu
maigetsu	
mainen	hima deshita

10.2.7 Adverb

			chiisai desu
kore	wa	chotto	takakatta desu
sore	(ga)	totemo	
kono uchi	(mo)		kirei desu
			kirei deshita

sono shin'bun	o (wa) (mo)	chotto	yomimashoo karimasu	

kono eiga ano zasshi	wa (mo)	amari chittomo	muzukashiku arimasen omoshiroku arimasen deshita suki de wa arimasen suki ja arimasen deshita	
kore	o (wa) (mo)		tabemasen nomimasen deshita	

anata	wa (mo)	zuibun	erai desu chiisakatta desu	
Nikkoo Nara			shizuka desu kirei deshita	yo ne nee
gohan	o (mo)		tabemashita kaimashita	
watakushi Suujii san	wa (ga) (mo)	tokidoki taitei itsumo sugu mata	ikimasu kikimashita	

eiga terebi			omoshiroi desu omoshirokatta desu	
ten'ki	wa (ga) (mo)	tokidoki taitei itsumo mada	ii desu yokatta desu	
nihon'go baiorin			heta desu muzukashii desu	
heya			kirei desu kitanakatta desu	
hon on'gaku koocha	o (wa) (mo)	moo	yomimashita kikimashita nomimashita	

10.2.8 Sentence Interjective

Ano kissaten wa kirei ja arimasen. *Demo,* on'gaku ga ii desu.

Ten'ki ga warui desu. *Demo,* Asakusa e ikimasu.

Kyoo wa Tookyoo e ikimashita. *Demo,* ashita wa ikimasen.

Watakushi wa piano ga heta desu. *Demo,* Buraun san wa joozu desu.

On'gaku ga daisuki desu. *Dakara,* maiban kikimasu.

Kono kamera wa yasukatta n desu. *Dakara,* kaimashita.

Ten'ki ga warukatta n desu. *Dakara,* ryokoo shimasen deshita.

Jin'ja wa totemo shizuka deshita. *Sore ni,* kirei deshita.

Kono hon wa tsumaranakatta desu. *Sore ni,* takakatta desu.

Doitsugo to furan'sugo o naraimashita. *Sore ni,* nihon'go mo naraimashita.

10.3 QUESTION AND ANSWER

10.3.1 Alternate question

a.

koocha	ga	oishii desu / suki desu		ocha	ga	oishii desu / suki	
piano	o	nomimasu / hikimasu		baiorin	o	nomimasu / hikimasu	
toshokan	de	karimasu	ka,	gakkoo	de	karimasu	ka?
nihon'go	de	hanashimasu		eigo	de	hanashimasu	
uchi	ni	imasu		kissaten	ni	imasu	
Yooroppa	e kara	kaerimasu		Amerika	e kara	kaerimasu	

b.

koocha	wa	oishii desu / suki desu		mazui desu / kirai desu	
		nomimasu		nomimasen	
toshokan	de	karimasu	ka,	hon'ya de kaimasu	ka?
nihon'go	de	hanashimasu		kakimasu	
Yooroppa	e kara	kaerimasu		Chuugoku e ikimasu	
uchi	ni	imashoo		dekakemashoo	

10.3.2 Propositional question "Won't you......?"

(anata mo) | (issho ni)	....	de	....	o	nomi*masen* tabe*masen* kaki*masen* narai*masen* hanashi*masen* kai*masen* mi*masen* machi*masen* sagashi*masen*	ka?

| (anata mo) \| (issho ni) | .... | de | .... | o | shimasen
yomimasen
kikimasen
hikimasen
karimasen
ben'kyoo shimasen
ken'butsu shimasen | ka? |
| | .... | e
kara | | | ikimasen
kimasen
kaerimasen
hairimasen
dekakemasen
ryokoo shimasen | |

10.3.3 *Hai (Ee), iie* response

Ryokoo wa tanoshikatta desu ka? .... { Hai, tanoshikatta desu. / Iie, tanoshiku arimasen deshita.

Ryokoo wa tanoshiku arimasen deshita ka? .... { Hai, tanoshiku arimasen deshita. / Iie, tanoshikatta desu.

Anata wa on'gaku o kikimasu ka? .... { Ee, kikimasu. / Iie, kikimasen.

Anata wa amari on'gaku o kikimasen ne? .... { Hai, kikimasen. / Iie, kikimasu (yo).

Kono hen wa shizuka desu ka? .... { Hai, shizuka desu. / Iie, shizuka ja arimasen.

Kono hen wa shizuka ja arimasen ne? .... { Ee, shizuka ja arimasen. / Iie, shizuka desu (yo).

Anata wa gitaa o hikimasu ka? .... { Hai, hikimasu. / Iie, hikimasen.

Kesa piano o hikimasen deshita ne? .... { Ee, hikimasen deshita. / Iie, hikimashita (yo).

10.4 AURAL COMPREHENSION

わたくしの　なまえは、なかむら　いくおです。　いま　がくせい
です。　がっこうは　とうきょうに　あります。スミスさんは　わたくし
の　ともだちです。　きのう、スミスさんと　いっしょに　ぎんざへ
いきました。　しょくどうで　てんぷらを　たべました。　スミスさんは
てんぷらが　だいすきです。　スミスさんは　にほんごが　じょうずでは
ありませんが、ときどき　にほんの　えいがを　みます。　きのうも
みました。　それから、きっさてんへも　いきました。　あまり　しずか
じゃありませんでしたが、きれいでした。　おんがくも　ききました。
にほんの　きっさてんは　とても　いいです。

LESSON 11

11.1 USEFUL EXPRESSIONS

Doozo ohairi kudasai.
"Please come in." This expression is a polite equivalent of (*Doozo*) *haitte kudasai.*

Kokakoora wa ikaga desu ka /
"How about Coca-Cola?" "Would you like some Coke?" ~ *wa ikaga desu ka?* is often used to ask if someone would like to have something. The less polite equivalent would be ~ *wa doo desu ka?*

Ee, itadakimasu.
"Yes, thank you." This expression is used to accept an offer of any kind. *Ee* (or *hai*) may be omitted.

Iie, kekkoo desu.
"No, thank you." This expression is used to decline an offer of any kind.

11.2 DIALOG

— Ishii's visiting Minoru —

Ishii : Minoru kun,*¹ imasu ka /   (Knocking at the door)

Minoru : A, Ishii san   Doozo ohairi kudasai.

Ishii : Ee, arigatoo.

Minoru : Atsui*² deshoo*³. Kokakoora wa ikaga desu ka /

Ishii : Ee, itadakimasu.

Minoru : Ame ga takusan*⁴ furimasu nee. Ashita mo ten'ki ga warui deshoo ka /

Ishii : Ashita wa tabun ii deshoo. Rajio de soo iimashita yo.

Minoru : Soo desu ka /

Ishii : Anata wa suiei ga suki deshoo*⁵ / Ashita boku to*⁶ issho ni umi e

ikimasen ka /

Minoru : Suiei wa suki desu ga, ashita wa tsugoo*⁷ ga warui n desu.

Ishii : Dooshite desu ka /

Minoru : Kon'ban kuni e kaerimasu.

Ishii :   Kuni e / Anata no uchi wa Tookyoo deshoo[*8]/

Minoru :   Iie, Hokkaidoo desu.

Ishii :   Oya, soo desu ka. Jaa, gokazoku[*9] wa min'na Hokkaidoo desu[*8] ka /

Minoru :   Chichi[*10] to haha wa Sapporo ni imasu ga, ani to ane wa Tookyoo desu[*8].

Ishii :   Kyonen[*11] no fuyu,[*12] Hokkaidoo e ryokoo shimashita ga, totemo samukatta desu.

Minoru :   Yoru wa toku ni samukatta deshoo.[*13] Ima wa aki desu ga, asa ya yoru wa kitto moo samui desu yo /

11.3 PATTERN SENTENCES

11.3.1

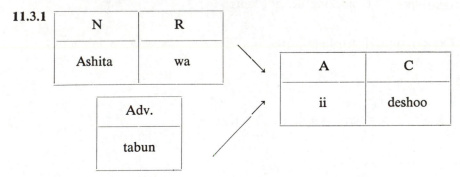

"[It] will probably be good tomorrow."

11.3.2

N	R		A	C
Yoru	wa		samukatta	deshoo

"It must have been cold at night."

11.3.3

N	R		N	C
Uchi	wa		Tookyoo	deshoo

"[Your] house must be in Tōkyō."

11.4 NOTES

11.4.1 *-Kun* in *Minoru kun* is a dependent Nominative that is used in the same way as *-san* in *Yamada san*. The *-kun*, however, is used normally by men, while *-san* can be used by both men and women. *-Kun* may not be used with the name of a person who is superior to the speaker. It is commonly used among friends, classmates, etc.

11.4.2 *Atsui* "hot," *samui* "cold," *atatakai* "warm," and *suzushii* "cool" are not usually used with the word *ten'ki* "weather." *Ten'ki* is used with *ii, warui, subarashii,* etc. *Ten'ki ga ii desu,* but never *ten'ki ga atsui desu.*

Atsui desu.	"It is hot."
Kyoo wa amari suzushiku arimasen.	"It is not very cool today."
Kinoo wa atatakakatta desu.	"It was warm yesterday."
Yoru samuku arimasen deshita ka?	"Wasn't it cold at night?"

11.4.3 *Deshoo* is the OO form of the Copula *desu.* While *desu* makes a statement definite or confirmative, *deshoo* functions to make it suppositional, presumptive uncertain, less confirmative, etc., and is often expressed as "I suppose," "will (probably) be."

Atsui desu.	"It's hot."
Atsui deshoo.	"It must be hot."
Itoo san wa gakusei desu.	"Mr. Itō is a student."
Itoo san wa gakusei deshoo.	"I presume that Mr. Itō is a stduent." "Mr. Itō will (probably) be a student."

Deshoo follows an Adjective, a Nominative, an adjectival Nominative or a Verb. (Verb plus *deshoo* will be introduced in later volumes.)

Adjective   Nominative   adjectival Nominative   + *desu* ⟶ Adjective   Nominative   adjectival Nominative   + *deshoo*

Kon'ban wa atatakai deshoo.	"It will be warm tonight."
Ten'ki wa warui deshoo.	"The weather will (probably) be bad."
Minoru kun wa on'gaku ga suki deshoo.	"Minoru will (probably) like music."

Deshoo and *desu yo* are often confused by foreigners because of the similarity of sounds. However, there is a difference in intonation and juncture. Train yourself to be able to distinguish them.

11.4.4 *Takusan* is an Adverb meaning "many," or "much."

154

Ame ga takusan furimasu nee.	"It rains a lot, doesn't it?"
Yuki ga takusan furimashita.	"It snowed a lot."
Otera ga takusan arimasu.	"There are many (Buddhist) temples."
Koohii o takusan nomimashita.	"[I] drank a lot of coffee."

The opposite word for *takusan* is *sukoshi* "a few," or "a little."

11.4.5 When the *deshoo,* the OO form of the Copula *desu,* is said with a rising intonation, that is *deshoo?,* it is a question asking for the hearer's agreement to the statement like *desu ne?.* But *deshoo?* bears a little more uncertainty.

Compare:

Anata wa suiei ga suki desu ka ?	"Do you like swimming?"
Anata wa suiei ga suki desu ne ?	"You like swimming, don't you?"
Anata wa suiei ga suki deshoo ?	"You probably like swimming, don't you?"

11.4.6 *To* in *boku to* is a Relational meaning "with (someone)." This Relational usually occurs before a Verb and after either a personal name or a Nominative that represents an animate object. Occasionally *issho ni* "together" is used with *to.*

Itoo san to hanashimashita.	"[I] talked with Mr. Itō."
Watashi to issho ni ikimashoo.	"Let's go together with me."
Ishii san wa Keiko san to kekkon shimashita.	"Mr. Ishii married Keiko."

The Relational *wa* or *mo* may occur after *to,* forming multiple Relationals.

Anata to wa hanashimasen.	"[I] won't talk with you."
Ishii san to mo ikimashita.	"[I] went [there] with Mr. Ishii, too."

11.4.7 *Tsugoo ga warui (desu)* is used idiomatically to mean "circumstances do not permit (one's doing such and such)." The opposite expression *tsugoo ga ii (desu)* is "circumstances permit (one's doing such and such)," or "something suits one's convenience."

(Go)*tsugoo wa doo desu ka ?	"Are you available?"
Ee, ii desu.	"Yes, I am."
Chotto tsugoo ga warui n desu.	"I am not available."

* See 11.4.9.

11.4.8 *Anata no uchi wa Tookyoo deshoo?* means "your home is in Tōkyō, isn't it?" In expressing "something or someone is in a place," *~ ni arimasu* or *~ ni imasu* may be replaced by *desu,* and the Copula *desu* is common when referring to locations of buildings, houses, etc.

Eki wa doko ni arimasu ka ?
Eki wa doko desu ka ?

"Where is the station?"

Boku no uchi wa Yokohama desu.

"My house is in Yokohama."

Minoru kun wa ima gakkoo desu.

"Minoru is at school now."

11.4.9 Like *o-* as in *ohima* "leisure time," the prefix *go-* may occur at the beginning of some Nominatives to show "politeness." In normal style speech, the use of this word is conventionally limited. Both *o-* and *go-* are common in women's speech.

Compare:

kazoku	....	plain word for "family," so you can use *kazoku* either to refer to someone else's family or to your own in less formal or ordinary speech
(go)kazoku	....	this word may be used only to refer to someone else's family in polite speech
shujin	....	(my) husband; (my) master
goshujin	....	(someone else's) husband; (someone else's) master: *go-* is mandatory
kyoodai	....	(my) brother(s) and/or sister(s)
(go)kyoodai	....	(someone else's) brother(s) and/or sister(s)

Note that *go-* is not indispensable in mentioning someone else's family members but it may be added when politeness is required.

11.4.10 *Chichi* "father," *haha* "mother," *ani* "older brother," *ane* "older sister," etc. are used to refer to the speaker's own family members. As partly explained in Note 11.4.9, depending upon whether you are referring to your own family members or to someone else's, different terms will be used in Japanese. Here are some more examples:

when referring to your family members:		when referring to someone else's family members:
chichi	"father"	otoosan
haha	"mother"	okaasan
ani	"older brother"	oniisan
ane	"older sister"	oneesan
otooto	"younger brother"	otootosan
imooto	"younger sister"	imootosan
kodomo	"child"	kodomosan *or* okosan
shujin	"husband"	goshujin

kanai	"wife"	okusan
kazoku	"family"	(go)kazoku
kyoodai	"brothers and/or sisters"	(go)kyoodai

Otoosan wa ogen'ki desu ka?	"How is your father?"
Hai, chichi wa gen'ki desu.	"Yes, my father is fine."
Goshujin wa sen'sei deshoo?	"Isn't your husband a teacher?"
Ee, shujin wa sen'sei desu.	"Yes, he is a teacher."

11.4.11 *Kyonen* is a time Nominative meaning "last year."

rainen "next year"	kotoshi "this year"	kyonen "last year"

These time Nominatives are used without any Relationals following except *wa* and *mo*.

Kyonen Hokkaidooe ryokoo shimashita.	"[I] took a trip to Hokkaidō last year."
Rainen mo Yooroppa e ikimasu.	"[I] am going to Europe next year, also."

11.4.12 *Fuyu* is a Nominative meaning "winter." Like *kyoo* "today," *kon'getsu* "this month," *fuyu* "winter," and the other names of seasons can be used without any Relational following it. Here are the names of the four seasons:

haru "spring"	natsu "summer"	aki "fall"	fuyu "winter"

Natsu doko e ikimashoo ka?	"Where shall we go in the summer?"
Yama ka umi e ikimashoo.	"Let's go to the mountains or the seaside."

11.4.13 As explained in Note 11.4.3, an Adjective may occur before the Copula *deshoo*. When the perfect tense form or the TA form of an Adjective occurs with *deshoo,* it is the presumptive to the past: "something or someone must have been such and such."

Adjective(-*katta*) + *desu* ⟶ **Adjective(-*katta*)** + *deshoo*

Yoru wa toku ni samukatta deshoo.	"It must have been especially cold in the evening."
Ano mise no koohii wa oishikatta deshoo.	"The coffee of that shop must have been good."
Kinoo wa ten'ki ga yokatta deshoo.	"The weather must have been good yesterday."
Kono mizu wa tsumetakatta deshoo.	"I suppose this water was cold."

11.5 VOCABULARY

Dialog

Minoru	....	N	man's first name
-kun	....	Nd	equivalent of -san (used by men) (see 11.4.1)
atsui	....	A	is hot (see 11.4.2)
deshoo	....	C	OO form of desu (see 11.4.3)
Kokakoora	....	N	Coca-cola
ikaga	....	Ni	how? (polite equivalent of doo)
ame	....	N	rain
takusan	....	Adv.	a lot (see 11.4.4)
furimasu	....	V	(rain or snow) fall (normal form of furu)
tabun	....	Adv.	probably; perhaps
rajio	....	N	radio
soo	....	Adv.	so; in that way
iimashita	....	V	said (TA form of iimasu ←— iu)
suiei	....	N	swimming
to	....	R	with (someone) (see 11.4.6)
umi	....	N	sea; seaside
tsugoo	....	N	convenience (see 11.4.7)
kuni	....	N	country; home (town; country)
Hokkaidoo	....	N	Hokkaidō Prefecture (northern island of Japan)
oya	....	SI	oh!; oh?; my!
(go)kazoku	....	N	(someone else's) family (see 11.4.9)
min'na	....	N	all; everyone
chichi	....	N	(my) father (see 11.4.10)
haha	....	N	(my) mother
Sapporo	....	N	capital city of Hokkaidō
ani	....	N	(my) older brother
ane	....	N	(my) older sister
kyonen	....	N	last year
fuyu	....	N	winter
samukatta	....	A	was cold (weather) (TA form of samui)
aki	....	N	autumn; fall
kitto	....	Adv.	surely; no doubt

Notes

atatakai	. . . .	A	is warm
suzushii	. . . .	A	is cool
yuki	. . . .	N	snow
sukoshi	. . . .	Adv.	a little (see 11.4.4)
Yokohama	. . . .	N	the name of a city
go-	. . . .	(prefix)	(see 11.4.9)
shujin	. . . .	N	(my) husband
goshujin	. . . .	N	someone else's husband
kyoodai	. . . .	N	sister(s) and/or brother(s)
otoosan	. . . .	N	(someone else's) father (see 11.4.10)
okaasan	. . . .	N	(someone else's) mother
oniisan	. . . .	N	(someone else's) older brother
oneesan	. . . .	N	(someone else's) older sister
otooto	. . . .	N	(my) younger brother
imooto	. . . .	N	(my) younger sister
kodomo	. . . .	N	child
okosan	. . . .	N	(someone else's) child
kanai	. . . .	N	my wife
okusan	. . . .	N	(someone else's) wife
kotoshi	. . . .	N	this year
rainen	. . . .	N	next year
haru	. . . .	N	spring
natsu	. . . .	N	summer
yama	. . . .	N	mountain
tsumetakatta	. . . .	A	was cold (thing) (TA form of *tsumetai*)

11.6 HIRAGANA PRACTICE

11.6.1 Recognize the difference or similarity between two characters in each of the following pairs:

きや‥‥‥きゃ	しゆ‥‥‥しゅ	ちよ‥‥‥ちょ
きゆ‥‥‥きゅ	しよ‥‥‥しょ	にや‥‥‥にゃ
きよ‥‥‥きょ	ちや‥‥‥ちゃ	にゆ‥‥‥にゅ
しや‥‥‥しゃ	ちゆ‥‥‥ちゅ	によ‥‥‥にょ

ひや……ひゃ	りゆ……りゅ	じよ……じょ
ひゆ……ひゅ	りよ……りょ	びや……びゃ
ひよ……ひょ	ぎや……ぎゃ	びゆ……びゅ
みや……みゃ	ぎゆ……ぎゅ	びよ……びょ
みゆ……みゅ	ぎよ……ぎょ	ぴや……ぴゃ
みよ……みょ	じや……じゃ	ぴゆ……ぴゅ
りや……りゃ	じゆ……じゅ	ぴよ……ぴょ

11.6.2 Read and write the following:

じんじゃ	しゅじん	じゃあ	おちゃ
としょかん	じむしょ	でんしゃ	きょねん

11.7 DRILLS

11.7.1 Pronunciation Drill

Minoru kun   warui   umi   kun   uchi   fuyu   fune   Furan'su

Suiei ga suki desu.   Takusan furimasu.

11.7.2 Pattern Drill

1. Atsui deshoo.

2. Ashita mo ten'ki ga warui deshoo ka?

3. Ashita wa tabun ii deshoo.

4. Anata wa suiei ga suki deshoo?

5. Ashita boku to issho ni umi e ikimasen ka?

6. Anata no uchi wa Tookyoo deshoo?

7. Gokazoku wa min'na Hokkaidoo desu ka?

8. Yoru wa toku ni samukatta deshoo.

11.7.3 Transformation Drill

1. Kyoo wa *atsui desu*.   ⟶   Kyoo wa *atsui deshoo*.

2. Anata wa suiei ga suki desu.   ⟶   Anata wa suiei ga suki deshoo.

3. Minoru kun wa gekusei desu.   ⟶   Minoru kun wa gakusei deshoo.

4. Ashita wa ten'ki ga warui desu.   ⟶   Ashita wa ten'ki ga warui deshoo.

5. Kon'ban suzushii desu.   ⟶   Kon'ban suzushii deshoo.

6. Ano kata wa goshujin desu.   ⟶   Ano kata wa goshujin deshoo.

7. Chichi to haha wa gen'ki desu. ⟶ Chichi to haha wa gen'ki deshoo.

8. Hokkaidoo no fuyu wa samui desu. ⟶ Hokkaidoo no fuyu wa samui deshoo.

9. Ashita mo atatakai desu. ⟶ Ashita mo atatakai deshoo.

10. Yuki ga kirai desu. ⟶ Yuki ga kirai deshoo.

11. Soo desu. ⟶ Soo deshoo.

11.7.4 Transformation Drill

1. Kinoo wa *samukatta* desu. ⟶ Kinoo wa *samukatta deshoo*.

2. Yoru wa suzushikatta desu. ⟶ Yoru wa suzushikatta deshoo.

3. Kesa wa ten'ki ga yokatta desu. ⟶ Kesa wa ten'ki ga yokatta deshoo.

4. Kono rajio wa yasukatta desu. ⟶ Kono rajio wa yasukatta deshoo.

5. Sono Kokakoora wa tsumetakatta desu. ⟶ Sono Kokakoora wa tsumetakatta deshoo.

6. Kesa wa atatakakatta desu. ⟶ Kesa wa atatakakatta deshoo.

7. Kotoshi no natsu wa atsukatta desu. ⟶ Kotoshi no natsu wa atsukatta deshoo.

8. Tsugoo ga warukatta desu. ⟶ Tsugoo ga warukatta deshoo.

9. Suiei wa tanoshikatta desu. ⟶ Suiei wa tanoshikatta deshoo.

11.7.5 Transformation Drill

1. Anata wa suiei ga suki *desu ne*? ⟶ Anata wa suiei ga suki *deshoo*?

2. Tsugoo wa ii desu ne? ⟶ Tsugoo wa ii deshoo?

3. Gokazoku wa gen'ki desu ne? ⟶ Gokazoku wa gen'ki deshoo?

4. Soo desu ne? ⟶ Soo deshoo?

5. Nikkoo wa kirei desu ne? ⟶ Nikkoo wa kirei deshoo?

6. Ima Hokkaidoo wa samui desu ne? ⟶ Ima Hokkaidoo wa samui deshoo?

7. Kono mizu wa tsumetai desu ne? ⟶ Kono mizu wa tsumetai deshoo?

8. Anata no uchi wa Hawai desu ne? ⟶ Anata no uchi wa Hawai deshoo?

9. Anata wa Tookyoo Daigaku no gakusei desu ne? ⟶ Anata wa Tookyoo Daigaku no gakusei deshoo?

10. Ashita wa isogashii desu ne? ⟶ Ashita wa isogashii deshoo?

11.7.6 Transformation Drill

1. Anata no uchi wa Tookyoo *ni arimasu* ka? → Anata no uchi wa Tookyoo *desu* ka?

2. Kazoku wa min'na Hokkaidoo *ni imasu*. ⟶ Kazoku wa min'na Hokkaidoo *desu*.

3. Eki wa doko ni arimasu ka? ⟶ Eki wa doko desu ka?

4. Chichi wa koko ni imasu. ⟶ Chichi wa koko desu.

5. Shujin wa ima kuni ni imasu. ⟶ Shujin wa ima kuni desu.

6. Jisho ya hon wa toshokan ni arimasu. ⟶ Jisho ya hon wa toshokan desu.

7. Ani wa ima daigaku ni imasu. ⟶ Ani wa ima daigaku desu.

8. Rajio wa boku no heya ni arimasu. ⟶ Rajio wa boku no heya desu.

11.7.7 E-J Expansion Drill

1. Umi e ikimasen ka?
   with me ...... Watakushi to umi e ikimasen ka?

2. Gakkoo de hanashimashita.
   with a teacher ...... Sen'sei to gakkoo de hanashimashita.

3. Amerika kara kaerimashita ka?
   with whom? ...... Dare to Amerika kara kaerimashita ka?

4. Kyonen ryokoo shimashita.
   with students ...... Gakusei to kyonen ryokoo shimashita

5. Eiga o mimashita.
   together with Keiko ...... Keiko san to issho ni eiga o mimashita.

6. Kyonen kekkon shimashita.
   to my husband ...... Shujin to kyonen kekkon shimashita.

7. Kissaten e hairimasen deshita.
   with Mr. Brown ...... Buraun san to kissaten e hairimasen deshita.

8. Ban'gohan o tabemasu ka?
   together with whom? ...... Donata to issho ni ban'gohan o tabemasu ka?

9. Kuni e kaerimasu.
   with my family ...... Kazoku to kuni e kaerimasu.

10. Kaimono o shimashita.
    together with my mother ...... Haha to issho ni kaimono o shimashita.

11.7.8 Expansion Drill

1. Ikimasen ka? .... Ikimasen ka?

   yama e .... Yama e ikimasen ka?

   issho ni .... Issho ni yama e ikimasen ka?

   boku to .... Boku to issho ni yama e ikimasen ka?

   natsu .... Natsu boku to issho ni yama e ikimasen ka?

   kotoshi no natsu .... Kotoshi no natsu boku to issho ni yama e ikimasen ka?

2. Furimasu yo. . . . . Furimasu yo.

    takusan . . . . Takusan furimasu yo.

    ame ga . . . . Ame ga takusan furimasu yo.

    kitto . . . . Kitto ame ga takusan furimasu yo.

    ashita wa . . . . Ashita wa kitto ame ga takusan furimasu yo.

3. Ii deshoo. . . . . Ii deshoo.

    ten'ki ga . . . . Ten'ki ga ii deshoo.

    tabun . . . . Tabun ten'ki ga ii deshoo.

    raigetsu mo . . . . Raigetsu mo tabun ten'ki ga ii deshoo.

4. Iimashita yo. . . . . Iimashita yo.

    soo . . . . Soo iimashita yo.

    rajio de . . . . Rajio de soo iimashita yo.

    kesa . . . . Kesa rajio de soo iimashita yo.

11.7.9 Response Drill (family words)

1. *Otoosan* wa ogen'ki desu ka?
    hai . . . . . . Hai, *chichi* wa gen'ki desu.

2. Gokazoku wa Tookyoo desu ka?
    hai . . . . . . Hai, kazoku wa Tookyoo desu.

3. Okusan wa sen'sei desu ka?
    iie . . . . . . Iie, kanai wa sen'sei de wa arimasen.

4. Gokyoodai wa doko ni imasu ka?
    Hokkaidoo . . . . . . Kyoodai wa Hokkaidoo ni imasu.

5. Oniisan wa gakusei desu ka?
    hai . . . . . . Hai, ani wa gakusei desu.

6. Oneesan no namae wa Kazuko san desu ka?
    hai . . . . . . Hai, ane no namae wa Kazuko desu.

7. Goshujin wa ima doko ni imasu ka?
    Doitsu . . . . . . Shujin wa ima Doitsu ni imasu.

8. Imootosan wa on'gaku ga suki desu ka?
    hai . . . . . . Hai, imooto wa on'gaku ga suki desu.

9. Okaasan wa piano o hikimasu ka?
    iie . . . . . . Iie, haha wa piano o hikimasen.

10. Okosan wa ima uchi ni imasu ka?
    iie . . . . . . Iie, kodomo wa ima uchi ni imasen.

11. Otootosan no namae wa nan desu ka?
    Ikuo . . . . . . Otooto no namae wa Ikuo desu.

11.7.10 Review Drill (negative response)

1. Kinoo ame ga furimashita ka? ...... Iie, kinoo ame ga furimasen deshita.

2. Anata wa suiei ga suki deshoo? ...... Iie, watashi wa suiei ga suki de wa arimasen.

3. Kyonen no natsu wa atsukatta desu ka? .... Iie, kyonen no natsu wa atsuku arimasen deshita.

4. Kazoku wa Hokkaidoo desu ka? ...... Iie, kazoku wa Hokkaidoo ja arimasen.

5. Itoo san to hanashimashita ka? ...... Iie, Itoo san to hanashimasen deshita.

6. Rajio de soo iimashita ka? ...... Iie, rajio de soo iimasen deshita.

7. Chuugokugo o hanashimasu ka? ...... Iie, chuugokugo wa hanashimasen.

8. Kinoo wa samukatta deshoo? ...... Iie, kinoo wa samuku arimasen deshita.

9. Haru wa suki deshoo? ...... Iie, haru wa suki ja arimasen.

10. Kyoo wa suzushii desu ka? ...... Iie, kyoo wa suzushiku arimasen.

11.8 EXERCISES

11.8.1 Express the following ideas in Japanese:

1. The weather will probably be good tomorrow morning.

2. It rained a lot last night.

3. It must have been very warm this morning.

4. Your family is in the States, isn't it?

5. The trip will certainly be pleasant.

6. That coffee must be cold.

11.8.2 Carry on the following conversations in Japanese:

1. — Is Mr. Ishii in (at home)?

    — Yes. Please come in.

    — Thank you. It's hot today, isn't it?

    — Yes, it is. How about a Coke?

    — No, thank you.

2. — Where is your home town? (=Where are you from?)

    — Sapporo.

    — Oh, really? I like Hokkaidō very much. It must be very cool there now.

— Yes. Summer in Hokkaidō is wonderful. But I don't like the winters there.

— Why?

— We have a lot of snow in winter.

11.8.3 Answer the following questions in Japanese:

1. Anata no uchi wa ima doko desu ka?

2. Anata no kuni wa doko desu ka?

3. Gokazoku wa min'na soko ni imasu ka?

4. Anata no kuni wa fuyu atatakai desu ka?

5. Anata no kuni de wa haru to natsu, ame ga takusan furimasu ka?

6. Kyonen ka kotoshi kuni e kaerimashita ka?

LESSON 12

12.1 USEFUL EXPRESSIONS

Doozo okamainaku.

"Please do not go to any trouble." "Don't bother."

Ocha o moo ippai doozo.

"Please have another cup of tea." Another example would be: *Isu o doozo,* "Please have a seat."

12.2 DIALOG

— About the family —

Mrs. Yamada: Ocha wa ikaga desu ka /

Ikuo: Doozo okamainaku. Ima Minoru kun wa rusu desu ka /

Mrs. Yamada: Ee, gomen nasai ne / Watakushi no tomodachi ga eiga no kippu o

san*[1]mai*[2] kuremashita.*[3] Dakara, kyoo kodomotachi*[4] wa min'na

dekakemashita.

Ikuo: Soo desu ka.

Mrs. Yamada: Ikuo san, kyoodai wa nan'nin*[2] desu ka /

Ikuo: Ani to ane to otooto to imooto ga hitori*[2] zutsu*[5] imasu.

Mrs. Yamada: Oniisan ya oneesan wa ikutsu*[6] desu ka /

Ikuo: Nijuu yon'sai*[2] to hatachi*[2] desu.

Mrs. Yamada: Otootosan'tachi wa mada chiisai n deshoo /

Ikuo: Ee, too to yattsu desu.

Mrs. Yamada: Soo desu ka. Jaa, otootosan to imootosan ni*[7] kono ehon o issatsu*[2]

zutsu agemashoo.*[8]

Ikuo :   Doomo sumimasen.   Kon'ban otoototachi ni yarimashoo.[3][8]   Tokoro

de, ima nan'ji[2] desu ka /

Mrs. Yamada :   San'ji desu.

Ikuo :   Jaa, sorosoro shitsurei shimasu.

Mrs. Yamada :   Soo desu ka /   Demo, ocha o moo[9] ippai[2] doozo.

Ikuo :   Ee, itadakimasu.

12.3   PATTERN SENTENCES

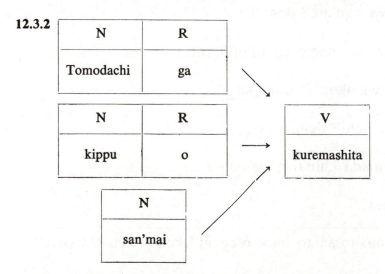

12.3.1

N	R
Otootosan	ni

N	R
ehon	o

V
agemashoo

"I think I'll give a picture book to [your] younger brother."

12.3.2

N	R
Tomodachi	ga

N	R
kippu	o

N
san'mai

V
kuremashita

"A friend [of mine] gave me (us) three tickets."

12.4 NOTES

12.4.1 *San* is the numeral meaning "three." Here is a list of the ordinary numerals:

0	rei; zero		100	hyaku
1	ichi		200	nihyaku
2	ni		300	san'byaku**
3	san		400	yon'hyaku
4	shi; yon; (yo-)*		500	gohyaku
5	go		600	roppyaku**
6	roku		700	nanahyaku
7	shichi; nana		800	happyaku**
8	hachi		900	kyuuhyaku
9	ku; kyuu		1,000	sen
10	juu		2,000	nisen
11	juuichi		3,000	san'zen**
12	juuni		4,000	yon'sen
13	juusan		5,000	gosen
14	juushi; juuyon; (juuyo-)*		6,000	rokusen
15	juugo		7,000	nanasen
16	juuroku		8,000	hassen**
17	juushichi; juunana		9,000	kyuusen
18	juuhachi		10,000	ichiman
19	juuku; juukyuu		20,000	niman
20	nijuu		30,000	san'man
21	nijuuichi		40,000	yon'man
⋮	⋮		50,000	goman
30	san'juu		60,000	rokuman
40	yon'juu; shijuu		70,000	nanaman
50	gojuu		80,000	hachiman
60	rokujuu		90,000	kyuuman
70	shichijuu; nanajuu		100,000	juuman
80	hachijuu		⋮	⋮
90	kyuujuu; kujuu		1,000,000	hyakuman

* *Yo-* for "four" is never used independently. It is always followed by a counter. (see 12.4.2)
** Phonetic changes or irregular combinations.

12.4.2 *San'mai* is the combination of the numeral *san* "three" and *-mai*, the counter for thin and flat objects. When you count things or people, there is usually an individual dependent Nominative called "counter" for each of them. The counter is selected according to the shape, classification, etc., of the item you count. The counter is attached to the numeral and formulates the "number" which is a Nominative. The counters appearing in this lesson are as follows:

-mai ...... the counter for thin and flat objects like paper, tickets, sliced things, dishes, etc. The numbers with *-mai* are formed regularly.

-nin ...... the counter for people. Note that the numbers for people are formed irregularly. *Hitori* and *futari* are native numbers. (see 12.4.6)

-sai ...... the counter for age. *Hatachi* is used for "twenty years old."

-satsu ...... the counter for books, magazines, notebooks, etc.

-ji ...... the counter indicating "o'clock."

-peeji ...... the counter meaning "page."

The following two counters are drilled in Lesson 1, Vol. II.

-hai ...... the counter for cupfuls, glassfuls, spoonfuls, etc.

-hon ...... the counter for long and slender objects like thread, pencils, cigarettes, bottles, pillars, belts, neckties, etc.

Number \ Counter		-mai	-nin	-sai	-satsu	-ji	-peeji	-hai	-hon
1	ichi		hitori	issai	issatsu		ippeeji	ippai	ippon
2	ni		futari						
3	san							san'bai	san'bon
4	yon / yo-		yo-	yon-	yon-	yo-	yon-	yon-	yon-
5	go								
6	roku							roppai / rokuhai	roppon
7	shichi / nana								
8	hachi			hassai / hachisai	hassatsu / hachisatsu		happeeji / hachipeeji	happai / hachihai	happon / hachihon
9	kyuu / ku			kyuu-	kyuu-	ku-	kyuu-	kyuu-	kyuu-
10	juu			jissai / jussai	jissatsu / jussatsu		jippeeji / juppeeji	jippai / juppai	jippon / juppon
(1) how many? or (2) what?	nan-	(1)	(1)	(1)	(1)	(2)	(1) (2)	nan'bai (1)	nan'bon (1)

(Blank columns indicate regular combinations of numerals and counters.)

There are two types of counters: (1) tells "how many," number of objects, and (2) tells a specific point or place from among those in a numerical sequence. Therefore, *nan-* before a counter of the first group means "how many," and *nan-* before a counter of the second group means "what."

(1)	nan'mai	"how many (sheets of paper, etc.)?"
	nan'nin	"how many (people)?"
	nan'sai	"how many years old?"
(2)	nan'ji	"what time?"
(1) & (2)	nan'peeji	"how many pages?" "what page?"

As you see in the above, the counters with the initials /s/, /h/, /k/, or /t/ become *ss, pp, kk,* or *tt* respectively after ONE and TEN. /h/, and /k/ become *pp,* and *kk* respectively after SIX and sometimes after EIGHT. /s/, /h/, and /k/ may become *z, b,* and *g* respectively after THREE and *nan.*

The numbers are quantity Nominatives that may be used without any Relational following them. Usually a quantity Nominative occurs immediately before the Predicate, between the Predicate Modifier with which the quantity is concerned and the Predicate.

$$\text{Nominative} + \begin{Bmatrix} o \\ ga \\ wa \end{Bmatrix} + \text{Predicate} \longrightarrow \text{Nominative} + \begin{Bmatrix} o \\ ga \\ wa \end{Bmatrix} + \begin{Bmatrix} \textbf{number} \\ \textbf{or} \\ \textbf{quantity Nominative} \end{Bmatrix} + \text{Predicate}$$

Kippu o nan'mai kaimashita ka?	"How many tickets did [you] buy?"
San'mai kaimashita.	"[I] bought three (tickets)."
Gakusei wa nan'nin imasu ka?	"How many students are there?"
Gonin imasu.	"There are five (students)."
Hon ga nan'satsu arimasu ka?	"How many books are there?"
Issatsu arimasu.	"There is one (book)."
Ima nan'ji desu ka?	"What time is it now?"
Yoji desu.	"It is four o'clock."
Ima nan'sai desu ka?	"How old are [you] now?"
Juuhassai desu.	"[I] am eighteen."

12.4.3 *Kuremashita* is a Verb meaning "(someone) gave (something) to me or us." The Japanese are rather sensitive in the use of words expressing "giving," or "receiving." Different words should be used according to "who-gives-whom" and "who-gets-from-whom." The differences in these usages come from differences in social status or age, or the degree of respect or politeness that exists between one person who gives and the other who receives.

Agemasu, yarimasu, kuremasu, all mean "give." There are, however, clear distinctions in their usage.

170

Agemasu and *yarimasu*:

1. When something is given to a third party (See Diagram 1A & 1B.):

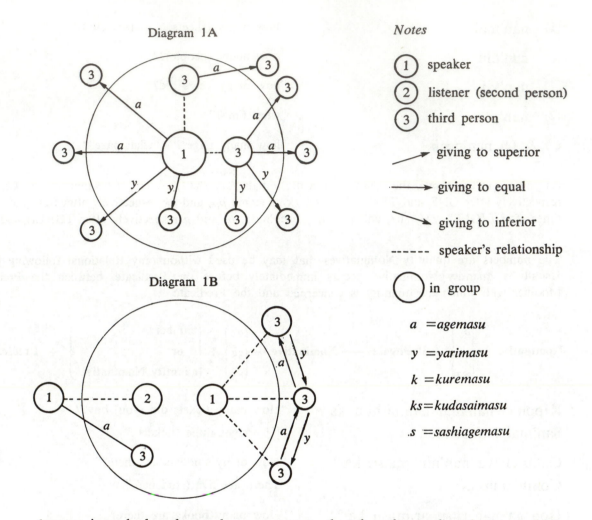

Diagram 1A

Diagram 1B

Notes

① speaker

② listener (second person)

③ third person

↗ giving to superior

→ giving to equal

↘ giving to inferior

------ speaker's relationship

◯ in group

a =*agemasu*

y =*yarimasu*

k =*kuremasu*

ks=*kudasaimasu*

.s =*sashiagemasu*

Agemasu is used when the speaker or someone other than the speaker gives to a third person unless the recipient is a member of the giver's "in-group" (persons he is closely associated with, such as family, peer group, etc.) or someone who is definitely inferior in age, social status, etc.

Watakushi wa tomodachi ni hon o agemashita.	"I gave a book to a friend of mine."
Watakushi wa sen'sei ni hon o agemashita.	"I gave a book to my teacher."
Chichi ga Yamamoto san ni hon o agemashita.	"My father gave a book to Mr. Yamamoto."
Ishii sen'sei wa okusan ni hon o agemashita.	"Mr. Ishii gave a book to his wife."

Even when the recipient is inferior to the giver in age, social status, etc., if he (the recipient) is a member of the listener's "in-group" and the listener is not inferior to the speaker, *agemasu* is used.

Watakushi wa Ishii sen'sei no okosan ni hon o agemasu.	"I will give a book to Mr. Ishii's child."
Ano gakusei wa Watanabe san no otootosan ni hon o agemasu.	"That student is going to give a book to Mr. Watanabe's younger brother."

Yarimasu is used only when the recipient is a member of the giver's "in-group" and is younger than the giver, or is definitely inferior in age, social status, etc.

Watakushi wa imooto ni hon o yarimashita.	"I gave a book to my younger sister."
Tanaka san wa inu ni gohan o yarimashita.	"Mr. Tanaka gave food to the dog."

2. When something is given to the listener (See Diagram 2.):

Diagram 2

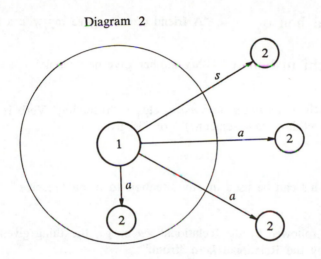

At this stage, avoid using *yarimasu* when you are talking about giving something to your listener, even when the recipient is younger or inferior in social status or is a member of your "in-group." When the recipient-listener is a person outside of your "in-group" to whom you want to show deference, you should use *sashiagemasu*. (*Sashiagemasu* will not be drilled until Lesson 1, Vol. II.)

To a friend:	Minoru san, anata ni hon o agemasu.	"Minoru, I'll give you a book."
To a child:	Kazuko san, anata ni hon o agemasu.	"Kazuko, I'll give you a book."

Kuremasu and *kudasaimasu* are used when something is given to the speaker or to a member of his "in-group." *Kuremasu* is used when the giver is equal or inferior in social standing, age, etc., and also *kuremasu* is used even when the giver is older or superior, if the giver is a member of the speaker's "in-group" and the listener is not. If the giver is someone outside of the "in-group" and older than or superior to the recipient in social standing, etc., *kudasaimasu* is used. However, *kudasaimasu* will not be drilled until Lesson 1, Vol. II. (See Diagram 3.)

Diagram 3

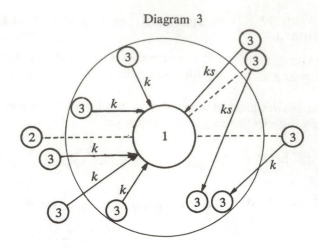

Tomodachi ga watakushi ni hon o kuremashita.	"A friend of mine gave me a book."
Tomodachi ga kanai ni hon o kuremashita.	"A friend of mine gave my wife a book."
Haha wa watakushitachi ni hon o kuremashita.	"My mother gave us a book."

Just like "giving" Verbs, such as *agemasu, kuremasu*, etc., a "receiving" Verb is *moraimasu*, which means "get, or receive (something from someone)," or "is given."

moraimasu (⟵ *morau*)

    "Someone receives." This can be used in any situation to mean "receive," "is given," or "get (from someone)."

The person who receives is followed by the Relational *wa* or *ga*, the thing given is followed by *o*, and the person who gives by the Relational *kara* "from."

Recipient $\begin{matrix} wa \\ (ga) \end{matrix}$ + giver + *kara* + Nominative (object) *o* + *moraimasu*

Kinoo tomodachi kara eiga no kippu o moraimashita.	"[I] got movie tickets from a friend of mine yesterday."
Dare kara moraimashita ka?	"From whom did you get [it]?"

Such Verbs as *naraimasu* "learn," *karimasu* "borrow," *kikimasu* "hear," *kaimasu* "buy" can also be applied to the above pattern.

watashi wa tomodachi kara ⎰eigo o naraimashita / jisho o karimashita / kippu o kaimashita / sore o kikimashita⎱ "I ⎰learned English / borrowed a dictionary / bought tickets / heard it⎱ from a friend of mine"

12.4.4 *-Tachi* in *kodomotachi* is a dependent Nominative that turns the word *kodomo* "child" into the plural "children." This is always used with words that indicate animate objects, particularly human beings.

kodomo	"child"	......	kodomotachi	"children"
gakusei	"student"	......	gakuseitachi	"students"

Note that in Japanese the plural form of a word, except a pronoun, is not mandatory even when you are referring to more than one (being). *Kodomo* may refer to "a child" or "children," and *hon* may mean "a book" or "books." The plural forms of pronouns, such as *watakushi anata*, etc., however, should be identified with the *-tachi*.

wata(ku)shi	"I"	......	wata(ku)shitachi	"we"
boku	"I"	......	bokutachi	"we"
atashi	"I"	......	atashitachi	"we"
anata	"you"	......	anatatachi	"you"
kimi*	"you"	......	kimitachi	"you"
ano kata	"that person"	......	ano katatachi	"those people"

* *Kimi* is used by men. This should not be used to a superior.

Sometimes *-tachi* is used to refer to a group of persons, only one of them being represented.

otooto to imooto ...... otoototachi

"(my) younger brother and younger sister"   "(my) younger brother et al"

Yamada san to Itoo san to Suzuki san ga kimashita. ...... Yamada san'tachi ga kimashita.

"Mr. Yamada, Mr. Itō, and Mr. Suzuki came."   "Mr. Yamada and some other people came."

12.4.5 *-Zutsu* is a dependent Nominative that is often used after a number or a numeral. It means "each" or "respectively."

Ani to ane ga hitori zutsu imasu.   "I have one older brother and one older sister."

Hon to zasshi o nisatsu zutsu kaimashita.   "[I] bought two books and two magazines (respectively)."

Kami o ichimai zutsu agemasu.   "[I] will give one sheet of paper to each of you."

12.4.6 *Ikutsu* is an interrogative Nominative meaning "how many?" In addition to the numbers introduced in Note 12.4.2, there is another group of numbers that will be called "native numbers." The native numbers are limited to one through ten, as shown below:

1	hitotsu	2	futatsu	3	mittsu	4	yottsu	5	itsutsu
6	muttsu	7	nanatsu	8	yattsu	9	kokonotsu	10	too

Ikutsu is the interrogative counterpart of the native numbers. These native numbers occur without any counter following them, and are used to count age (as well as a numeral plus -*sai*), or things like apples, pears, pebbles, coins, balls, candy, etc., that have no particular counters.

The usage of the native numbers is the same as that of the numbers.

Otootosan wa ima ikutsu desu ka?	"How old is [your] younger brother?"
Yottsu desu.	"He is four years old."
Okashi o hitotsu tabemashita.	"[I] ate a piece of candy."

12.4.7 *Ni* in *otootosan ni agemashoo* is a Relational meaning that the preceding word is the recipient of an action. It is often expressed in English equivalents as "to (someone)" as an indirect object. In the pattern of "giving," the giver is followed by *ga* or *wa*, the thing given is followed by *o*, and the recipient by *ni*. Note that the giver and the recipient are normally animate in Japanese.

$$\text{Giver} + \begin{Bmatrix} ga \\ wa \end{Bmatrix} + \text{recipient} + ni + \text{object} + o + \begin{cases} agemasu \\ yarimasu \\ kuremasu \end{cases}$$

Verbs that may occur in this sentence pattern are not necessarily those of "giving," but also Verbs such as *iimasu* "say," *shimasu* in *den'wa o shimasu* "make a phone call," and *hanashimasu* "talk or speak."

Anata ni kore o agemasu.	"[I] will give this to you."
Sen'sei ga boku ni kami o ichimai kuremashita.	"The teacher gave me a sheet of paper."
Otooto ni soo iimashita.	"[I] said so to my younger brother."
Tomodachi ni den'wa (o) shimashita ka?	"Did [you] make a phone call to [your] friend?"

12.4.8 *Agemashoo* here means "I think I shall give." The OO form of a Verb, *-mashoo,* may be used as a suggestion or a proposal of performance which concerns only the speaker, in addition to such a use as is introduced in Note 4.4.7, as a suggestion or a proposal of performance in which both the speaker and the hearer are to be involved. In other words, the subject of a sentence of this connotation is always "I."

Okosan ni kore o agemashoo.	"I think I'll give this to [your] child."
Watashi ga ikimashoo.	"I think I'll go."
Kon'ban anata ni den'wa o shimashoo.	"I think I'll call you up tonight."

12.4.9 *Moo* used immediately before a number or a numeral usually means "more" in "one more cup of tea," or "two more (volumes of) books." When *moo* means "already," the accent shifts from *moo͞* to *͞moo.*

Moo issatsu yomimasen ka?	"Won't you read another (one more) volume (book, etc.)?"
Tomodachi ga moo gonin kimasu.	"Five more friends [of mine] are coming."
Moo gonin kimashita.	"Five people have already come."

12.5 VOCABULARY

Dialog

rusu	....	N	is out; is not at home
kippu	....	N	ticket
san'mai	....	N	three sheets (see 12.4.2)
kuremashita	....	V	gave (me) (TA form of *kuremasu* ←— *kureru*) (see 12.4.3)
-tachi	....	Nd	(turns the preceding animate Nominative into plural)
nan'nin	....	Ni	how many (people)? (see 12.4.2)
hitori	....	N	one (person) (see 12.4.2)
-zutsu	....	Nd	each (see 12.4.5)
ikutsu	....	Ni	how old?; how many (objects)? (see 12.4.6)
nijuu yon'sai	....	N	twenty-four years old (see 12.4.2)
hatachi	....	N	twenty years old (see 12.4.2)
too	....	N	ten (see 12.4.6)
yattsu	....	N	eight (see 12.4.6)
ni	....	R	to (a person) (see 12.4.7)
ehon	....	N	picture book
issatsu	....	N	one (book) (see 12.4.2)
agemashoo	....	V	I think I'll give (OO form of *agemasu* ←— *ageru*) (see 12.4.3 & 12.4.8)
yarimashoo	....	V	I think I'll give (OO form of *yarimasu* ←— *yaru*) (see 12.4.3 & 12.4.8)
tokoro de	....	SI	by the way; incidentally
nan'ji	....	Ni	what time? (see 12.4.2)
san'ji	....	N	three o'clock
moo	....	Adv.	more (see 12.4.9)
ippai	....	N	a cupful of (see 12.4.2)
doozo	....	SI	please

Notes

-mai	....	Nd	sheet (of) (counter for something thin and flat) (see 12.4.2)
-nin	....	Nd	(counter for people) (see 12.4.2)
-sai	....	Nd	year(s) (old) (see 12.4.2)
-satsu	....	Nd	volume (counter for books, etc.) (see 12.4.2)
-ji	....	Nd	o'clock (see 12.4.2)
-peeji	....	Nd	page (see 12.4.2)
-hai	....	Nd	cupfuls; glassfuls (see 12.4.2)
-hon	....	Nd	(counter for pencils, bottles, etc.) (see 12.4.2)

futari	....	N	two (persons) (see 12.4.2)
nan-	....	Ni	how many ~ ?; what ~ ? (see 12.4.2)
agemasu	....	V	give (normal form of *ageru*) (see 12.4.3)
yarimasu	....	V	give (normal form of *yaru*) (see 12.4.3)
kuremasu	....	V	give (me) (normal form of *kureru*) (see 12.4.3)
moraimasu	....	V	receive; get (normal form of *morau*) (see 12.4.3)
kara	....	R	from (a person) (see 12.4.3)
kimi	....	N	you (used by men)
kami	....	N	paper
hitotsu	....	N	one (see 12.4.6)
futatsu	....	N	two
mittsu	....	N	three
yottsu	....	N	four
itsutsu	....	N	five
muttsu	....	N	six
nanatsu	....	N	seven
kokonotsu	....	N	nine
okashi	....	N	candy; sweets; confections

12.6 HIRAGANA PRACTICE

12.6.1 Recognize the difference in each of the following pairs:

かた [kata] ····· かった [katta]   きと [kito] ····· きっと [kitto]

また [mata] ····· まった [matta]   そと [soto] ····· そっと [sotto]

12.6.2 Read and write the following:

さっぽろ　　ざっし　　　あつかった　きっぷ

ちっとも　　いっぱい　　いっさつ　　きっさてん

みっつ　　　よっつ　　　やっつ　　　むっつ

いそがしかったです。　　ちょっと　まってください。

12.6.3 Recognize the difference in each of the following pairs:

お	……おう	[oo]	と	……とう	[too]
こ	……こう	[koo]	ど	……どう	[doo]
ご	……ごう	[goo]	の	……のう	[noo]
そ	……そう	[soo]	ほ	……ほう	[hoo]
ぞ	……ぞう	[zoo]	ぼ	……ぼう	[boo]
も	……もう	[moo]	じょ	……じょう	[joo]
よ	……よう	[yoo]	ちょ	……ちょう	[choo]
ろ	……ろう	[roo]	ひょ	……ひょう	[hyoo]
きょ	……きょう	[kyoo]	びょ	……びょう	[byoo]
ぎょ	……ぎょう	[gyoo]	みょ	……みょう	[myoo]
しょ	……しょう	[shoo]	りょ	……りょう	[ryoo]

12.6.4 Read and write the following:

ひこうき	とうきょう	しょくどう
きょうしつ	ほっかいどう	べんきょうします
おとうと	いもうと	いきましょうか
こうちゃ	どうして	りょこうしました
どうぞ	おとうさん	
もう	にっこう	

12.7 DRILLS

12.7.1 Pronunciation Drill

ikutsu	futatsu	itsutsu	yattsu
issatsu	mittsu	muttsu	kokonotsu
hitotsu	yottsu	nanatsu	hitotsu zutsu

178

12.7.2 Pattern Drill

1. Watakushi no tomodachi ga eiga no kippu o san'mai kuremashita.

2. Ikuo san, kyoodai wa nan'nin desu ka?

3. Ani to ane to otooto to imooto ga hitori zutsu imasu.

4. Oniisan ya oneesan wa ikutsu desu ka?

5. Jaa, otootosan to imootosan ni kono ehon o issatsu zutsu agemashoo.

6. Kon'ban otoototachi ni yarimashoo.

7. Ima nan'ji desu ka?

12.7.3 E-J Drill (numbers and numerals)

1. *three tickets* .... san'mai
2. *four people* .... yonin
3. *five books* .... gosatsu
4. *eleven years old* .... juuissai
5. *nine pages* .... kyuupeeji
6. *eight pieces of candy* .... yattsu
7. *nine children* .... kunin *or* kyuunin
8. *one student* .... hitori
9. *four o'clock* .... yoji
10. *five pieces of candy* .... itsutsu
11. *page four* .... yon'peeji
12. *seven sheets of paper* .... nanamai *or* shichimai
13. *nine o'clock* .... kuji
14. *how many magazines?* .... nan'satsu
15. *how old?* .... ikutsu *or* nan'sai
16. *what time?* .... nan'ji
17. *how many people?* .... nan'nin
18. *how many pieces of candy?* .... ikutsu
19. *what page or how many pages?* .... nan'peeji

12.7.4 Expansion Drill

1. Agemasu. ...... Agemasu.
   kippu o ...... Kippu o agemasu.
   eiga no ...... Eiga no kippu o agemasu.
   anata ni ...... Anata ni eiga no kippu o agemasu.
   watashi wa ...... Watashi wa anata ni eiga no kippu o agemasu.

2. Agemashoo. ...... Agemashoo.
   rajio o ...... Rajio o agemashoo.
   otootosan ni ...... Otootosan ni rajio o agemashoo.
   anata no ...... Anata no otootosan ni rajio o agemashoo.

3. Yarimashita. ...... Yarimashita.

okashi o	. . . . . .	Okashi o yarimashita.
kodomotachi ni	. . . . . .	Kodomotachi ni okashi o yarimashita.
boku wa	. . . . . .	Boku wa kodomotachi ni okashi o yarimashita.

4. Kuremasen deshita. . . . . . . Kuremasen deshita.

Kokakoora o	. . . . . .	Kokakoora o kuremasen deshita.
watashi ni	. . . . . .	Watashi ni Kokakoora o kuremasen deshita.
chichi wa	. . . . . .	Chichi wa watashi ni Kokakoora o kuremasen deshita.

5. Kuremashita. . . . . . . Kuremashita.

kami to en'pitsu o	. . . . . .	Kami to en'pitsu o kuremashita.
watakushitachi ni	. . . . . .	Watakushitachi ni kami to en'pitsu o kuremashita.
sen'sei wa	. . . . . .	Sen'sei wa watakushitachi ni kami to en'pitsu o kuremashita.

6. Naraimasu ka? . . . . . . Naraimasu ka?

nihon'go o	. . . . . .	Nihon'go o naraimasu ka?
donata kara	. . . . . .	Donata kara nihon'go o naraimasu ka?
anata no otoosan wa	. . . . .	Anata no otoosan wa donata kara nihon'go o naraimasu ka?

7. Yarimasu. . . . . . . Yarimasu.

gohan o	. . . . . .	Gohan o yarimasu.
inu ni	. . . . . .	Inu ni gohan o yarimasu.
otooto ga	. . . . . .	Otooto ga inu ni gohan o yarimasu.

8. Moraimashita. . . . . . . Moraimashita.

okane o	. . . . . .	Okane o moraimashita.
okusan kara	. . . . . .	Okusan kara okane o moraimashita.
Yamada san no	. . . . . .	Yamada san no okusan kara okane o moraimashita.

9. Kuremasu ka? . . . . . . Kuremasu ka?

nani o	. . . . . .	Nani o kuremasu ka?
watashitachi ni	. . . . . .	Watashitachi ni nani o kuremasu ka?
oneesan wa	. . . . . .	Oneesan wa watashitachi ni nani o kuremasu ka?

10. Hanashimashoo. . . . . . . Hanashimashoo.

sore o	. . . . . .	Sore o hanashimashoo.
goshujin ni	. . . . . .	Goshujin ni sore o hanashimashoo.

11. Iimashita. ...... Iimashita.

    soo ...... Soo iimashita.

    boku ni ...... Boku ni soo iimashita.

    tomodachi ga ...... Tomodachi ga boku ni soo iimashita.

12. Den'wa shimasu. ...... Den'wa shimasu.

    anata ni ...... Anata ni den'wa shimasu.

    kon'ban ...... Kon'ban anata ni den'wa shimasu.

13. Kakimashita. ...... Kakimashita.

    tegami o ...... Tegami o kakimashita.

    haha ni ...... Haha ni tegami o kakimashita.

    shujin ga ...... Shujin ga haha ni tegami o kakimashita.

12.7.5 Transformation Drill

1. Anata ni kore o *agemasu*. ⟶ Anata ni kore o *agemashoo*.
2. Watashi ga hanashimasu. ⟶ Watashi ga hanashimashoo.
3. Inu ni okashi o yarimasu. ⟶ Inu ni okashi o yarimashoo.
4. Okusan ni soo iimasu. ⟶ Okusan ni soo iimashoo.
5. Ashita no asa dekakemasu. ⟶ Ashita no asa dekakemashoo.
6. Suujii san kara kamera o kaimasu. ⟶ Suujii san kara kamera o kaimashoo.
7. Watakushi wa koohii o nomimasu. ⟶ Watakushi wa koohii o nomimashoo.
8. Yamamoto san ni den'wa shimasu. ⟶ Yamamoto san ni den'wa shimashoo.
9. Asahi Shin'bun o yomimasu. ⟶ Asahi Shin'bun o yomimashoo.
10. Boku wa jazu o kikimasu. ⟶ Boku wa jazu o kikimashoo.
11. Yamamoto sen'sei kara naraimasu. ⟶ Yamamoto sen'sei kara naraimashoo.

12.7.6 Expansion Drill

1. Eiga no kippu ga arimasu. .... Eiga no kippu ga arimasu.

    kyuumai .... Eiga no kippu ga *kyuumai* arimasu.

    uchi ni .... Uchi ni eiga no kippu ga kyuumai arimasu.

2. Kodomo ga imasu. .... Kodomo ga imasu.

    hachinin .... Kodomo ga hachinin imasu.

    niwa ni .... Niwa ni kodomo ga hachinin imasu.

3. Okashi o agemashoo.   ....   Okashi o agemashoo.

   itsutsu zutsu   ....   Okashi o itsutsu zutsu agemashoo.

   okosan ni   ....   Okosan ni okashi o itsutsu zutsu agemashoo.

4. Jisho o kaimashita.   ....   Jisho o kaimashita.

   nisatsu   ....   Jisho o nisatsu kaimashita.

   Tookyoo de   ...   Tookyoo de jisho o nisatsu kaimashita.

   kinoo   ...   Kinoo Tookyoo de jisho o nisatsu kaimashita.

5. Rekoodo o moraimashita. ....   Rekoodo o moraimashita.

   rokumai   ...   Rekoodo o rokumai moraimashita.

   Watanabe san kara   ...   Watanabe san kara rekoodo o rokumai moraimashita.

   sen'getsu   ....   Sen'getsu Watanabe san kara rekoodo o rokumai moraimashita.

6 Eigo no zasshi o kuremasu. ....   Eigo no zasshi o kuremasu.

   nisatsu   ....   Eigo no zasshi o nisatsu kuremasu.

   ane ga   ....   Ane ga eigo no zasshi o nisatsu kuremasu.

   ashita   ....   Ashita ane ga eigo no zasshi o nisatsu kuremasu.

7. Nihon'go no hon o yomimasu. .   Nihon'go no hon o yomimasu.

   rokupeeji zutsu   ...   Nihon'go no hon o rokupeeji zutsu yomimasu.

   maiban   ....   Maiban nihon'go no hon o rokupeeji zutsu yomimasu.

   boku wa   ....   Boku wa maiban nihon'go no hon o rokupeeji zutsu yomimasu.

8. Soo kikimashita.   ....   Soo kikimashita.

   Buraun san kara   ....   Buraun san kara soo kikimashita.

   gakkoo de   ....   Gakkoo de Buraun san kara soo kikimashita.

   kinoo   ....   Kinoo gakkoo de Buraun san kara soo kikimashita.

12.7.7 Combination Drill

1. Ehon o agemashoo.
   Nisatsu zutsu agemashoo. ⟶ Ehon o nisatsu zutsu agemashoo.

2. Rekoodo o kaimashita.
   Gomai kaimashita. ⟶ Rekoodo o gomai kaimashita.

3. Okashi o tabemashita ka?
   Ikutsu tabemashita ka? ⟶ Okashi o ikutsu tabemashita ka?

4. Sen'sei ga imasu.
   Kunin imasu. ⟶ Sen'sei ga kunin imasu.

5. Zasshi o moraimashita.
   Rokusatsu moraimashita. } ⟶ Zasshi o rokusatsu moraimashita.

6. Kippu o yarimashoo.
   Nanamai zutsu yarimashoo. } ⟶ Kippu o nanamai zutsu yarimashoo.

7. Kono zasshi o yomimashita.
   Juurokupeeji yomimashita. } ⟶ Kono zasshi o juurokupeeji yomimashita.

12.7.8 Mixed Drill

Watakushi wa *Yamamoto san* ni kippu o *agemashita*.

1. watakushi wa haha ni   ...... Watakushi wa haha ni kippu o agemashita.

2. ani ga otooto ni   ...... Ani ga otooto ni kippu o yarimashita.

3. Imooto ga Yamamoto san ni   ...... Imooto ga Yamamoto san ni kippu o agemashita.

4. watakushi wa ane ni   ...... Watakushi wa ane ni kippu o agemashita.

5. Yamamoto san ga watakushi ni   ...... Yamamoto san ga watakushi ni kippu o kuremashita.

6. tomodachi ga imooto ni   ...... Tomodachi ga imooto ni kippu o kuremashita.

7. watakushi wa imooto ni   ...... Watakushi wa imooto ni kippu o yarimashita.

8. Yamamoto san ga Sumisu san ni ...... Yamamoto san ga Sumisu san ni kippu o agemashita.

9. chichi ga watakushi ni   ...... Chichi ga watakushi ni kippu o kuremashita.

10. Yamamoto san ga chichi ni   ...... Yamamoto san ga chichi ni kippu o kuremashita.

12.7.9 Response Drill

1. Okosan wa nan'nin desu ka?
   rokunin   ...... Kodomo wa rokunin desu.

2. Imootosan wa ikutsu desu ka?
   yattsu   ...... Imooto wa yattsu desu.

3. Oniisan wa ima nan'sai desu ka?
   hatachi   ...... Ani wa ima hatachi desu.

4. Inu ni okashi o ikutsu yarimashita ka?
   mittsu   ...... Inu ni okashi o mittsu yarimashita.

5. Kono hon o nan'peeji yomimashita ka?
   juusan'peeji   ...... Kono hon o juusan'peeji yomimashita.

6. Oneesan wa kippu o nan'mai kaimasu ka?
   nanamai   ...... Ane wa kippu o nanamai kaimasu.

12.8 EXERCISES

12.8.1 Insert appropriate numbers or numerals in the blanks, according to the given English words:

1. Eiga no kippu o (   ) kaimashita.   (four)

2. Zasshi o (   ) yomimashita.   (five)

3. Ima (   ) desu.   (nine o'clock)

4. Kodomo ga (   ) imasu.   (two)

5. Yamada san wa (   ) desu ka?   (how old)

   (   ) desu.   (twenty-one years old)

12.8.2 Make appropriate questions which will lead to the following answers:

1. Itsutsu zutsu moraimashita.
2. Hai, hachimai arimasu.
3. Iie, kyuusatsu kuremashita.
4. Juuji desu yo.
5. Gakusei ga kunin imashita.
6. Juuhassai desu.
7. Nijuumai agemashita.
8. Nanasatsu kuremasu.
9. Okashi ga hitotsu arimasu.
10. Happeeji yomimashita.

12.8.3 Rearrange each group of the following words into a good Japanese sentence:

1. kono   dare   o   agemasu   ni   kippu   ka
2. zutsu   o   kodomotachi   okashi   mittsu   ni   yarimashoo
3. oniisan   nani   anata   ka   kuremashita   o   wa   ni
4. ka   hon   kinoo   de   nan'satsu   toshokan   yomimashita   o

12.8.4 Complete each sentence, inserting, in each blank, one of the following words:

age(*masu*),   kure(*masu*),   yari(*masu*),   morai(*masu*),   ni,   o,   kara,   ga

1. Inu (   ) okashi (   ) (   )mashoo.
2. Imootosan kara nani (   ) (   )mshita ka?
3. Tomodachi (   ) zasshi (   ) nisatsu kuremashita.
4. Chichi wa boku (   ) jidoosha (   ) (   )mashita.
5. Okosan (   ) ehon (   ) (   )mashoo.
6. Watakushi (   ) Minoru kun ni rekoodo (   ) (   )mashita.

12.8.5 Read the following paragraph and translate into English:

Boku wa Ikuo desu. Boku wa Tookyoo no daigaku no gakusei desu. Kazoku wa min'na Kyooto ni imasu. Kazoku wa chichi to haha to ane to imooto desu. Ane wa Kyooto no daigaku no gakusei desu. Imooto wa mada kokonotsu desu. Boku wa imooto ga suki desu. Dakara, tokidoki imooto ni okashi ya hon o yarimasu. Boku wa tokidoki kazoku ni tegami o kakimasu. Chichi ya haha mo tegami o kuremasu. Kotoshi no natsu, boku wa Kyooto no uchi e kaerimasu.

12.8.6 Write about your family.

LESSON 13

— Review —

13.1 PATTERN

13.1.1 Copula - presumptive

(2)		(1)	
asa kotoshi rainen kyoo		atsui samui isogashii	
haru	(wa) (mo)	atatakai subarashii	
aki		suzushii	
kyonen kinoo kesa sen'getsu yoru		atatakakatta suzushikatta isogashikatta subarashikatta	
natsu		atsukatta	
fuyu		samukatta	deshoo deshoo ?
koocha		tsumetai oishii mazukatta	
nihon'go		muzukashii yasashikatta	
kono hon eiga	wa (mo)	omoshiroi yokatta tanoshii	
kyookai ano kata no uchi		shizuka	
Yooroppa Kyooto umi yama		kirei	
anata goshujin		Sumino san sen'sei gakusei	
Minoru kun		rusu gozon'ji	
oneesan no namae		Kazuko	

13.1.2 Copula *desu* replacing *ni arimasu* and *ni imasu*

(2)			(1)	
chichi				
otoosan				
haha				
okaasan				
oniisan		niwa		
ani		heya		
oneesan		gakkoo		
ane		kyookai		imasu
kyoodai		uchi		imasen
kazoku		gaikoku		imashita
kodomotachi		kuni		imasen deshita
okosan		koko		
otooto	wa	Tookyoo		
imootosan	(ga)	Amerika	ni	
kanai	(mo)			
okusan				
shujin				
goshujin				
min'na				
terebi				
rajio		heya		
shin'bun		uchi		arimasu
Ryooan'ji		Kyooto		arimasen
Chuuzen'jiko		Nikkoo		arimashita
jin'ja		soko		arimasen deshita
Sapporo		Hokkaidoo		

(2)			(1)	
……		……		
……		……		desu
……	wa	……		deshita
……	(ga)	……		deshoo
……	(mo)	……		ja arimasen
……		……		de wa arimasen deshita

13.1.3

$$\left.\begin{array}{l}\text{Giver}\\\text{Actor}\end{array}\right\} + \left\{\begin{array}{l}wa\\ga\\mo\end{array}\right\} + \text{recipient} + ni + \text{object} + o + \left\{\begin{array}{l}agemasu\\yarimasu\\kuremasu\\iimasu\\hanashimasu, \text{ etc.}\end{array}\right.$$

Giver / Actor	wa (ga) (mo)	recipient	ni	object	o	verb
Minoru kun		min'na		okashi		
watakushi		kimi		kamera		
haha		sen'sei		hon		agemasu
Buraun san		anata no okusan		eiga no kippu		
ano gakusei		okosan				
Sumino san		inu		okashi		
boku		otooto		ehon		yarimashita
ane		imooto		Kokakoora		
chichi		kodomotachi		kore		
	wa	imooto	ni	zasshi	o	
Minoru kun	(ga)	watakushi		rajio		
tomodachi	(mo)	watakushitachi		rekoodo		kuremasu
kimi		boku		kippu		
Kazuko san		ani		sore		
		min'na		okane		
		kanai				
shujin		Watanabe san		tegami		kakimashita
kanai		kyoodai		hen'ji		
kodomo		chichi		den'wa	(o)	shimasu
boku		kimi				iimasu
		min'na		soo		hanashimasu

13.1.4

$$\text{Recipient} + \left\{\begin{array}{l}wa\\ga\\mo\end{array}\right\} + \text{person} + kara + \text{object} + o + \left\{\begin{array}{l}moraimasu\\karimasu\\kikimasu\\kaimasu\\naraimasu\end{array}\right.$$

Recipient	wa (ga) (mo)	person	kara	object	o	verb
watakushi		tomodachi		kamera		
Yamamoto san		Ishii san		jisho		moraimasu
kodomo		otoosan		okashi		
ane		sen'sei		tegami		
	wa		kara	kamera	o	
	(ga)			zasshi		karimashita
boku	(mo)	anata		nihon'go no hon		kaimasu
Suzuki san		Ueki san		taipuraitaa		
gakusei		sen'sei		sore		kikimashita
				gaikokugo		naraimasu

13.1.5 Quantity expressions

a.

(go)kazoku		hitori	
(go)kyoodai		futari	
kodomo(san)		san'nin	imasu
okosan	ga	yonin	(desu)
ani	(wa)	gonin	
oniisan	(mo)	rokunin/nananin	
ane		hachinin	
oneesan		kunin/kyuunin	
otooto(san)		juunin	ikimasu
imooto(san)		juuichinin	kimasu

	ga wa mo	issatsu	arimasu
		nisatsu	
		san'satsu	
zasshi		yon'satsu	
hon		gosatsu	agemasu
ehon		rokusatsu	yarimasu
jisho	o wa mo	nanasatsu/shichisatsu	kuremasu
		hachisatsu/hassatsu	moraimasu
		kyuusatsu	kaimasu
		jissatsu/jussatsu	yomimasu
		juuissatsu	karimasu

	ga wa mo	ichimai	arimasu
		nimai	
		san'mai	
kami		yon'mai/yomai	
shin'bun		gomai	agemasu
rekoodo		rokumai	yarimasu
kippu	o wa mo	shichimai/nanamai	kuremasu
		hachimai	moraimasu
		kyuumai/kumai	kaimasu
		juumai	
		juuichimai	

		ippeeji/ichipeeji	
		nipeeji	
		san'peeji	
		yon'peeji	
hon	o	gopeeji	yomimasu
		rokupeeji	
		nanapeeji/shichipeeji	
		happeeji/hachipeeji	
		kyuupeeji	
		jippeeji/juppeeji	

chichi		issai
otoosan		nisai

		san'sai	
		yon'sai	
		gosai	
haha		rokusai	
okaasan		shichisai/nanasai	
ani		hassai/hachisai	
oniisan		kyuusai	
ane		jissai/jussai	
oneesan		juuissai	
imooto	wa	hatachi	desu
otooto	(ga)	hitotsu	deshita
kodomo	(mo)	futatsu	
kanai		mittsu	
okusan		yottsu	
shujin		itsutsu	
goshujin		muttsu	
Watanabe san		nanatsu	
Minoru kun		yattsu	
		kokonotsu	
		too	
		ichiji	
		niji	
		san'ji	
		yoji	
		goji	
ima	(wa)	rokuji	desu
		shichiji	
		hachiji	
		kuji	
		juuji	
		juuichiji	
		juuniji	
ishi	ga (wa) (mo)	hitotsu futatsu mittsu yottsu	arimasu
okashi	o (wa) (mo)	itsutsu muttsu nanatsu yattsu kokonotsu too	kaimasu

↓

gokazoku kyoodai	wa ga	nan'nin	imasu desu ikimasu	
jisho zasshi	wa ga o wa	nan'satsu	arimasu yomimasu	
kippu kami	wa ga o wa	nan'mai	arimasu kaimasu	ka ?
okashi ishi	wa ga o wa	ikutsu	arimasu kaimasu	
goshujin okusan	wa	nan'sai ikutsu	desu	
ima	(wa)	nan'ji	desu	

b.

Buraun san chichi		Suujii san haha		zasshi hon		issatsu	agemashoo
otooto kanai	to	imooto kodomo	ni	kippu rekoodo	o	ichimai	yarimasu
kimi ani min'na kodomotachi imoototachi		boku ane		okashi		hitotsu	kuremasu

zutsu (between ichimai column and verbs)

c.

ehon jisho	o	moo	nisatsu	agemasu yarimasu kuremasen ka ?
kami kippu			nimai	agemasu
okashi			hitotsu	tabemasu

d.

ame yuki	ga (wa) (mo)		furimasu
rekoodo on'gaku Kokakoora hon okashi	o (wa) (mo)	takusan sukoshi	kaimasu kikimasu nomimasu yomimasu tabemasu agemasu

jin'ja					
otera					
gakkoo					arimasu
rekoodo		ga	takusan		
ehon		(wa)	sukoshi		
kippu		(mo)			
jidoosha					
hito					
kodomo					imasu

13.1.6 Relational *to* "with"

watakushi			umi e ikimasu
boku			uchi e kaerimasu
Yamamoto san			
imooto	to	(issho ni)	Kyooto o ken'butsu shimasu
tomodachi			eki de machimasu
kodomotachi			
min'na			ban'gohan o tabemasu

13.2 AURAL COMPREHENSION

a.　ぼくの　かぞくは　ごにんです。　ちちと　ははと　いもうとと

おとうとと　ぼくです。　みんな　とうきょうに　います。　ぼくたちは

まえ、　ならに　いましたが、　ならは　あまり　すきではありませんで

した。

ちちは　がっこうの　せんせいです。　ははは　ぴあのが　じょうず

です。　まいばん　ひきます。　いもうとは　ここのつです。　おとうとは

じゅうにさいです。　いもうとは　ほんが　だいすきです。　だから、

ぼくは　まいげつ　いっさつずつ　いもうとに　ほんを　やります。

せんげつは　がいこくの　えほんを　やりました。　ちょっと　たかかっ

たですが、　とても　きれいです。

b.　　きのう、　おとうとが　ともだちから　えいがの　きっぷを　にまい
もらいました。　おとうとは　ぼくに　にまい　くれました。　ぼくは
あした　かずこさんと　いっしょに　いきます。　ぼくは　えいがや
おんがくが　だいすきですが、　とくに　あめりかの　えいがが　すきです。
この　えいがも　おもしろいでしょう。

LESSON 14

14.1 GENERAL INTRODUCTION TO JAPANESE WRITING SYSTEM

Japan had no writing system before *kanji* (Chinese characters) were introduced from China. After the Japanese started to use *kanji* to write their language two types of pronunciation were gradually developed in Japan.

One method was to attach Japanese meanings to certain *kanji* and use Japanese pronunciation for these *kanji*. Such pronunciation is called *kun* pronunciation. The other method was to pronounce the *kanji* according to their original Chinese sounds, with Japanese modification. Such pronunciation is called *on* pronunciation.

However, various *kanji* were introduced to Japan at various times, and the original Chinese pronunciations of them differed, depending upon the time and place of origin. Thus, not only the southern Chinese sounds were introduced but also the northern sounds. Not only the Chinese pronunciations of one period were introduced but also those of other periods. This explains why there are generally at least two Japanese pronunciations for each *kanji*. *Kanji* are generally used for meanings, but some *kanji* are used as phonetic symbols without any meaning attached. The number of *kanji* used merely as phonetic symbols was gradually narrowed down to a few that represented certain Japanese sounds. Eventually the Japanese syllabary called *kana* replaced *kanji* as phonetic symbols.

Two types of *kana* were developed: *hiragana* and *katakana*. *Katakana* were developed on the basis of adopting just one portion of *kanji*, and *hiragana* were developed on the basis of modifying the shape of *kanji*.

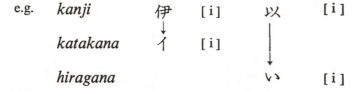

Today, *kana* and about two thousand *kanji* are used in the writing of Japanese. *Kanji* and *kana* are combined in writing. Usually Nominatives, Verb Base, and Adjective Base are written in *kanji*, and Sentence Interjectives, Pre-Nominatives, Relationals, Adverbs, Copula and Sentence Particles are written in *kana*. It is the readings of *kanji*, the orthographic arrangement of *kana* and the suggested *kanji-kana* combinations that the student is to learn. They look rather cumbersome but they are not as chaotic as the English orthographic system.

14.2 HIRAGANA

In the postwar writing system of Japan, there are forty-six simple *hiragana* symbols and twenty-five variations. Since these *hiragana* have been practiced lesson by lesson, students are required to be able to recognize and produce all the *hiragana* at this stage. The following explanations are given only to systematize *hiragana* writing arrangements.

14.2.1 Simple Hiragana

Chart 1

gyoo*2 \ dan*1	/a/	/i/	/u/	/e/	/o/	zero*3
a	あ	い	う	え	お	
ka /k/	か	き	く	け	こ	
sa /s/	さ	し	す	せ	そ	
ta /t/	た	ち	つ	て	と	
na /n/	な	に	ぬ	ね	の	
ha /h/	は	ひ	ふ	へ	ほ	
ma /m/	ま	み	む	め	も	
ya /y/	や	(い)*4	ゆ	(え)	よ	
ra /r/	ら	り	る	れ	ろ	
wa /w/	わ	(ゐ)	(う)	(ゑ)	を	
n' /n'/						ん

*1 *Kana* are classified into five *dan* according to the vowel final. Thus, あ、か、さ、た、な、は、ま、や、ら、and わ belong to /a/ *dan*.

*2 *Kana* are also divided according to the consonant initial. The /t/ group of symbols is called, for instance, *ta gyoo* and た、ち、つ、て and と are grouped as the *ta gyoo* sounds.

*3 Zero means that there is no vowel final.

*4 *Hiragana* in parentheses indicates that either it is not in current use or it is identical with *a gyoo* symbols both in shape and in pronunciation.

14.2.2 Two-dots Hiragana

There are twenty *hiragana* that represent voiced sounds. *Ga gyoo, za gyoo,* and *da gyoo* correspond to *ka gyoo, sa gyoo,* and *ta gyoo* respectively. *Ba gyoo* corresponds to *ha gyoo* in shape but it is not the voiced counterpart of *ha gyoo*.

Voiced *hiragana* have two dots at the upper right-hand corner of the corresponding *hiragana*.

194

Chart 2

gyoo \ dan	/a/	/i/	/u/	/e/	/o/
ga /g/	が	ぎ	ぐ	げ	ご
za /z/	ざ	じ	ず	ぜ	ぞ
da /d/	だ	ぢ*	づ*	で	ど
ba /b/	ば	び	ぶ	べ	ぼ

* See 14.4.6.

14.2.3 One-circle Hiragana

Chart 3

gyoo \ dan	/a/	/i/	/u/	/e/	/o/
pa /p/	ぱ	ぴ	ぷ	ぺ	ぽ

They are the voiceless counterparts of *ba gyoo*.

14.2.4 A syllable composed of a consonant plus や、ゆ、or よ

Contracted sounds, such as /kya/, /syu/, /ryo/ etc., are represented by the combination of a *hiragana* of *i dan* and や、ゆ、or よ.

Usually the second symbol /ya/, /yu/, or /yo/ is written in a small character.

Chart 4

	/ya/	/yu/	/yo/		/ya/	/yu/	/yo/
/k/	きゃ	きゅ	きょ	/r/	りゃ	りゅ	りょ
/s/	しゃ	しゅ	しょ	/g/	ぎゃ	ぎゅ	ぎょ
/t/	ちゃ	ちゅ	ちょ	/z/	じゃ	じゅ	じょ
/n/	にゃ	にゅ	にょ	/b/	びゃ	びゅ	びょ
/h/	ひゃ	ひゅ	ひょ	/p/	ぴゃ	ぴゅ	ぴょ
/m/	みゃ	みゅ	みょ				

Note that the above combinations are written differently when a Japanese sentence is written vertically.

Compare: きゃく …… きゃく   しょり …… しょり   りゅう …… りゅう

14.2.5 How to write Hiragana

There is a slight difference between printed and hand-written *hiragana*.

Compare:

Chart 5   Stroke Order

a	あ	あ	ー	ナ	あ		te	て	て	て		
i	い	い	い	い			to	と	と	ヽ	と	
u	う	う	′	う			na	な	な	ー	ナ	な	
e	え	え	′	ラ	え		ni	に	に	し	じ	に
o	お	お	ー	お	お		nu	ぬ	ぬ	し	ぬ	
ka	か	か	フ	カ	か		ne	ね	ね	し	ね	
ki	き	き	ー	ニ	き	き	no	の	の	の		
ku	く	く	く				ha	は	は	し	に	は
ke	け	け	し	に	け		hi	ひ	ひ	ひ		
ko	こ	こ	ヽ	こ			fu	ふ	ふ	′	う	ふ	ふ
sa	さ	さ	ー	さ	さ		he	へ	へ	へ		
shi	し	し	し				ho	ほ	ほ	し	に	ほ
su	す	す	ー	す			ma	ま	ま	ー	ニ	ま
se	せ	せ	ー	ナ	せ		mi	み	み	み	み	
so	そ	そ	ヽ	ッ	そ		mu	む	む	ー	も	む
ta	た	た	ー	ナ	た	た	me	め	め	し	め	
chi	ち	ち	ー	ち			mo	も	も	し	も	も
tsu	つ	つ	つ				ya	や	や	つ	や	や

yu	ゆ	ゆ	い	ゆ
yo	よ	よ	゛	よ
ra	ら	ら	、	ら
ri	り	り	い	り
ru	る	る	る	
re	れ	れ	し	れ

ro	ろ	ろ	ろ	
wa	わ	わ	し	わ
o	を	を	ち	を
n'	ん	ん	ん	
ga	が	が	カ	が
pa	ぱ	ぱ	は	ぱ

14.3 KATAKANA

With certain exceptions the use of *katakana*, in the postwar standard Japanese writing system, is limited to those names or words that are foreign in origin. Despite the increasing trend of using foreign words in everyday Japanese, *katakana* are considered secondary writing symbols. Therefore, this text is so arranged that the student learns *katakana* as they appear in lessons. The chart of *katakana* below is only for reference. It is suggested that the student consult Charts 6 through 10 whenever he encounters new *katakana* in this text.

14.3.1 Simple Katakana

Chart 6

gyoo \ *dan*	/a/	/i/	/u/	/e/	/o/	zero
a	ア	イ	ウ	エ	オ	
ka /k/	カ	キ	ク	ケ	コ	
sa /s/	サ	シ	ス	セ	ソ	
ta /t/	タ	チ	ツ	テ	ト	
na /n/	ナ	ニ	ヌ	ネ	ノ	
ha /h/	ハ	ヒ	フ	ヘ	ホ	
ma /m/	マ	ミ	ム	メ	モ	
ya /y/	ヤ	(イ)	ユ	(エ)	ヨ	
ra /r/	ラ	リ	ル	レ	ロ	
wa /w/	ワ	(ヰ)	(ウ)	(ヱ)	ヲ	
n' /n'/						ン

14.3.2 Two-dots Katakana

Chart 7

gyoo \ dan	/a/	/i/	/u/	/e/	/o/
ga /g/	ガ	ギ	グ	ゲ	ゴ
za /z/	ザ	ジ	ズ	ゼ	ゾ
da /d/	ダ	(ヂ)	(ヅ)	デ	ド
ba /b/	バ	ビ	ブ	ベ	ボ

14.3.3 One-circle Katakana

Chart 8

gyoo \ dan	/a/	/i/	/u/	/e/	/o/
pa /p/	パ	ピ	プ	ペ	ポ

14.3.4 A syllable composed of a consonant plus ヤ、ユ、or ヨ

Chart 9

	/ya/	/yu/	/yo/		/ya/	/yu/	/yo/
/k/	キャ	キュ	キョ	/g/	ギャ	ギュ	ギョ
/s/	シャ	シュ	ショ	/z/	ジャ	ジュ	ジョ
/t/	チャ	チュ	チョ	/b/	ビャ	ビュ	ビョ
/n/	ニャ	ニュ	ニョ	/p/	ピャ	ピュ	ピョ
/h/	ヒャ	ヒュ	ヒョ				
/m/	ミャ	ミュ	ミョ				
/r/	リャ	リュ	リョ				

14.3.5 How to write Katakana

Chart 10 Stroke Order

a	ア	ア	⁻	ア	te	テ	テ	⁻ ニ テ
i	イ	イ	ノ	イ	to	ト	ト	l ト
u	ウ	ウ	`	゛ ウ	na	ナ	ナ	⁻ ナ
e	エ	エ	⁻	ー エ	ni	ニ	ニ	⁻ ニ
o	オ	オ	⁻	ナ オ	nu	ヌ	ヌ	フ ヌ
ka	カ	カ	フ	カ	ne	ネ	ネ	` ナ オ ネ
ki	キ	キ	⁻	ニ キ	no	ノ	ノ	ノ
ku	ク	ク	ノ	ク	ha	ハ	ハ	ノ ハ
ke	ケ	ケ	ノ	ト ケ	hi	ヒ	ヒ	⁻ ヒ
ko	コ	コ	フ	コ	fu	フ	フ	フ
sa	サ	サ	⁻	ナ サ	he	へ	へ	へ
shi	シ	シ	`	シ	ho	ホ	ホ	⁻ ナ オ ホ
su	ス	ス	フ	ス	ma	マ	マ	フ マ
se	セ	セ	⁻	セ	mi	ミ	ミ	` ニ ミ
so	ソ	ソ	`	ソ	mu	ム	ム	ム ム
ta	タ	タ	ノ	ク タ	me	メ	メ	ノ メ
chi	チ	チ	ノ	ー チ	mo	モ	モ	⁻ ニ モ
tsu	ツ	ツ	`	゛ ツ	ya	ヤ	ヤ	フ ヤ

yu	ユ	ユ	フ	ユ
yo	ヨ	ヨ	フ	ヲ ヨ
ra	ラ	ラ	ー	ラ
ri	リ	リ	＼	リ
ru	ル	ル	ノ	ル
re	レ	レ	レ	

ro	ロ	ロ	㇐	㇆ ロ
wa	ワ	ワ	＼	ワ
o	ヲ	ヲ	ー	ニ ヲ
n'	ン	ン	＼	ン
ga	ガ	ガ	フ カ	ガ
pa	パ	パ	ノ	ハ パ

14.4 POSTWAR REVISED ORTHOGRAPHY

The following are the rules of the postwar revised Japanese orthography.

14.4.1 Long Vowels of Hiragana

Long vowels are written by adding one *a gyoo hiragana* to its preceding vowel.

(1) Long vowels of *a dan kana*, such as あ、か、さ、た、な、は、ま、や、ら、わ、が、 etc., are written by adding あ to the *kana* as follows:

あ あ [aa], さ あ [saa], は あ [haa], ま あ [maa]

(2) Long vowels of *i dan kana*, such as い、き、し、ち、に、ひ、み、り、ぎ、 etc., are written by adding い to the *kana* as follows:

いい [ii], おおきい [ookii], おいしい [oishii], ちいさい [chiisai]

(3) Long vowels of *u dan kana*, such as う、く、す、つ、ぬ、ふ、む、ゆ、る、ぐ、 etc., are written by adding う to the *kana* as follows:

すう [suu], ふつう [futsuu], ぎゅうにゅう [gyuunyuu]

(4) Long vowels of *e dan kana*, such as え、け、せ、て、ね、へ、め、れ、げ、 etc., are written by adding い to the *kana* as follows:

えいが [eiga], えいご [eigo], がくせい [gakusei], とけい [tokei], たいてい [taitei]

But the following words are exceptions:

ええ [ee], ねえ [nee], おねえさん [oneesan]

(5) Long vowels of *o dan kana*, such as お、こ、そ、と、の、ほ、も、よ、ろ、ご、etc., are written by adding う to the *kana* as follows:

おう [oo], そう [soo], どう [doo], もう [moo]

But there are some exceptions:

おおきい [ookii], おおい [ooi], とおい [tooi],

とおる [tooru], とおり [toori], こおる [kooru], etc.

14.4.2 Long Vowels of Katakana

In writing *katakana*, long vowels are shown by writing a bar after the *katakana*. When lines are written horizontally, as is done in this textbook, the bar is horizontal. When the lines are written vertically, the bar is written vertically.

コーヒー [koohii], デパート [depaato], ヨーロッパ [Yooroppa]

14.4.3 Single-Consonant Syllables of Hiragana and Katakana

Single-consonant syllables, such as *t* in *ki-t-to*, *k* in *ga-k-ko-o*, *p* in *i-p-pa-i*, *s* in *i-s-sho*, etc., are expressed by つ [tsu] in *hiragana* and ツ [tsu] in *katakana*. Either つ or ツ is usually written in a small letter.

きっぷ [kippu], ざっし [zasshi], きっと [kitto], クラシック [kurashikku]

14.4.4 Relationals *wa* and *e*

Relationals *wa* and *e* are written as は and へ. But Relationals は and へ have to be pronounced as *wa* and *e* respectively.

とうきょうへ きます。	[Tookyoo e kimasu.]
どこへ いきましたか。	[Doko e ikimashita ka?]
これは なんですか。	[Kore wa nan desu ka?]
わたくしは おんがくが だいすきです。	[Watakushi wa on'gaku ga daisuki desu.]

14.4.5 Relational *o*

The Relational *o* is written as を.

おちゃを のみましょう。	[Ocha o nomimashoo.]
なにを しましたか。	[Nani o shimashita ka?]

14.4.6   Use of ぢ and づ

In ordinary cases, じ and ず are written for *ji* and *zu* respectively.   But in the following cases, ぢ and づ are used instead:

(1) When two or more words make a compound, and the initial syllable of the second or the third word is *ji* or *zu* but was originally *chi* or *tsu,* it should be written as ぢ or づ.

It is quite common that a simple *kana* becomes two-dots *kana* when placed after another word, thus forming a compound.

$$\text{はな [hana]} + \text{ち [chi]} \longrightarrow \text{はなぢ [hanaji]}$$

(2) When *ji* follows *chi* or *zu* follows *tsu* in one word, the *ji* and *zu* are written as ぢ and づ.

ちぢむ [chijimu], つづく [tsuzuku]

14.4.7   Foreign words

Conventionally, some of the foreign words carry sounds close to the original sounds, when they are used in Japanese.   In those cases, *katakana* combinations different from those introduced in 14.3.4 may occur.   Here are some of them:

e.g.	カリフォルニア	[Kari*fo*runia]	"California"
	ディック	[*Di*kku]	"Dick"
	フォーク	[*fo*oku]	"fork"
	フィラデルフィア	[*Fi*raderu*fi*a]	"Philadelphia"

14.5   MARKS

(1) The small circle [。] indicates the end of a sentence or an utterance.

これを　あげます。   [Kore o agemasu.]

(2) The mark [、] indicates a pause.

さあ、いきましょう。   [Saa, ikimashoo.]

(3) Quotations are indicated by 「　　」.

「きれいですねえ」と　いいました。   ["Kirei desu nee" to iimashita.]

202

14.6 KANA EXERCISES

14.6.1 Make a pair by filling in the blank in *hiragana*:

Example: おとうと ―（いもうと）

ちち　　―（　　　　　）　　ごしゅじん―（　　　　　）
あに　　―（　　　　　）　　しゅじん　―（　　　　　）
おとうさん―（　　　　　）　　せんせい　―（　　　　　）
おねえさん―（　　　　　）

14.6.2 Fill in the blank with its antonym in *hiragana*:

Example: むずかしいです―（やさしいです）

おもしろいです―（　　　　　）　　うるさいです　―（　　　　　）
きたないです　―（　　　　　）　　へたです　　　―（　　　　　）
おいしいです　―（　　　　　）　　いそがしいです―（　　　　　）
あたたかいです―（　　　　　）　　おおきいです　―（　　　　　）
いいです　　　―（　　　　　）　　だいきらいです―（　　　　　）
すきです　　　―（　　　　　）　　たかいです　　―（　　　　　）
ちかいです　　―（　　　　　）　　あついです　　―（　　　　　）

14.6.3 Read the following *katakana*:

クラシック　　　テレビ　　　カメラ　　　ジャズ
アメリカ　　　　パン　　　　レポート　　ポピュラー
レコード　　　　デパート　　スージー　　フォーク
スミス　　　　　イギリス　　ヨーロッパ　スプーン
タイプライター　フランス　　コーヒー　　ナイフ
ビール　　　　　マッチ　　　ブラウン　　ページ
コカコーラ　　　ピアノ　　　レストラン　バイオリン
ラジオ　　　　　ビフテキ　　メリーランド　ギター
ロシア　　　　　ドイツ　　　ハワイ　　　カリフォルニア

14.6.4 Write your name in *katakana*:

e.g. トーマス・ブラウン　　　　　"Thomas Brown"

LESSON 15

— Review Exercise —

15.1 EXERCISES

15.1.1 What would you say when:

1. you greet someone in the afternoon?

2. you greet someone at night?

3. you leave someone who you think will not see you again within the same day?

4. you want to ask someone if he understands something?

5. you want to say you understand what someone said?

6. you want to answer you do not understand what someone said?

7. you want someone to listen carefully?

8. you want someone to wait a minute?

9. you want to thank someone?

10. someone thanks you or apologizes to you?

11. you want to apologize?

12. you want to express regret or disappointment?

13. you apologize to someone for what you have done to him?

14. you visit someone else's home and inform him that you are at the door of his house?

15. you greet someone who has come to visit your home?

16. you want to ask someone to speak in Japanese?

17. you accept something to drink or to eat offered by someone?

18. you have finished (are through) drinking or eating something offered by someone?

19. you want to ask someone to read something?

20. you want to ask someone to write something?

21. you have returned home?

22. someone of your family has come home while you are at home?

23. you ask someone to do something for you?

24. you want to congratulate?

25. someone goes out somewhere?

26. you go out somewhere?

27. you want someone to say once more?

28. you have kept someone waiting?

29. you greet someone in the morning?

30. you are introduced to someone?

31. you are about to leave the place you visited?

32. you want to tell someone to come again?

33. you want to ask someone how he is?

34. you want to tell someone that you are fine (thanks to him)?

35. you want to ask someone politely if he is familiar with it?

36. you want to tell someone to enter?

37. you offer someone Coke?

38. you want to tell someone not to trouble himself for you?

39. you offer a guest another cup of tea?

40. you do not accept the above offer?

41. you leave someone at night who you think will not see you again within the same day?

42. you want to be excused for a moment?

43. you want to ask someone to open (the book on) page five?

44. you want to ask someone to close the book?

15.1.2 Transform the code sentence according to the given English sentences:

A. Watanabe san wa sen'sei desu.

   1. Mr. Watanabe was a teacher.

   2. Mr. Watanabe is not a teacher.

   3. Mr. Watanabe must be a teacher.

   4. Mr. Watanabe was not a teacher.

B. Ano eiga wa omoshiroi desu.

   1. That movie is not interesting.

   2. That movie must be interesting.

   3. That movie must have been interesting.

   4. That movie was interesting.

C. Buraun san ni den'wa o shimasu.

   1. Let's telephone Mr. Brown.

   2. I didn't telephone Mr. Brown.

   3. I phoned Mr. Brown.

   4. Won't you phone Mr. Brown?

15.1.3 Insert an appropriate Relational in each blank.

1. Gakkoo (   ) ikimasu.

2. Sumino san (   ) hon desu.

3. Eiga (   ) mimashoo.

4. Eki (   ) machimasu.

5. Watakushi (   ) gakusei desu.

6. Kore (   ) dare (   ) jidoosha desu ka?

7. Dono shin'bun (   ) omoshiroi desu ka?

8. Boku (   ) rekoodo ja arimasen.

9. Anata wa dore (   ) moraimashita ka?

10. Niwa (   ) tori (   ) imasu yo.

11. Okaasan (   ) uchi (   ) imashita.

12. Kodomo ga inu (   ) okashi (   ) yarimashita.

13. Anata (   ) kurashikku (   ) kikimasu ka?
    "Do you listen to classical music also (as well as jazz, popular music)?"

14. Anata (   ) suiei (   ) suki desu ka?
    "Do you like swimming also (as well as other people)?"

15. Otootosan (   ) wa zasshi (   ) agemashita.

16. Kon'ban kyoodai ni (   ) tegami (   ) kakimashoo.
    "This evening, I think I will write a letter to my brothers too (as well as to someone else)."

17. Buraun san (   ) Amerika (   ) kimashita.
    "Mr. Brown came from the States."

18. Jazu (   ) popyuraa ga daisuki desu.
    "I like jazz, popular music, etc."

19. Kyooto (   ) Nikkoo o ken'butsu shimashita.
    "He saw Kyōto or Nikkō."

20. Haha wa boku (   ) okane (   ) kuremashita.

21. Kon'getsu (   ) ikimasen (   ), raigetsu (   ) ikimasu.

22. Asa (   ) yoru (   ) suzushii deshoo?

   "It will be cool in the morning and at night, won't it?"

23. Eigo (   ) furan'sugo (   ) naraimasu.

   "I'll learn English or French."

24. Den'sha (   ) ikimasu ka?

   "Are you going by train?"

25. Kazuko san (   ) den'wa (   ) hanashimashita.

   "I talked with Kazuko on the phone."

26. Kore (   ) takakatta desu (   ), are (   ) yasukatta n desu yo.

27. Shujin (   ) yomimasen deshita.

   "My husband didn't read it either."

28. Otooto (   ) issho ni kissaten (   ) koocha (   ) nomimashita.

29. Watakushi (   ) yama (   ) suki desu.

15.1.4 Correct errors.

1. Inu ni okashi o kuremashita.

2. Issho ni uchi o kaerimashoo.

3. Tomodachi o eigo no zasshi ni agemasu.

4. Sen'sei to gakusei ga kyooshitsu de arimasu.

5. Ashita haha ni tegami o kakimashita.

6. Koko ni Kazuko san ni machimashoo.

7. Kore wa amari kirei desu nee.

8. Rainen Nihon ni ken'butsu shimashita.

9. Sono kissaten wa chittomo shizuka desu.

10. Imooto to otooto ga hitotsu zutsu imasu.

11. Watakushi wa mae Meriiran'do Daigaku o nihon'go de naraimasu.

12. Kinoo no eiga wa totemo omoshiroi desu yo.

13. Watashi wa sen'sei de hon o moraimashita.

14. Boku wa jazu ga suki desu ga, kurashikku ga suki desu.

15. Kodomo ni den'sha no kippu o nisatsu yarimashita.

16. Hikooki ni Yooroppa o ikimasen deshita.

17. Kimi wa suiei o joozu desu nee.

15.1.5 Write down an appropriate answer to each of the following questions:

A. 1. Anata no gokazoku wa nan'nin desu ka?

   2. Otoosan ya okaasan wa anata to issho ni imasu ka?

   3. Kyoodai wa nan'nin desu ka?

   4. Oniisan (oneesan, imootosan, *or* otootosan) wa ikutsu desu ka?

B. 1. Anata no kuni wa doko desu ka?

   2. Kuni no oten'ki wa doo desu ka?

   3. Natsu wa atsui deshoo?

   4. Ame ga takusan furimasu ka?

   5. Fuyu yuki ga furimasu ka?

C. 1. Anata wa raigetsu ryokoo shimasu ka?

   2. Doko e ikimasu ka?

   3. Soko wa tooi desu ka?

   4. Nan de ikimasu ka?

   5. Dare to issho ni ikimasu ka?

D. 1. Anata wa mae doitsugo (furan'sugo, roshiago, chuugokugo, *or* eigo) o naraimashita ne?

   2. Doko de naraimashita ka?

   3. Donata kara naraimashita ka?

   4. Sore wa muzukashikatta desu ka, yasashikatta desu ka?

   5. Roshiago wa naraimasen deshita ka?

   6. Anata wa itsumo nanigo o hanashimasu ka?

15.1.6 Make appropriate questions that will lead to the following answers:

1. Sen'getsu ryokoo shimashita.

2. Kuji desu.

3. Imooto wa ima yattsu desu.

4. Ano kata wa Yamamoto sen'sei desu yo.

5. Iie, moraimasen deshita.

6. Pan'ya wa soko ni arimasu.

7. Eiga wa omoshirokatta desu.

8. Kore wa Katoo san no heya desu.

9. Nisatsu zutsu agemashita.

208

10. Den'sha de uchi e kaerimashita.

11. Kodomo wa futari imasu.

12. Hai, totemo oishikatta desu.

13. Kore ga yokatta desu.

14. Inu to tori ga imashita.

15. Iie, kirei deshita yo.

16. San'mai arimashita.

17. Iie, pan'ya ja arimasen deshita.

18. Maigetsu Kan'da de hon o kaimasu.

19. Hai, hashi de wa tabemasen. Naifu to fooku de tabemasu.

15.1.7 Complete each sentence by inserting, in each blank, one of the Sentence Interjectives listed below. (Use each word only once.)

demo, dakara, sore ni, soshite, sore kara, ee, iie, hai

1. Boku wa gakusei desu. (   ), ani wa gakusei ja arimasen.

2. Watakushi wa kyonen Doitsu e ikimashita. (   ), Furan'su e ikimashita.

3. Sumisu san wa jazu ga suki desu. (   ), popyuraa mo daisuki desu yo.

4. "Oniisan wa itsumo gyuunyuu o nomimasu ka?" "(   ), itsumo nomimasu."

5. "Kotoshi no fuyu wa yuki ga furimasen deshita ka?" "(   ), furimasen deshita."

6. Kinoo wa isogashikatta n desu. (   ), yoru mo jimusho ni imashita.

7. Kinoo Nikkoo o ken'butsu shimashita. (   ), yoru uchi e kaerimashita.

8. "Ano kissaten wa kirei desu ka?" "(   ), chittomo kirei ja arimasen."

15.2 HIRAGANA EXERCISES

15.2.1 Insert appropriate *hiragana* in each blank:

1. こども ___ _____ です。
   wa   yattsu

2. なに ___ かいますか。
   o

3. _____ ですか。
   soo

4. _____、これ ___ たべま _____。
   jaa   o   shoo

5. やまもとさん ___ にっこうに いました。

                wa

6. _____ おいしくありません。

   chittomo

7. _____、 わかりません。

      iie

8. _____ すみません。

   doomo

9. _____ ___ のみました。

  ocha   o

10. _____ ならいました。

  moo

11. _____。

    sayoonara

12. きのう どこ ___ いきましたか。

            e

13. _____、 _____ で えいが ___ みましたよ。

  soosoo   Tookyoo   o

14. とても つめた _____ です。

          katta

15. _____ おかまいなく。

  doozo

16. _____ に _____ かえりません。

  issho   wa

17. だれが _____ ___ _____ しましたか。

        Kyooto   e   ryokoo

15.2.2 Read the following sentences:

1. うちへ かえりません。
2. でんえんは あまり きれいじゃありません。
3. あそこで かいましょう。
4. よるは さむかったでしょう。
5. ごはんを たべますか。
6. おんがくも ちっとも よくありません。
7. きのう てんきが よくありませんでした。
8. うちは とうきょうでしょう？
9. わたくしは べんきょうが すきです。

10. おとうとさんに　えほんを　あげましょう。

11. まるぜんは　ちょっと　とおいです。

12. あれも　せんせいの　へやです。

13. りょうあんじへは　いきませんでした。

14. ともだちが　きっぷを　さんまい　くれました。

15. この　ほんは　とても　おもしろかったです。

16. デパートに　けいこさんが　いました。

17. スミスさんは　がくせいでした。

18. まえは　すきじゃありませんでした。

15.2.3 Write the following sentences in *hiragana*:

1. Nani o tabemasu ka?

2. Yamamoto san wa umi ga suki desu.

3. Eki de ano hito o machimashoo.

4. Kuni e kaerimasen.

5. Soko mo Katoo sen'sei no jimusho desu yo.

6. Gin'koo ni Kazuko san ga imashita.

7. Amari suki ja arimasen.

8. Soko wa atatakakatta deshoo.

9. Watanabe san wa mae Tookyoo Daigaku no gakusei deshita.

10. Imooto san ni zasshi o agemashoo.

11. Nikkoo e wa ikimasen deshita.

12. Nihon'go wa totemo omoshirokatta desu yo.

13. Ame ga takusan furimashita.

14. Kono jisho mo chittomo yoku arimasen.

15. Chuuzen'jiko wa Nikkoo deshoo?

16. Kinoo wa samuku arimasen deshita.

17. Ano kissaten wa amari shizuka de wa arimasen.

18. Watakushi no gakkoo wa chotto tooi desu.

19. Mizu o nomimashoo ka?

20. Kippu o gomai moraimashita.

APPENDIX I

ABBREVIATIONS

A	. . . .	Adjective	*takai, isogashii, yoi*
Adv.	. . . .	Adverb	*totemo, tokidoki, tabun*
B	. . . .	Base	
C	. . . .	Copula	*desu, deshita, deshoo*
D	. . . .	Derivative	
Dv	. . . .	verbal Derivative	*-masu, -masen, -mashita, -mashoo*
E	. . . .	Predicate Extender	*(ja) arimasen, (-ku) arimasen*
I	. . . .	Inflection	
N	. . . .	Nominative	
Na	. . . .	adjectival Nominative	*kirei, shizuka, gen'ki*
Nd	. . . .	dependent Nominative	*-kata, -hen, -mai, -san*
Ni	. . . .	interrogative Nominative	*doko, ikutsu, itsu, nani*
N	. . . .	ordinary Nominative	*gakkoo, kami, ashita, gomai*
NM	. . . .	Nominative Modifier	*watakushi no (hon), sono (hito)*
P	. . . .	Predicate	
PC	. . . .	Pre-Copula	*n (desu)*
PM	. . . .	Predicate Modifier	(Adverb, time Nominative, N+R, number)
PN	. . . .	Pre-Nominative	*kono, sono, ano, dono*
R	. . . .	Relational	
Rc	. . . .	clause Relational	*(-masu) ga, ... (desu) ga, ...*
Rp	. . . .	phrase Relational	*no, to, ya, wa, mo, ga, o, e, ni, de*
S	. . . .	Sentence	
SI	. . . .	Sentence Interjective	*hai, ee, iie, jaa, soshite, dakara, demo, a*
SP	. . . .	Sentence Particle	*ka, yo, ne, nee*
V	. . . .	Verb	*ikimasu, yomimasu, furimasu, arimasu*

APPENDIX II

SENTENCE STRUCTURE

$$S = SI + PM \left\{ \begin{array}{l} (NM)^{*1} \left\{ \begin{array}{l} PN \\ N + (R)^{*2} \\ Adv.^{*3} \\ P^{*4} \end{array} \right\}^{*5} + N + (R) \\ (Adv.) + Adv. + (R) \\ P^{*6} + (R) \end{array} \right\} // P \left\{ \begin{array}{l} V\{B + I + D\} \\ A\{B + I + D\} \\ (NM) + N + (R) + C \end{array} \right\} + (R) + (E)^{*7} + (PC)^{*8} + (C)^{*9} \right\} + SP$$

*1   (NM) = NM optional

*2   (R) = R optional

*3   Adv. is only followed by Na such as *kirei*, adverbially used N such as *san'nin, kyoo*, or place N such as *ushiro, ue*.

*4   limited to final-clause Predicate such as *iku, itta*.

*5   { } = specification or limitation

*6   limited to TE, KU, TARI, Stem forms. R is obligatory for TARI, Stem forms, but optional for TE, KU forms.

*7   (E) = E optional

*8   (PC) = PC optional

*9   (C) = C optional

APPENDIX III

RELATIONALS

Relational		Lesson	Functions	Example Sentences
de	Rp	4	place of action [in; at; on, etc.]	*Gakkoo de naraimashita.*
de	Rp	9	means [by means of; with]	*Den'sha de kaerimashoo.*

Relational		Lesson	Functions	Example Sentences
e	Rp	3	direction [to]	*Umi e ikimasen ka?*
ga	Rp	4	subject	*Den'wa ga arimasu.*
ga	Rc	7	reversal reasoning [but; although]	*Ten'ki ga warukatta desu ga, dekakemashita.*
			[and]	*Sono eiga o mimashita ga, omoshirokatta desu.*
ka	Rp	9	[or]	*Koohii ka ocha o nomimashoo.*
kara	Rp	9	place of departure [from]	*Doko kara kimashita ka?*
		12	source [from]	*Tomodachi kara moraimashita.*
mo	Rp	5	inclusion [also; too]	*On'gaku mo suki desu.* *Kyooto e mo ryokoo shimashita.*
		8	[(not) either]	*Rekoodo mo yoku arimasen.* *Uchi ni mo imasen.*
ni	Rp	4	location [in; at; on, etc.]	*Soko ni arimasu.*
		12	indirect object [to (a person)]	*Anata ni agemashoo.*
no	Rp	5	qualification or modification of Nominative [of; in, etc.]	*Kore wa watakushi no heya desu.* *Nihon'go no hon o kaimasu.* *Gin'za no mise de kaimashita.*
o	Rp	3	direct object	*Terebi o mimasu ka?*
to	Rp	4	exhaustive listing [and]	*Kami to en'pitsu o kaimashita.*
		11	involvement [with]	*Okusan to issho ni kimasen ka?*
wa	Rp	5	topic	*Kore wa hon desu.* *Kinoo wa Nikkoo ni imashita.*
		8	in negation	*On'gaku wa kikimasen.* *Osake wa suki ja arimasen.*
		9	contrast	*Ima wa suki desu ga, mae wa kirai deshita.*
ya	Rp	9	sample listing [and (the like)]	*Kyooto ya Nara e ikimashoo.*

APPENDIX IV

CONJUGATION TABLE

— Normal Form —

1. Verb

Lesson	Form	Imperfect Affirmative	Imperfect Negative	Perfect Affirmative	Perfect Negative	OO form
a	12	agemasu (ageru)	agemasen	agemashita	agemasen deshita	agemashoo
a	4	arimasu	arimasen	arimashita	arimasen deshita	(arimashoo)
b	9	ben'kyoo (o) shimasu (suru)	ben'kyoo (o) shimasen	ben'kyoo (o) shimashita	ben'kyoo (o) shimasen deshita	ben'kyoo (o) shimashoo
c	5	chigaimasu (chigau)	chigaimason	chigaimashita	chigaimasen deshita	(chigaimashoo)
d	9	dekakemasu (dekakeru)	dekakemasen	dekakemashita	dekakemasen deshita	dekakemashoo
d	9	den'wa (o) shimasu (suru)	den'wa (o) shimasen	den'wa (o) shimashita	den'wa (o) shimasen deshita	den'wa (o) shimashoo
f	11	furimasu (furu)	furimasen	furimashita	furimasen deshita	(furimashoo)
h	8	hairimasu (hairu)	hairimasen	hairimashita	hairimasen deshita	hairimashoo
h	5	hanashimasu (hanasu)	hanashimasen	hanashimashita	hanashimasen deshita	hanashimashoo
h	8	hikimasu (hiku)	hikimasen	hikimashita	hikimasen deshita	hikimashoo
i	11	iimasu (iu)	iimasen	iimashita	iimasen deshita	iimashoo
i	3	ikimasu (iku)	ikimasen	ikimashita	ikimasen deshita	ikimashoo
i	4	imasu (iru)	imasen	imashita	imasen deshita	imashoo
k	3	kaerimasu (kaeru)	kaerimasen	kaerimashita	kaerimasen deshita	kaerimashoo
k	3	kaimasu (kau)	kaimasen	kaimashita	kaimasen deshita	kaimashoo

Lesson	Form	Imperfect Affirmative	Imperfect Negative	Perfect Affirmative	Perfect Negative	OO form
k	4	kaimono (o) shimasu (suru)	kaimono (o) shimasen	kaimono (o) shimashita	kaimono (o) shimasen deshita	kaimono (o) shimashoo
	4	kakimasu (kaku)	kakimasen	kakimashita	kakimasen deshita	kakimashoo
	7	karimasu (kariru)	karimasen	karimashita	karimasen deshita	karimashoo
	9	kekkon (o) shimasu (suru)	kekkon (o) shimasen	kekkon (o) shimashita	kekkon (o) shimasen deshita	kekkon (o) shimashoo
	9	ken'butsu (o) shimasu (suru)	ken'butsu (o) shimasen	ken'butsu (o) shimashita	ken'butsu (o) shimasen deshita	ken'butsu (o) shimashoo
	8	kikimasu (kiku)	kikimasen	kikimashita	kikimasen deshita	kikimashoo
	3	kimasu (kuru)	kimasen	kimashita	kimasen deshita	kimashoo
	12	kuremasu (kureru)	kuremasen	kuremashita	kuremasen deshita	(kuremashoo)
m	4	machimasu (matsu)	machimasen	machimashita	machimasen deshita	machimashoo
	4	mimasu (miru)	mimasen	mimashita	mimasen deshita	mimashoo
	12	moraimasu (morau)	moraimasen	moraimashita	moraimasen deshita	moraimashoo
n	5	naraimasu (narau)	naraimasen	naraimashita	naraimasen deshita	naraimashoo
	3	nomimasu (nomu)	nomimasen	nomimashita	nomimasen deshita	nomimashoo
r	9	ryokoo (o) shimasu (suru)	ryokoo (o) shimasen	ryokoo (o) shimashita	ryokoo (o) shimasen deshita	ryokoo (o) shimashoo
s	4	sagashimasu (sagasu)	sagashimasen	sagashimashita	sagashimasen deshita	sagashimashoo
	3	shimasu (suru)	shimasen	shimashita	shimasen deshita	shimashoo
t	3	tabemasu (taberu)	tabemasen	tabemashita	tabemasen deshita	tabemashoo

| | Form | Imperfect | | Perfect | | OO form |
Lesson		Affirmative	Negative	Affirmative	Negative	
w	5	wasuremasu (wasureru)	wasuremasen	wasuremashita	wasuremasen deshita	wasuremashoo
y	12	yarimasu (yaru)	yarimasen	yarimashita	yarimasen deshita	yarimashoo
	7	yomimasu (yomu)	yomimasen	yomimashita	yomimasen deshita	yomimashoo

Forms in parentheses are not to be used at this stage.

2. Verbal Derivative

Dictionary Form	Stem Form	TA Form	OO Form
-masu	-mase(n)*	-mashita	-mashoo

* (n) will be explained in later volumes.

Tense

| Imperfect | | Perfect | | OO Form |
Affirmative	Negative	Affirmative	Negative	
-masu	-masen	-mashita	-masen deshita	-mashoo

3. Adjective

Adjectives introduced in Learn Japanese Vol. I are as follows:

atatakai	11	kitanai	8	subarashii	9	urusai	8
atsui	11	mazui	8	suzushii	11	warui	7
chiisai	7	muzukashii	7	takai	7	yasashii	7
chikai	7	oishii	8	tanoshii	9	yasui	7
erai	7	omoshiroi	7	tooi	7	yoi	7
ii	7	ookii	7	tsumaranai	7		
isogashii	8	samui	11	tsumetai	11		

Any Adjective in Japanese inflects as shown in the charts below:

Dictionary Form	TA Form	KU Form
taka*i*	taka*katta*	taka*ku*

Tense

Imperfect		Perfect	
Affirmative	Negative	Affirmative	Negative
-i	-ku arimasen	-katta	-ku arimasen deshita

4. Copula

Dictionary Form	TA Form	OO Form
desu	deshita	deshoo

Tense

Imperfect		Perfect		OO Form
Affirmative	Negative	Affirmative	Negative	
desu	ja arimasen de wa arimasen	deshita	ja arimasen deshita de wa arimasen deshita	deshoo

APPENDIX V

DIALOG — English Equivalent

3.2   — After class, leaving the classroom —

Mr. Yamada: Miss Ishii, are you going [back] home soon?

Miss Ishii: No, I am not going [back] soon.

Mr. Yamada: Where are you going?

Miss Ishii: I am going to Kanda.

Mr. Yamada: To Kanda?

Miss Ishii:	Yes, I am going to buy books.
Mr. Yamada:	After that, what are you going to do?
Miss Ishii:	I will have a meal at a restaurant. Then I will go [back] home. How about you?
Mr. Yamada:	I am going [back] soon.
Miss Ishii:	Are you coming to school tomorrow?
Mr. Yamada:	Yes, I come to school every day. Well, hurry back.
Miss Ishii:	I am going.

4.2 — On the street —

Mr. Ueki:	Is there a telephone in this vicinity?
Mr. Suzuki:	There is one over there, you see.
Mr. Ueki:	Well, excuse me for a moment. I'll come [back] soon.

* * * * *

Mr. Ueki:	Sorry to have kept you waiting.
Mr. Suzuki:	Don't mention it. Well, shall we go [now]?
Mr. Ueki:	Yes, let's go. Oh, there's Mr. Yamada. Hello, Mr. Yamada.
Mr. Yamada:	Hi.
Mr. Suzuki:	Hello.
Mr. Ueki:	I saw you at the station yesterday. Where did you go?
Mr. Yamada:	I went to Shinjuku. And, I did some shopping at the department store. Oh, by the way, Keiko and Kazuko were in the department store.
Mr. Ueki:	Is that so?
Mr. Suzuki:	Mr. Yamada, do you have some free time now?
Mr. Yamada:	Yes.
Mr. Suzuki:	Mr. Ueki and Mr. Itō are coming to my house now. Let's eat supper together at my home.
Mr. Yamada:	Yes, thank you.

5.2 — In front of Prof. Nakamura's office —

Miss Koyama:	Prof. Nakamura, this is Mr. Smith. Mr. Smith was a student at the University of Maryland before.
Mr. Smith:	How do you do?
Prof. Nakamura:	I'm glad to meet you.
Mr. Smith:	Is this your room?
Prof. Nakamura:	Yes, it is.
Mr. Smith:	Is that one over there your room, too?
Prof. Nakamura:	No, that isn't. That is Prof. Katō's room.
Mr. Smith:	Is that Prof. Katō's room? My Japanese language teacher was Prof. Katō.
Prof. Nakamura:	No wonder, your Japanese is excellent.

Mr. Smith:	No, it's still poor. But, I like the study of foreign languages. I also studied German here [at the university].
Prof. Nakamura:	Who was your teacher?
Mr. Smith:	I forgot his name. (Looking at his watch) Oh, it's noon, isn't it? I'd better be leaving now.
Prof. Nakamura:	Really? Well, come again.
Mr. Smith:	Yes, I'll come again.

7.2 — Books, magazines, and newspapers —

Bill: Susie, at which bookstore do you usually buy books?

Susie: I buy them at the Maruzen Book Store in most cases. It is a little far [from here], but it is very good. How about you?

Bill: I borrow them at the school library in most cases. That book is quite big! Was it expensive?

Susie: No, it was inexpensive.

Bill: Did you already read it?

Susie: Yes, I did.

Bill: How was it?

Susie: It was very interesting. Won't you read it, too?

Bill: Thank you.

Susie: Here you are. (Looking at a magazine in Bill's hand) That is a Japanese magazine, isn't it? Are magazines in Japanese easy or difficult?

Bill: They are easy. So, I sometimes read Japanese magazines and newspapers.

Susie: Good! (Great! Remarkable! Excellent! . . . .)

8.2 — Going to a coffee shop —

Yamamoto: Aren't you Mr. Watanabe?

Watanabe: Oh! Mr. Yamamoto. How are you?

Yamamoto: Fine, thank you. And you?

Watanabe: I am fine, too.

Yamamoto: Are you busy now?

Watanabe: No, I am not very busy.

Yamamoto: Won't you stop for a while and have some tea in that area?

Watanabe: Yes. Shall we go into that coffee shop over there?

Yamamoto: The coffee of that [coffee] shop is not good at all. Besides, the music is not good either. Let's go to the Denen.

Watanabe: Is the Denen far?

Yamamoto: No, it is not. It is near from here.

Watanabe: Then, let's go there.

220

Yamamoto: The Denen is not too pretty, but it is quiet. Besides, their musical records are very good. Do you like music, too?

Watanabe: Yes, I like classical music very much. But, I don't listen to jazz and popular music very often.

Yamamoto: I don't like jazz either. Now, here we are. Let's go in.

9.2 — Going sightseeing —

Mr. Sumino: You weren't home yesterday, were you?

Miss Brown: No, I wasn't. But, how do you happen to know?

Mr. Sumino: I phoned you in the morning and at night, but there was no answer.

Miss Brown: I'm sorry about that. I was in Nikkō yesterday.

Mr. Sumino: You were? When did you leave?

Miss Brown: I left here yesterday morning. And I came back this morning.

Mr. Sumino: Did you go by car?

Miss Brown: No, I went by train from Asakusa.

Mr. Sumino: Do you like (Buddhist) temples and (Shintō) shrines and the like?

Miss Brown: Yes, I didn't particularly like them before, but now I like them very much.

Mr. Sumino: Did you go to Chūzenji Lake, also?

Miss Brown: Yes, I did. But the weather was not good. Therefore, it wasn't very enjoyable.

Mr. Sumino: That was too bad. I took a trip to Kyōto last month.

Miss Brown: Then, did you visit the Ryōanji temple? The stone garden [over] there is wonderful, isn't it?

Mr. Sumino: I didn't go to the Ryōanji temple. But I am going to Kyōto again this month or next month.

Miss Brown: How nice!

11.2 — Ishii's visiting Minoru —

Ishii: Minoru, are you home? (knocking at the door)

Minoru: Oh, Mr. Ishii, please come in.

Ishii: Thank you.

Minoru: It must be hot. [You must feel hot.] Would you care for a Coke?

Ishii: Yes, thank you.

Minoru: It rains a lot, doesn't it? Do you suppose that the weather will be bad tomorrow, too?

Ishii: It will probably be good tomorrow. They said so on the radio, you know.

Minoru: Really?

Ishii: You like swimming, don't you? Won't you go to the beach with me tomorrow?

Minoru: I like swimming, but I can not go to the beach tomorrow (the circumstances won't permit me to go to the beach tomorrow).

Ishii: Why is that?

Minoru: I am going home tonight.

Ishii: To your home? Isn't your home in Tōkyō?

Minoru: No. It's in Hokkaidō.

Ishii: Oh, is that so? Then, are your family all in Hokkaidō?

Minoru: My father and mother are in Sapporo, but my older brother and older sister are in Tōkyō.

Ishii: I took a trip to Hokkaidō last winter; it was very cold.

Minoru: It must have been particularly cold at night. It's fall now, but it will certainly be cold already in the morning and at night now.

12.2 — About the family —

Mrs. Yamada: How about tea?

Ikuo: Please don't go to any trouble. Is Minoru out now?

Mrs. Yamada: Yes, I am sorry. A friend of mine gave me three movie tickets. So, all my children went out [to see the movie] today.

Ikuo: Did they?

Mrs. Yamada: Ikuo, how many brothers and/or sisters do you have?

Ikuo: I have an older brother, an older sister, a younger brother and a younger sister, respectively.

Mrs. Yamada: How old are your older brother and older sister?

Ikuo: They are twenty-four and twenty.

Mrs. Yamada: Aren't your younger brother and your younger sister still little?

Ikuo: Yes, they are ten and eight.

Mrs. Yamada: Are they? Then, I will give one each of these picture books to your younger brother and sister.

Ikuo: Thank you very much. I think I will give [them] to my younger brother and sister this evening. By the way, what time is it now?

Mrs. Yamada: It's three.

Ikuo: Then, I'd better be leaving now.

Mrs. Yamada: Really? But, please have another cup of tea.

Ikuo: Yes, I will.

APPENDIX VI

GLOSSARY

* Numbers refer to lessons in which the words first occur.
* Numerals and numeral-counter combinations are not listed in this section. See Notes 12.4.1 and 12.4.2.

(A)

a	SI	4	oh; ah
aa	N	7	that way
agemasu	V	12	give (normal form of *ageru*) (see 12.4.3)
aki	N	11	autumn; fall

amari	Adv.	8	(not) very much; (not) very often (see 8.4.2)
ame	N	11	rain
Amerika	N	3	the United States of America; America
anata	N	3	you
ane	N	11	(my) older sister
ani	N	11	(my) older brother
ano	PN	7	that over there (see 7.4.2)
are	N	5	that one over there (see 5.4.8)
arimasen	E	8	(see 8.4.1 & 8.4.3)
arimasu	V	4	is situated (normal form of *aru*) (see 4.4.4)
asa	N	9	morning
asagohan	N	4	breakfast; morning meal
Asahi Shin'bun	N	7	Asahi Newspaper
Asakusa	N	9	a place in downtown Tōkyō
ashita	N	3	tomorrow (see 3.4.15)
asoko	N	4	that place over there; over there (see 4.4.5)
atashi	N	7	I (used by women) (see 7.4.6)
atatakai	A	11	is warm
atsui	A	11	is hot (see 11.4.2)

(B)

baiorin	N	8	violin
ban	N	9	evening; night
ban'gohan	N	4	supper; evening meal
ben'kyoo	N	5	study
ben'kyoo (o) shimasu	V	9	study (normal form of *ben'kyoo (o) suru*)
bifuteki	N	3	beefsteak
biiru	N	3	beer
boku	N	7	I (used by men) (see 7.4.6)
Buraun	N	9	Brown
byooin	N	7	hospital

(C)

chichi	N	11	(my) father
chigaimasu	V	5	differ; is different
chiisai	A	7	is small; is little (in size)
chikai	A	7	is near
chittomo	Adv.	8	(not) at all (see 8.4.2)
chotto	Adv.	7	a little; for a while (see 8.4.4)

Chuugoku	N	5	China
chuugokugo	N	5	Chinese language
Chuuzen'jiko	N	9	Lake Chūzenji in Nikkō

(D)

daigaku	N	5	university; college
daikirai	Na	8	dislike very much
daisuki	Na	8	like very much
dakara	SI	7	so; therefore
dame	Na	8	no good
dare	Ni	5	who? (see 5.4.15)
de	R	4	at; in (see 4.4.8)
de	R	9	by means of (see 9.4.6)
dekakemasu	V	9	go out; set out (normal form of *dekakeru*)
demo	SI	5	but; however
Den'en	N	8	name of a coffee shop
den'sha	N	9	electric train; streetcar
den'wa	N	4	telephone
den'wa (o) shimasu	V	9	make a phone call (normal form of *den'wa* (*o*) *suru*)
depaato	N	4	department store
deshita	C	5	TA form of *desu* (see 5.4.7)
deshoo	C	11	OO form of *desu* (see 11.4.3)
desu	C	5	(see 5.4.4)
de wa arimasen	C	8	formal equivalent of *ja arimasen* (see 8.4.1)
Doitsu	N	5	Germany
doitsugo	N	5	German language
doko	Ni	3	what place?; where?
donata	Ni	5	who? (polite equivalent of *dare*) (see 5.4.15)
dono	PN	7	which? (see 7.4.2)
doo	N	7	how? (see 7.4.9)
doori de	SI	5	no wonder!; indeed!
dooshite	Adv.	9	how?; why? (see 9.4.4)
doozo	SI	12	please
dore	Ni	5	which one? (see 5.4.3)

(E)

e	R	3	to (a place) (see 3.4.3)
ee	SI	3	yes (see 3.4.7)
ehon	N	12	picture book

eiga	N	4	movie
eigo	N	5	English language
eki	N	4	station
en'pitsu	N	5	pencil
erai	A	7	is great; is remarkable

(F)

fooku	N	9	fork
fune	N	9	boat; ship
Furan'su	N	5	France
furan'sugo	N	5	French language
furimasu	V	11	(rain or snow) fall (normal form of *furu*)
futari	N	12	two (persons) (see 12.4.2)
futatsu	N	12	two
fuyu	N	11	winter

(G)

ga	R	4	(see 4.4.3)
ga	Rc	7	but; although (see 7.4.5)
gaikoku	N	9	foreign country; abroad
gaikokugo	N	5	foreign language
gakkoo	N	3	school
gakusei	N	5	student
(o)gen'ki	Na	8	healthy; in good spirits
-getsu	Nd	9	month
gin'koo	N	5	bank
Gin'za	N	3	Ginza Street or a shopping center of Tōkyō
gitaa	N	8	guitar
-go	Nd	5	language (see 5.4.11)
go-	(prefix)	11	(see 11.4.9)
gohan	N	3	meal; boiled rice
goshujin	N	11	someone else's husband
gozon'ji	N	9	know
gyuunyuu	N	3	cow's milk

(H)

haha	N	11	(my) mother
hai	SI	3	yes (formal equivalent of *ee*) (see 3.4.7)
-hai	Nd	12	cupfuls; glassfuls (see 12.4.2)
hairimasu	V	8	go in (normal form of *hairu*)

haizara	N	4	ashtray
hanashimasu	V	5	speak; talk (normal form of *hanasu*)
haru	N	11	spring
hashi	N	9	chopsticks
hatachi	N	12	twenty years old (see 12.4.2)
Hawai	N	3	Hawaii
-hen	Nd	4	area; vicinity
hen'ji	N	9	reply
heta	Na	5	unskillful; poor (at) (see 5.4.12)
heya	N	5	room
hikimasu	V	8	play (instruments, such as piano, organ, violin, guitar, etc.)
hikooki	N	9	airplane
(o)hima	Na	4	free time
hiragana	N	9	the Japanese cursive syllabary
(o)hiru	N	5	noon (it sometimes means "lunch")
hirugohan	N	4	lunch; noon meal
hito	N	5	person
hitori	N	12	one (person) (see 12.4.2)
hitotsu	N	12	one (see 12.4.6)
Hokkaidoo	N	11	Hokkaidō Prefecture (northern island of Japan)
hon	N	3	book
-hon	Nd	12	(counter for pencils, bottles, etc.) (see 12.4.2)
hon'ya	N	7	book store (see 7.4.3)

(I)

Igirisu	N	5	England
ii	A	7	is good (see 7.4.4)
iie	SI	3	no (see 3.4.7)
iimasu	V	11	say (normal form of *iu*)
ikaga	Ni	11	how? (polite equivalent of *doo*)
ikimasu	V	3	go (normal form of *iku*)
Ikuo	N	3	boy's first name
ikutsu	Ni	12	how old?; how many (objects)? (see 12.4.6)
ima	N	4	now (see 9.4.1)
imasu	V	4	exist (normal form of *iru*) (see 4.4.4)
imooto	N	11	(my) younger sister
inu	N	4	dog
ishi	N	9	stone

Ishii	N	3	family name
isogashii	A	8	is busy
issho ni	PM	4	together; with [me, us, etc.]
Itoo	N	4	family name
itsu	Ni	9	when? (see 9.4.1)
itsumo	Adv.	7	always; usually (see 7.4.1)
itsutsu	N	12	five

(J)

jaa	SI	3	well
ja arimasen	C	8	negative of *desu* (see 8.4.1)
jazu	N	8	jazz
-ji	Nd	12	o'clock (see 12.4.2)
jidoosha	N	9	automobile
jimusho	N	5	office
jin ja	N	9	*Shintō* shrine
jisho	N	3	dictionary
joozu	Na	5	skillful; proficient; good (at) (see 5.4.12)

(K)

ka	SP	3	(see 3.4.5)
ka	R	9	or (see 9.4.14)
kaerimasu	V	3	go back; come back (normal form of *kaeru*)
kaimasu	V	3	buy (normal form of *kau*)
kaimono	N	4	shopping
kaimono (o) shimasu	V	4	do shopping (normal form of *kaimono (o) suru*)
kakimasu	V	4	write (normal form of *kaku*)
kamera	N	3	camera
kameraya	N	7	camera shop; camera dealer
kami	N	12	paper
kanai	N	11	my wife (see 11.4.10)
Kan'da	N	3	Kanda Street or book center of Tōkyō
(o)kane	N	4	money
kara	R	9	from (a place) (see 9.4.7); from (a person) (see 12.4.3)
Kariforunia	N	5	California
karimasu	V	7	borrow (normal form of *kariru*)
-kata	Nd	5	person (see 5.4.2)
Katoo	N	5	family name
kazoku	N	11	family (see 11.4.9)

Kazuko	N	4	girl's first name
Keiko	N	4	girl's first name
kekkon (o) shimasu	V	9	marry (normal form of *kekkon (o) suru*)
ken'butsu (o) shimasu	V	9	see the sights of; visit (transitive Verb) (normal form of *ken'butsu (o) suru*)
késa	N	9	this morning
kikimasu	V	8	listen to; hear (normal form of *kiku*) (*Kikimasu* is a transitive Verb: the Relational *o* occurs with this Verb to show a direct object. *Jazu o kikimasu.*)
kimasu	V	3	come (normal form of *kuru*)
kimi	N	12	you (used by men)
kinoo	N	4	yesterday (see 9.4.1)
kippu	N	12	ticket
kirai	Na	5	dislike (see 5.4.12)
kirei	Na	8	pretty; clean (*Kirei* is not an Adjective but an adjectival Nominative. Adjectives never end in *-ei*.)
kissaten	N	8	coffee shop
kitanai	A	8	is dirty; is unclean; is messy
kitto	Adv.	11	surely; no doubt
kodomo	N	11	child (see 11.4.10)
Kokakoora	N	11	Coca-cola
koko	N	4	this place; here
kokonotsu	N	12	nine
kon'ban	N	9	tonight
kon'getsu	N	9	this month
kono	PN	7	this (see 7.4.2)
koo	N	7	in this way
koocha	N	8	black tea
koohii	N	3	coffee
kore	N	5	this one (see 5.4.8)
kotoshi	N	11	this year
Koyama	N	5	family name
-kun	Nd	11	equivalent of *-san* (used by men) (see 11.4.1)
kuni	N	11	country; home (town; country)
kurashikku	N	8	classical music
kuremasu	V	12	give (me) (normal form of *kureru*)
kyonen	N	11	last year
kyoo	N	3	today

kyoodai	N	11	sister(s) and/or brother(s)
kyookai	N	9	church
kyooshitsu	N	5	classroom
Kyooto	N	9	old capital of Japan; Kyōto Prefecture

(M)

machimasu	V	4	wait (normal form of *matsu*) (Different from the English Verb "wait," *machimasu* is a transitive Verb; it follows the direct object Relational *o*.)
mada	Adv.	5	still
mae	N	5	before (see 9.4.1)
-mai	Nd	12	sheet (of) (counter for something thin and flat) (see 12.4.2)
maiasa	N	9	every morning
maiban	N	9	every night
maigetsu	N	9	every month
mainen	N	9	every year
mainichi	N	3	every day
Mainichi Shin'bun	N	7	Mainichi Newspaper
maishuu	N	9	every week
Maruzen	N	7	Maruzen Book Store
-masen	Dv	3	(see 3.4.8)
-mashita	Dv	4	TA form of -*masu* (see 4.4.9)
-mashoo	Dv	4	OO form of -*masu* (see 4.4.7)
-masu	Dv	3	(see 3.4.4)
mata	Adv.	5	again
matchi	N	4	match
mazui	A	8	tasteless; does not taste good
Meriiran'do	N	5	Maryland
mimasu	V	4	see (normal form of *miru*) (or "watch" as in "watch T.V.")
min'na	N	11	all; everyone
Minoru	N	11	man's first name
mise	N	8	shop; store
mittsu	N	12	three
mizu	N	3	water
mo	R	5	also; too (see 5.4.10)
mo	R	8	(not) either (see 8.4.5)
moo	Adv.	7	already (see 7.4.1)
moo	Adv.	12	more (see 12.4.9)

moraimasu	V	12	receive; get (normal form of *morau*) (see 12.4.3)
muttsu	N	12	six
muzukashii	A	7	is difficult

(N)

n (desu)	PC	7	(see 7.4.8)
naifu	N	9	knife
Nakamura	N	5	family name
namae	N	5	name
nan	Ni	5	what? (see 5.4.4)
nan-	Ni	12	how many ~ ?; what ~ ? (see 12.4.2)
nanatsu	N	12	seven
nani	Ni	3	what? (see 3.4.9)
nanigo	Ni	5	what language?
nan'ji	Ni	12	what time? (see 12.4.2)
nan'nin	Ni	12	how many (people)? (see 12.4.2)
Nara	N	9	old capital of Japan; Nara Prefecture
naraimasu	V	5	study; take lessons; is taught; learn (normal form of *narau*) (Note that *naraimasu* is not always equivalent to "learn.")
natsu	N	11	summer
ne	SP	5	(see 5.4.16)
nee	SP	5	(see 5.4.14)
-nen	Nd	9	year
ni	R	4	in; at (see 4.4.2)
ni	R	12	to (a person) (see 12.4.7)
Nihon	N	3	Japan
nihon'go	N	5	Japanese language
Nikkoo	N	9	city in Tochigi Prefecture (famous for the Tōshōgū Shrine)
-nin	Nd	12	(counter for people) (see 12.4.2)
niwa	N	9	garden
no	R	5	(see 5.4.6)
nomimasu	V	3	drink (normal form of *nomu*)

(O)

o	R	3	(see 3.4.12)
o-	(prefix)	4	(see 4.4.12)
ocha	N	3	(green) tea
oishii	A	8	is tasty; is good
okaasan	N	11	(someone else's) mother (see 11.4.10)

okashi	N	12	candy; sweets; confections
okosan	N	11	(someone else's) child (see 11.4.10)
okusan	N	11	(someone else's) wife (see 11.4.10)
omoshiroi	N	7	is interesting
oneesan	N	11	(someone else's) older sister (see 11.4.10)
on'gaku	N	8	music
oniisan	N	11	(someone else's) older brother (see 11.4.10)
ookii	A	7	is big; is large
otoosan	N	11	(someone else's) father (see 11.4.10)
otooto	N	11	(my) younger brother
oya	SI	11	oh!; oh?; my!

(P)

pan	N	3	bread
pan'ya	N	7	bakery
-peeji	Nd	12	page
piano	N	8	piano
popyuraa	N	8	popular music

(R)

raigetsu	N	9	next month
rainen	N	11	next year
rajio	N	11	radio
rekoodo	N	8	record
repooto	N	5	a term paper; a report
resutoran	N	3	restaurant
Roshia	N	5	Russia
roshiago	N	5	Russian language
rusu	N	12	is out; is not at home
ryokoo (o) shimasu	V	9	travel; take a trip (see 9.4.5)
Ryooan'ji	N	9	Ryōanji Temple in Kyōto (famous for its stone garden)

(S)

saa	SI	8	now!
sagashimasu	V	4	look for (normal form of *sagasu*) (*Sagashimasu* is a transitive Verb; it follows the direct object Relational *o*.)
-sai	Nd	12	year(s) (old) (see 12.4.2)
(o)sake	N	4	Japanese rice wine; alcohol
samui	A	11	is cold (weather)
-san	Nd	3	Mr.; Mrs.; Miss (see 3.4.1)

Sapporo	N	11	capital city of Hokkaidō
-satsu	Nd	12	volume (counter for books, etc.) (see 12.4.2)
sen'getsu	N	9	last month (see 9.4.13)
sen'sei	N	5	teacher
shimasu	V	3	do (normal form of *suru*)
shin'bun	N	7	newspaper
shin'bun'ya	N	7	newsstand; newsdealer
Shin'juku	N	4	a district of Tōkyō
shizuka	Na	8	quiet
shokudoo	N	4	dining room (hall); cafeteria; eating place
shujin	N	11	(my) husband
-shuu	Nd	9	week
soko	N	4	that place; there
sono	PN	7	that (see 7.4.2)
soo	N	7	in that way; so
soo	Adv.	11	so; in that way
soosoo	SI	4	oh, yes; I remember (this is used when the speaker suddenly recalls something)
sore	N	5	that one (see 5.4.8)
sore kara	SI	3	afterwards; and (then)
sore ni	SI	8	besides; moreover
soshite	SI	3	and
subarashii	A	9	is wonderful
sugu	Adv.	3	soon (see 3.4.2)
suiei	N	11	swimming
suki	Na	5	like; fond of (see 5.4.12)
sukoshi	Adv.	11	a little (see 11.4.4)
Sumino	N	9	family name
Sumisu	N	5	Smith
supuun	N	9	spoon
Suujii	N	7	Susie
Suzuki	N	4	family name
suzushii	A	11	is cool

(T)

tabako	N	4	tobacco; cigarettes
tabakoya	N	7	tobacco shop
tabemasu	V	3	eat (normal form of *taberu*)

tabun	Adv.	11	probably; perhaps
-tachi	Nd	12	(turns the preceding animate Nominative into plural) (see 12.4.4)
taipuraitaa	N	3	typewriter
taitei	Adv.	7	generally; in most cases
takai	A	7	is expensive
takusan	Adv.	11	a lot (see 11.4.4)
tanoshii	A	9	is pleasant
(o)tearai	N	4	rest room (literal meaning is "hand-washing") (see 4.4.12)
tegami	N	4	letter (correspondence)
ten'ki	N	9	weather
ten'pura	N	3	*tempura*; Japanese fry; fritter
(o)tera	N	9	Buddhist temple
terebi	N	4	television
to	R	4	and (see 4.4.11)
to	R	11	with (someone) (see 11.4.6)
tokidoki	Adv.	7	sometimes; once in a while
tokoro de	SI	12	by the way; incidentally
toku ni	PM	9	particularly
tomodachi	N	5	friend
too	N	12	ten
tooi	A	7	is far
Tookyoo	N	3	capital of Japan
tori	N	4	bird; chicken (meat)
toshokan	N	7	(school or public) library
totemo	Adv.	7	very (see 7.4.1)
tsugoo	N	11	convenience (see 11.4.7)
tsumaranai	A	7	is uninteresting; is dull; is unimportant
tsumetai	A	11	is cold (thing)
(U)			
uchi	N	3	home; house
Ueki	N	4	family name
umi	N	11	sea; seaside
urusai	A	8	is noisy; is annoying
(W)			
wa	R	5	(see 5.4.3)
wa	R	8	(see 8.4.6)
warui	A	7	is bad

wasuremasu	V	5	forget (normal form of *wasureru*)
watakushi	N	5	I (the contracted form *watashi* may also be used)
Watanabe	N	8	family name

(Y)

ya	R	9	and (selective) (see 9.4.8)
-ya	Nd	7	-store; -dealer (see 7.4.3)
yama	N	11	mountain
Yamada	N	3	family name
Yamamoto	N	8	family name
yarimasu	V	12	give (normal form of *yaru*)
yasashii	A	7	is easy
yasui	A	7	is inexpensive
yattsu	N	12	eight
yo	SP	4	(see 4.4.6)
yoi	A	7	is good (see 7.4.4)
Yokohama	N	11	the name of a city
yomimasu	V	7	read (normal form of *yomu*)
Yomiuri Shin'bun	N	7	Yomiuri Newspaper
Yooroppa	N	9	Europe
yoru	N	9	night (see 9.4.1)
yottsu	N	12	four
yuki	N	11	snow

(Z)

zan'nen	Na	9	regrettable; disappointing
zasshi	N	7	magazine
zuibun	Adv.	7	extremely; quite (see 7.4.1)
-zutsu	Nd	12	each (see 12.4.5)

APPENDIX VII

INDEX TO NOTES